CURYE ON INGLYSCH

EARLY ENGLISH TEXT SOCIETY
SS. 8
1985

This book has been published with the help of a grant from the Canadian Federation for the Humanities, using funds provided by the Social Sciences and Humanities Research Council of Canada.

dur fort . saffron . and salt . sethe hyt a lytel
but not to stondyg . Chartrelbes of ßche .
Take colde þynge . hadok oþer hake ⁊
ye lyuers lß yo robßn͛ . ⁊ sethe hit Ise lle .
in Ißatur . pyke olkte ye bones . ⁊ grynde
smal þo ßche . Dralbe a lyoure of almaß
des . ⁊ bred lß͛ yo self broþ . ⁊ do ý to yi ßche.
igrolkndn . ⁊ sethe hýt . do ý to polbdur
fort . salt ⁊ saffron . ⁊ make hit stondyg
Ꝕlaunche almaundes . ⁊ grynde hem .
and dralbe hem up lß Ißatur . Ise lle
yi ryse clene . ⁊ do ý to sugur roche . and
salt . let hýt be stondyng . frye almaund͛
brolkne ⁊ flourche hýt ý lß . or lß sugur .
Ryse of ßche . orþe . lampraý in galeef .
Take a lampraý . ⁊ fle hým lß Ißyne ⁊
salt . and schalde hým in Ißatur . slýte
hým a lýte . at ye eyne kepe ye blode . put
hým on a spýte . ⁊ rost hý . ⁊ kepe Ißel þo
gres . grynde reyßyngus coraunce . Dra
Ise hé up lß Ißyne . ⁊ vinegre of galyn
ga . floure of canel . polbdur of clolkes .
⁊ do ý to reyßyngus coraunce . drAlbe

CURYE ON INGLYSCH

ENGLISH CULINARY MANUSCRIPTS
OF THE FOURTEENTH CENTURY
(INCLUDING THE *FORME OF CURY*)

EDITED BY

CONSTANCE B. HIEATT
AND
SHARON BUTLER

Published for

THE EARLY ENGLISH TEXT SOCIETY

by the

OXFORD UNIVERSITY PRESS

LONDON NEW YORK TORONTO

1985

Oxford University Press, Walton Street, Oxford OX2 6DP

London New York Toronto
Delhi Bombay Calcutta Madras Karachi
Kuala Lumpur Singapore Hong Kong Tokyo
Nairobi Dar es Salaam Cape Town
Melbourne Auckland
and associated companies in
Beirut Berlin Ibadan Mexico City Nicosia

Published in the United States
by Oxford University Press, New York

British Library Cataloguing in Publication Data
Curye on Inglysch: English culinary manuscripts
of the fifteenth century (including the forme
of cury)——(Early English Text Society.S.S.;8)
1. Cookery, English
I. Hieatt, Constance II. Butler, Sharon
III. Early English Text Society IV. Series
641.5942   TX717
ISBN 0-19-722409-1

Set by Joshua Associates, Oxford
Printed in Great Britain by
Richard Clay (The Chaucer Press) Ltd,
Bungay Suffolk

AUTHORS' PREFACE

The division of labour for this collaborative project has been a fairly even one. Sharon Butler has taken primary responsibility for the texts and Constance B. Hieatt for the editorial material. We have, however, done considerably more than simply checked each other's work: C. B. H. has also worked with the manuscripts, and S. B. has initiated or revised various parts of the editorial apparatus.

None of the work would have been possible without the assistance of the universities which are our employers, both in the form of leave and of financial aid, and the Social Sciences and Humanities Research Council of Canada (formerly the Canada Council), which has, at various times, provided both of us with funds necessary for work in England with the manuscripts and at various British libraries. Among the other institutions and organizations whose co-operation has been essential to our enterprise, we are especially in debt to the Department of Manuscripts of the British Library; the Division of Western Manuscripts of the Bodleian Library; and the manuscript divisions of the National Library of Wales, the New York Public Library, and the Library of the University of Durham. We are especially grateful to the British Library for permission to reproduce a page of BL MS Harleian 1605 as a frontispiece for this volume.

Among individuals to whom special thanks are owed, foremost is Dr Curt Bühler, owner of the only manuscript in private hands of those printed and collated here. We are very grateful to M. B. Parkes, of Keble College, Oxford, for his generosity in helping us solve an enormous number of palaeographical and dating problems; Dr I. A. Doyle of the University Library of Durham has also given us valuable help and advice in this and other areas, and we thank J. P. Hudson, Head of Large Collections of the British Library's Department of Manuscripts, for giving us his opinion on the date of MS Sloane 468.

Others who have helped us with one problem or another

include Brenda Thaon, of the Université de Montréal; Ian Short of Westfield College, the University of London; and Robin Jones of the Department of French, University of Western Ontario: all of whom gave assistance in unravelling problems connected with the French or Anglo-Norman background or sources. Several readers and consultants on both sides of the Atlantic offered helpful suggestions for correction or improvement, and we owe a special debt of gratitude to Norman Davis, Director, and Pamela Gradon, Editorial Secretary, of the E.E.T.S. for their patient assistance and encouragement. And, finally, we would like to thank Professor Donald Fry of the State University of New York, Stony Brook, for encouraging us to proceed with the work in the first place.

C. B. Hieatt,
University of Western Ontario

S. Butler,
University of Toronto

December 1982

TABLE OF CONTENTS

Table of Manuscript Sigla   ix

Introduction   1
    Section 1. The Fourteenth-Century Menu   1
    Section 2. Fourteenth-Century Recipes: Historical
                Development and Characteristics   6
    Section 3. Manuscript Sources   15
                a. Part I   16
                b. Part II   17
                c. Part III   19
                d. Part IV   20
                e. Part V   30
    Section 4. Variants and Editorial Principles   32

Select Bibliography   35

Fourteenth-Century Menus from MS Cosin v iii 11   39
    Part I: DIUERSA CIBARIA (63 recipes)   43
    Part II: DIUERSA SERVISA (92 recipes)   59
    Part III: UTILIS COQUINARIO (37 recipes)   81
    Part IV: THE FORME OF CURY (205 recipes)   93
    Part V: GOUD KOKERY (25 recipes)   147

Appendix A: Manuscripts Cited but not Given Sigla   157
Appendix B: Chart of Recipes in *The Forme of Cury*   158
Index and Glossary   167

TABLE OF MANUSCRIPT SIGLA

Note that these sigla are only for manuscripts frequently cited in notes and text; other manuscripts cited or used are listed in Appendix A.

A	London, BL Add. 5016
A1	London, BL Add. 32085
Ar	London, BL Arundel 334
As	Oxford, Bodleian Ashmole 1444
B	New York, [Morgan] Bühler 36
C	Durham, University Library Cosin v iii 11
D	Oxford, Bodleian Douce 257
H	London, BL Harl. 1605
He	London, BL Add. 46919
J	London, BL Cotton Julius D viii
L	Oxford, Bodleian Laud Misc. 553
P	Aberystwyth, National Library of Wales Peniarth 394 D
R	Oxford, Bodleian Rawlinson D 1222
Ro	London, BL Royal 12 C xii
S	London, BL Sloane 468
S1	London, BL Sloane 374
S2	London, BL Sloane 1108
S3	London, BL Sloane 442
W	New York, Public Library Whitney 1

INTRODUCTION

1. THE FOURTEENTH-CENTURY MENU

The recipes collected in this volume come from more than twenty manuscripts, few of which have ever been printed or collated before. The recipes themselves, although not all the manuscripts, date from the fourteenth century, the earliest period for which we have any such collections in English. However, the culinary traditions represented by these recipes and by the many historical feast menus of the fourteenth century and later, on which many of these dishes appear, were not born in that century, nor did they die with it. The menu of the English upper classes—the only one thought worth recording, of course—seems to have been much the same from the twelfth century well into the sixteenth. Some differences can be observed between fourteenth-century dishes and later recipes retaining the same names, but since we have only sparse evidence pre-dating the fourteenth century, it is only very tentatively that we can suggest what appear to be innovations of the time.

The only twelfth-century English recipes anyone has located to date are a few which occur rather casually in the *De Utensilibus* of Alexander Nequam,[1] written in Latin with Anglo-Norman and (a few) English glosses. All of Nequam's recipe suggestions are ones which can be found in fuller form in later medieval (and even Renaissance) sources: for example, stewed hen in cumin sauce, and fish boiled in wine and water and served with a 'green sauce' of various herbs. Our main sources of information about twelfth- and thirteenth-century English food are literary feast scenes, most of which are not very helpful because they describe the food as plentiful or 'of the best' without telling us exactly what was served. From

---

[1] In BL MS Cott. Titus D **xx**, ff. 1–16; printed in Thomas Wright, *A Volume of Vocabularies* (privately printed, 1857): two excerpts on food are printed, in translation, in Urban Tigner Holmes, Jr., *Daily Living in the Twelfth Century: Based on the Observations of Alexander Neckam in London and Paris* (Madison, Wisconsin, 1952).

Laȝamon's *Brut*, for example, we learn little more than that
game, especially venison, was as eagerly consumed at elegant
feasts in the thirteenth century as later.[1]

Some of the Anglo-Norman *chansons de geste* of the period
have casual references to food. In *Le Charroi de Nîmes*, a
twelfth-century work, Guillaume d'Orange reproaches King
Louis for forgetting—among other things—some splendid
venison Guillaume had served him, and somewhat later he
and his nephew Bertrand sit down to a meal of boar, crane,
wild goose, and peacocks with pepper sauce.[2] In the *Prise
d'Orange* the Saracen king Arragon serves Guillaume a similar
dinner.[3] All of these are items familiar in later menus and
recipes, but the accounts are not full-blown, item-by-item
descriptions of feasts; and they cannot be understood as complete menus.

The first fully detailed menu for an English feast is found
in the late thirteenth-century Anglo-Norman 'Treatise of
Walter of Bibbesworth', or, as it is described in one of the
manuscripts, 'la treytez ke moun sire Gauter de Bibelesworth
fist'.[4] The relevant verses, including some variants not found
in all manuscripts, read—with some emendation—as follows:

Un vallet de la novelerie
Qui vient de une graunt mangerie
De la feste nous ad countee,
Come lour service fust araee.
Sanz pain & vin ou cervoyse
Ne serra nuls a feste a eise,
Mes tous tres ny out ellyz,
Il aveyent mys a dyz.

[1] See, e.g., ll. 4038–52 in the edition of G. L. Brook and R. F. Leslie, Vol. 1,
EETS 250 (1963).
[2] Ed. Duncan McMillan (Paris, 1972), l. 219 and Laisse 30.
[3] Ls. 18 in *Les redactions en vers de la Prose d'Orange*, ed. Claude Regnier
(Paris, 1966), *AB* version.
[4] *Le Traité de Walter de Bibbesworth sur la langue française*, ed. Annie Owen
(University of Paris dissertation, 1929) is the most recent edition. It is not completely satisfactory, omitting, for example, a number of variants and glosses.
C. B. H. has, therefore, re-edited this passage from the nine manuscripts now in
British libraries and refers the reader to her article on this subject, '*Ore pur parler
de array de une graunt mangerye*: the Culture of the "Newe Get", ca. 1285', in
Acts of Interpretation: the Text in Its Contexts, 700–1600 (Norman, Oklahoma,
1982), pp. 219–33.

Mais au meins fait a saver
Du cours quil eurent a primer:
La teste du cengler armee
E le groign plein baneree;
Assez permy la mesoun,
De grese e de enfermeysoun,
Veneysoun oue le furmente.
Puis mainte autre diversete
Des gruwes, poouns, e cynes,
Chevereaus, purceaus, e gelynes.
Puis avoient conyns en gravee,
Trestout de zucre enfoundree,
Viaunde de Cypre e maumene,
Vin vermaile e blaunc a plente.
E puis tout autre foisoun de rost,
Cheascun de eus autre encost:
Feisaunz, ascyez, e perdriz,
Gryves, alouwes, e plovers rostis,
Merles, vis de coqs, & mauvys
Et des altres oiseaux que nomer ne puis;
Braoun, crespes, & fruture,
Oue zucre roset la temprure.
Et quant la table fu oustee,
Blaunche poudre oue la grosse dragee,
Maces, quibebes, clougilofrez,
E dautre espiecerye assez,
E oubleie a fuisoun.

(A fashionable yeoman who came from a great banquet has told us about the feast, how their service was ordered. Without bread and wine and ale, no one at a feast will be at ease, but the choicest of all three were provided there, he has told us. But it is worth knowing about the course which they had first: the head of a boar, larded, with the snout well garlanded, and enough for the whole household of venison fattened during the closed season. And then there were a great variety of cranes, peacocks, and swans, kids, pigs, and hens. Then they had rabbits in gravy, all covered with sugar, Viaunde de Cypre and Mawmenny, red and white wine in great plenty; and then quite a different multitude of roasts, each of them set next to another: pheasants, woodcocks, and partridges, fieldfares, larks, and roasted plovers, blackbirds, woodcocks, and song-thrushes, and other birds I cannot name; and fried meat, crisps, and fritters, with sugar mixed with rosewater. And when the table was taken away, sweet spice powder with large dragees, maces, cubebs, and enough spicerie, and plenty of wafers.)

4   CURYE ON INGLYSCH

There is absolutely no difference in the order of serving
here, and the general nature of the foods served, from what
can be observed in such later documents as menus of banquets
at the courts of Richard II and later monarchs[1] and literary
descriptions such as that of the feast near the beginning of
the alliterative *Morte Arthure*.[2] And almost identical menus
were recommended as late as the sixteenth century, in, for
example, Wynken de Worde's *Boke of Kervuynge*.[3]

This is, then, a fixed, definite, order of serving which pre-
vailed at least from the thirteenth to the sixteenth centuries,
although it may not appear particularly orderly to those who
are accustomed to beginning with soup or an *hors d'oeuvre*
and ending with something sweet. Actually, the menu generally did have something approximating soup at the very
beginning (pottages, of a vegetable nature) and ended with
small sweets (wafers, sugar-coated nuts and spices), but the
basic rationale was just a little different from our 'normal' one
today. It is perhaps best explained in the fifteenth-century dog-
gerel cookery collection known as the *Liber Cure Cocorum*;[4]
for a feast featuring various kinds of fowl, we are told,

> For a comyn rule in cure
> Now tas þys for a rewle fulle god,
> All hole futed fuylle in flud
> Gose before, and ay þou take
> þo grettis fyrst, savun gose and drake,
> Bothe of towne and of toþer,
> Also bakyn mete, my der brother,
> And most daynte, come byhynde:
> þys is a rewle mad in kynde.

(Morris ed., p. 55.)

[1] See, e.g., the menus printed in *Two Fifteenth Century Cookery Books*, ed.
Thomas Austin (EETS OS 91, 1888), pp. 57-64 and 67-9. A somewhat odd
exception occurs in the menu for the coronation feast of Henry VI, given in
Fabyan's Chronicle; each of the three courses is a full menu in miniature, beginning with heartier foods and ending with such delicacies as fritters: see *The Great
Chronicle of London*, ed. A. H. Thomas and I. D. Thornley (London, 1938),
pp. 152-3.
[2] ll. 176-238, in the edition ed. Valerie Krishna (New York, 1976), pp. 45-7.
[3] Printed in *The Babees Book* . . . , ed. F. J. Furnivall, EETS OS 32 (1868);
repr. Greenwood Press, N.Y., 1969.
[4] BL MS Sloane 1986, ff. 29^r-56^v; ed. R. Morris (London, 1862).

In other words, we are told that it is only *natural* to take the most substantial foods first, saving what is richer and/or more delicate for later in the meal. We follow the same principle in serving meats and vegetables before dessert, but we have lost the concept of serving non-sweet delicacies, such as small game birds, as part of 'dessert'. By medieval principles, they belonged in the last course, with or after such rich or sweet items as tarts and fritters. The substantial first course of the menu was the everyday, basic meal: in more austere households, such as that of Princess Cecill, mother of Edward IV—a highly devout lady who spent most of her day in private prayers or at services and had improving literature read aloud at meal times—dinner on meat days consisted mainly of boiled beef or mutton, with one roast added to the menu on Sundays, Tuesdays, Thursdays, and holidays. On Saturday, a fast-day in the fifteenth century, this household's dinner consisted of one serving of salt fish, one of fresh fish, and (out of Lent) butter.[1]

In more lavish establishments, the first course was still all that many members of the household were entitled to; the more delicate dishes were reserved for the higher ranks and honoured guests. Many of the royal 'household ordinances' spell out just how many servings of food and ale or wine each rank is entitled to. That not everyone had a right to taste every dish, even at a feast, is evident from extant records of provisions for actual feasts. For example, Dame Alice de Bryene, a gentlewoman whose carefully kept household records for the year from September 1412 to September 1413 we are lucky to have,[2] gave a harvest feast in August 1413 at which about 150 people were served: the two swans could not have gone very far, and most of the diners would have been lucky to get a taste of the twelve geese and twenty-four capons.

The lord (or lady) of the house was, however, expected to be generous in distributing tidbits of special dishes to others not similarly served. Thus the thirteenth-century 'household rules' attributed to Robert Grosseteste, Bishop of Lincoln,

[1] See *A Collection of Ordinances and Regulations for the Government of The Royal Household* (London, Society of Antiquaries, 1790), p. 38.
[2] *The Household Book of Dame Alice de Bryene*, trans. M. K. Dale and V. B. Redstone (Ipswich, 1931).

for the Countess of Lincoln, state, 'e comaundez ke vostre
esquele seyt issi replenie e tassee, e numeement des entremes,
ke curteysement puissez partir de vostre esquele a destre e a
senestre par tute vostre haute table, e la vus plarra, tut eyent
eus de mesmes co ke vus avez devaunt vus? (and order that
your dish be so refilled and heaped up, especially with the
light courses [i.e., the delicacies], that you may courteously
give from your dish to right and left to all at high table and
to whom else it pleases you that they have the same as you
had in front of you).[1] This no doubt explains why some
recipes, such as one for 'Checones in Critone' in BL MS
Arundel 334 (Ar), call for a quarter of a chicken for 'com-
mons' but 'a hole checkyn for a lorde'.

2. FOURTEENTH-CENTURY RECIPES:
HISTORICAL DEVELOPMENT AND
CHARACTERISTICS

But it is not only the order of service, and customs such as
serving the most prized dishes only to the higher-ranking
members of the household, which persisted over this period
of about five centuries. Characteristic dishes with distinctive
names, like 'Viaunde de Cypre' and 'Mawmenny', keep recur-
ring on menu after menu, from Walter of Bibbesworth's feast
to the menus suggested by Wynkyn de Worde, and in almost
every extensive recipe collection of the period. While a number of these dishes can also be found in French and Italian
collections of the period (see Bibliography), this is by no
means always the case. Anglo-Norman cookery featured
many dishes, including 'Viaunde de Cypre' and 'Mawmenny',
which do not appear in any French source. Later in the fourteenth century, a number of dishes unrecorded in France
which we suspect to be of Italian origin, such as 'Sambocade',
a tart flavoured with elderflowers, appear in some recipe
manuscripts, but it seems evident that Anglo-Norman cooks
made their own original contributions to English cuisine and
may have been, in turn, imitated on the Continent.[2]

[1] In *Walter of Henley*, ed. and trans. Dorothea Oschinsky (Oxford, 1971),
pp. 404–5.
[2] On the originality of Anglo-Norman cookery, see C. B. H.'s article 'The

For insight into the nature of the earlier Anglo-Norman cuisine inherited by fourteenth-century English cooks, we must turn to two Anglo-Norman groups of recipes transcribed early in the fourteenth century, which can be assumed to include recipes of thirteenth-century origin, found in BL MSS Royal 12 C xii (Ro), ff. 11^r-13^r, and Add 32085 (A1), ff. 117^r-119^r, the latter dating from the reign of Edward I.[1] Both of these groups are translated—in the second case in part— in a more extensive Middle English collection of the first quarter of the fourteenth century, BL MS Add. 46919 (He), ff. 19^r-24^v, a celebrated manuscript compiled under the direction of, and partly in the hand of, Friar William Herebert of Hereford.[2] Since a few of the recipes in this collection parallel ones found in a contemporary French collection,[3] it is instructive to compare French and English versions of the

Roast, or Boiled Beef of Old England', in *Book Forum* v (1980), 294-9. Only a few of the matters dealt with in that article are touched on here. There can be little doubt that some of the basic characteristics of aristocratic cookery in western Europe and England of the time came from the east, either via Spain and/or Italy or as direct importations by returning Crusaders. For example, the characteristic use of almond milk as a sauce base is not native to northern climes and is not a heritage from the Romans: while Apicius calls for toasted almonds fairly frequently, he has not a single recipe based on almond milk.

[1] The former was printed by Paul Meyer in *Bull. de la Société des Anciens Textes Français* (1893), 38-56.

[2] This heterogeneous collection includes, among other items, the 'Treatise' of Walter of Bibbesworth, poetry and prose by Nicholas Bozon, Latin hymns translated into English by Herebert, proverbs, Twici's work on hunting, and an amusing Anglo-Norman poem representing a mother's advice to her daughter on choosing a husband. The dialect of the recipes shows some signs of being that of the south-west midlands, but there are some forms not usually associated with that area, such as 'northern' *qw* for *wh* and *ane* for *one* and occasional 'south-eastern' *z* for initial *s*. Almost all of these culinary manuscripts have some odd mixtures of dialect forms, a notable example being the alternation of *eyren* with *egges* in a sizeable section of Douce 257. In general, however, they all seem to be written in what is basically a south-west midlands dialect. For full information on Add. 46919, see Paul Meyer, 'Notice et Extraits du MS. 8336 de la Bibliothèque de Sir Thomas Phillips à Cheltenham', *Romania* xiii (1884), 497-541; B. Schofield, 'The Manuscript of a Fourteenth Century Oxford Franciscan', *British Museum Quarterly* xvi (1952), 36-7; and the British Library *Catalogue of Additions to the Manuscripts 1946-1950*. (Note that catalogue descriptions of most of the other manuscripts used for this edition are scanty and, as far as dating is concerned, often of dubious accuracy.)

[3] i.e., the earliest MS of the work known as *Le Viandier de Taillevent*. This MS, which dates from *c.*1300, was published by Paul Aebischer, 'Un manuscrit valaisan du "Viandier" attribué à Taillevent', *Vallesia*, viii (1953), 73-100.

same dish. To give just one example, here are recipes for a popular dish which reappears in most later collections, from both sources (translations which follow are those of C. B. H.):

1. (French) *Brouet d'Alemagne*, de char de connins ou de poullale. Despeciez, metez surfrire en saing et oignuns menus; affinez amendez grant foison destrempez de vin et de boullon de beuef; faitez boullir avec vostre grain; affinez gingenbre, canelle, grene de paradis, girofle, nois mugetez; soit sur jaune, liant, deffait de verjus (of rabbit flesh or chicken. Cut into pieces and sauté in fat with minced onions. Draw up plenty of almonds with wine and beef bouillon, and put this to boil with your meat. Season with ginger, cinnamon, grain of paradise, cloves, nutmeg; it should be yellow, thick, with verjuice added.)

2. (English) *Bruet de Alemayne*. Milke of alemauns, itried clouwes de gylofree, quibibes, oyngnones ifried: & schal beon hot of clouwes & of quibibes; þe colour schal beon ȝoelu (milk of almonds, select cloves, cubebs, fried onions: and it shall be hot with cloves and cubebs. The colour should be yellow.)

The latter brief note does not spell out nearly as much of the procedure as does the French recipe, nor does it specify any meat or meat substitute to be put in the sauce. Evidently, this is a memorandum for cooks who know what kind of meat goes into a 'Bruet de Alemayne' and how to prepare it before adding the sauce. The five spices prescribed by the French recipe are reduced to two, but the cook is directed to add enough of these strong spices to make the effect *hot*. Most of the early French recipes simply call for an unspecified quantity of the same four or five spices, with no suggestion of fine discrimination in seasonings between recipes; the English ones, on the other hand, indicate significant differences. In contrast to the hot and sugarless 'Bruet de Alemayne', 'Maumenee' was to be spiced only with cloves, with sugar 'to abate the strength of the spice'. Ginger, balanced by sugar, is the only seasoning of several dishes, but 'Bruet Sarazineys Blanc' was to be highly seasoned with 'great plenty of ginger', without any sugar to soften its impact, while 'Bruet Salmene', which included galingale, cinnamon, and cloves, as well as ginger, required 'great plenty of sugar to abate the strength of the spices'.

The earliest English recipes, then, are terse, leaving a great deal up to the cook's basic knowledge, but nevertheless precise and discriminating in directions for seasoning and colouring.

As these recipes were passed down through succeeding genera-
tions, however, there was a tendency to spell out procedures
at greater and greater length and to add and/or vary ingredients. This process can be illustrated by some versions of the
originally Anglo-Norman favourite, 'Mawmenny', over a
period of somewhat more than a century.

(1) MS He, c.1325. Maumenee. Wyn; braun of chapoun ipolled al to
poudre, & soþþen do þryn to boillen wiþ þe wyn; alemauns igrounden
al druȝe & idon þryn, & poudre of clowes idon þryn; alemauns ifried
schulen beon idon þryn, & þer schal gret vlehs beon igrounden, & sucre
fort abaten þe streynþe of þe specerie; þe colour schal beon inde.

'Gret vlehs', the 'grosse char' of contemporary French collections, generally means boiled beef, pork, or mutton. Thus,
this recipe calls for ground, boiled meat, to be served in a
wine-based sauce thickened with finely ground capon meat
and almonds, seasoned with cloves and sugar—which means
mildly seasoned—with fried almonds added, no doubt for
flavour and texture.

(2) Bodl. MS Douce 257 (D), 1381. For to make maumene, tak þe
þyys oþer þe flesch of þe caponys. Seþe hem & kerf hem smal into a
morter & tak mylk of almandys wyþ broth of fresch buf, & do þe
flesch in þe mylk or in þe broth & do yt to þe fyre, & myng yt togedere
wyþ flour of rys oþere of wastelys als charchant als þe Blank de Sure,
& wyþ þe ȝolkys of eyryn for to make yt ȝolow, & safroun. & wan yt
ys dressyd in dysches wyþ Blank de Sure, straw vpon clowys of gelofre
& straw vpon powdre of galentyn, & serue yt forþe.

These directions are spelled out more clearly, making sure
that the capon is precooked, for example. But the capon is
now apparently the only meat in the recipe; beef broth has
been substituted for wine and extra thickening of rice flour
or bread crumbs is needed. The colour is no longer indigo,
but the far more common saffron yellow, and the seasonings,
which eliminate sugar and add 'powdre of galyntyn'—either
a mixed spice powder or a confusion with galingale—are
stronger, but scattered on top of the dish instead of mixed
into the sauce. There is no garnish of fried almonds.

(3) BL MS Add. 5016 (A), c.1425. Mawmenee. Take a potell of wyne
greke and ii pounde of sugur; take and claryfye the sugur with a quantite of wyne & drawe it thurgh a straynour in to a pot of erthe. Take
flour of rys and medle with sum of the wyne & cast togydre. Take

pynes with dates and frye hem a litell in grece oþer in oyle and cast
hem togydre. Take clowes & flour of canel hool and cast þerto. Take
powdour gynger, canel, clowes; colour it with saundres a lytel yf hit be
nede. Cast salt þerto, and lat it seeþ warly with a slowe fyre and not to
thyk. Take brawn of capouns yteysed oþer of fesauntes teysed small
and cast þerto.

This detailed recipe is about twice as long as that of a century earlier. The capon meat, for which pheasant is suggested
as a substitute, is a last-minute addition instead of the basis
of the sauce. Pine nuts and dates are substituted for the fried
almonds: the ground almonds have disappeared completely.
A specific (and large) quantity is specified for the wine, which
is a sweet variety, and for the sugar; ginger and cinnamon
have been added to the original clove spicing. The dish would
obviously be both sweeter and spicier than its predecessors.
And again the colour is changed: this time, the agent recommended is 'saundres', which would give a reddish-orange
effect.

We shall not take the space here to copy the recipe for
'Mawmene' which appears in BL MS Harl. 4016, c.1440.[1] It is
almost twice as long again, but, to summarize: it calls for a
strong, sweet wine with an equal amount of sugar; cinnamon;
pine nuts (not fried), and quinces preserved in sugar; to these
are added cloves, ground almonds, ale, teased flesh of pheasant, partridge or capon (now coming as last choice), with a
final seasoning and colouring of saffron, salt, and vinegar or
strong wine: we are warned to see 'that hit haue sugar right
ynough'. One may well doubt that an early fourteenth-
century diner would have identified this dish as 'Maumenee'.

This is one of many cases in which we can see that the later
the recipe, the sweeter and spicier it tends to be, although
this is not invariably the case. Some later versions are simply
expansions of the original, with or without errors in transcription. An example is a second recipe for 'Mawmenny' in MS
A, obviously a copy of the recipe in MS D, which expands
the recipe by several words but is otherwise fairly faithful to
its source—except for one remarkable scribal error: it renders
þyys 'thighs' as chese 'cheese', an ingredient called for in no
other 'mawmenny' recipe.

---

[1] It is printed in Austen, pp. 88-9.

Paul Aebischer, investigating the successive revisions of the *Viandier* recipes, found just such a tendency for each revision to be a little longer, spelling out procedures more carefully, sometimes suggesting additions or variations and sometimes miscopying the original. Thus, then, the length, wording, and type of ingredients called for can often give the experienced reader clues to the probable date of origin of a medieval French or English recipe, whatever the date of the manuscript in which it appears. It is easy to see, for example, that the recipes in MS Ar, a parchment quarto which probably dates from the second quarter of the fifteenth century, draw on at least two or three different sources, some markedly later than others, when we compare the length and ingredients of various recipes (many of which are repeated as many as three times in different forms), even though this manuscript tends to elaborate even its earliest recipes, specifying, for example, exactly which herbs to use where an earlier version may say 'put good herbes þerto'.

Such features are not, however, invariable tests for the relative dating of recipes. Some of them simply became confused in transmission, rather than elaborated. An example of this phenomenon is a recipe we first meet in MS He as 'Suade', a sauce featuring elderflowers.[1] Later in the same manuscript, after the scribe has switched sources from the collection of MS Ro to that of MS A1, we find an expanded version called 'Suot blanc', which calls for chicken or fish in a sauce of 'þilke floures'. When the same recipe turns up in the early fifteenth-century Bodley MS Laud Misc. 553 (L), it is somewhat shorter, apparently because the scribe did not understand that 'suot' was a form of an Anglo-Norman word for elder and had no idea what flower the recipe called for. The title is given as 'Sweteblanche', which would be unlikely to suggest anything but 'sweet and white' to a fifteenth-century English-speaker, and the flowers called for are 'þe floures of þe rede vyne'—perhaps suggested by the grapes called for as one of the ingredients of 'Suot blanc' in a translation of a

[1] Two thirteenth-century Anglo-Norman glossaries give what must be this word, however spelled, for Latin *sambucus* 'elder': in BL MS Harl. 978, f. 24ᵛ, the gloss is *sueþ*, and Bodl. MS Douce 88 gives *sue*. It appears in other Anglo-Norman MSS variously spelled, e.g. in MS A1 as *suet, sucche*, and *suge*, and in MS Ro as *swade*.

miswritten Anglo-Norman original. 'Suot blanc' tells us that
'these flowers' can be dried for use out of season, as elderflowers still are today, but this information is omitted in the
recipe in MS L—another indication that the scribe did not
know that elderflowers were involved.

A few other differences between fourteenth- and fifteenth-
century English recipes can be identified. Some very early
recipes include dried fruits, such as currants, but these were
usually reserved for fish-day and Lenten recipes. They occur
in the latter in notable abundance, no doubt in compensation
for the dairy products which, in addition to meat, were for-
bidden in Lent at this time. Many more dried fruits crop up
in fifteenth-century recipes (whether or not they are meatless)
and this tendency accelerates in the later sixteenth century,
when fresh and dried fruits seem to be called for in every
other recipe—but especially oranges and lemons, luxuries
new to England at this time.[1]

In general, then, fourteenth-century recipes are somewhat
plainer than later versions. While the recipes for special stews
may seem to call for spices much more frequently than most
modern counterparts would, the earliest recipes rarely call
for more than two or three in a particular dish, and the spices
most frequently called for are just those still in common use
today: pepper, ginger, cinnamon, cloves, nutmeg. Nor do the
extant household records suggest that these spices were used
lavishly or ubiquitously.

In Dame Alice de Bryene's reasonably elegant fifteenth-
century household, the only spice used on a scale which could

---

[1] See, e.g., 'A.W.''s *A Booke of Cookrye With the Serving in of the Table*
(London, 1591; repr. Walter J. Johnson, Inc., Amsterdam and Norwood, N.J.,
1976), where the first five recipes are all for stewed capon, with the following
additions: (1) currants, raisins, dates, onions, prunes, cloves, mace, pepper, verjuice; (2) lemons, white wine, rosewater, sugar, red currants, barberries, marrow,
verjuice, and sugar; (3) broth, verjuice, endive, lettuce or borage, dates, marrow,
cinnamon, orange peel, sugar, egg yolks, prunes; (4) marrow, broth, currants,
dates, prunes, mace, ginger, egg yolks, vinegar, sugar; (5) wine, oranges, cinnamon, sugar, and ginger. That citrus fruits were a very rare luxury indeed in England before the Renaissance may be judged by the fact that they are never called
for in medieval English recipes, and note that when Queen Eleanor of Castile,
homesick for the fruits of her native Spain, sent a ship to bring her some in 1289,
the total citrus cargo consisted of 15 lemons and 7 oranges; cf. John Carmi Par-
sons, *The Court and Household of Eleanor of Castile* (Toronto, 1977), p. 12,
n. 35.

be called lavish is mustard: one and a half bushels of mustard seed were consumed in the course of the year by a household which seemed to have averaged about twenty for meals, although the figures vary according to the number of guests. This is not a surprising amount of mustard for that number of people, since we know from various sources, including recipes, that mustard was a popular sauce for all sorts of food in medieval England. It usually accompanied herring, the principal staple in Lent, and was specified as an appropriate accompaniment for various meats and roast fowls; it was even added to the chutney-like preserve of fruits and vegetables called 'Compost' (modern French *compôte*). Mustard was cheap, since unlike most other spices it did not have to be imported.

The cheapest imported spices were pepper and ginger. Dame Alice paid 1*s.* 4*d.* a pound for ginger and 2*s.* 1*d.* for pepper, while cloves cost 3*s.* 4*d.* and cinnamon 4*s.* 6*d.* (p. 120). But the amounts of these spices actually purchased in the course of a year do not seem overwhelming in comparison with what a modern household would use: for example, five pounds of pepper for twenty people for a year means something like one teaspoon per person per week. Cinnamon, next to pepper the most used spice in Dame Alice's household despite its high price, was consumed at a rate which would allow about two and a half ounces a year per person (p. 104), perhaps in excess of the quantity used by families today, unless they happen to fancy cinnamon toast, but not enormously so.

Nor do the quantities of these spices recorded in Dame Alice's household accounts seem much out of line with those recorded for two rather more extravagant households of the thirteenth-century: those of Eleanor, Countess of Leicester,[1] and Richard de Swinfield, Bishop of Hereford.[2] While it is not as easy to calculate the number of people served in these households, the only item on the 'spice' budget which seems significantly higher for both than for Dame Alice's household almost two centuries later is sugar: for example, the bishop's

[1] See *Manners and Household Expenses of England in the Thirteenth and Fifteenth Centuries*, ed. H. T. Turner (Roxburghe Club, vol. 57, 1841).

[2] See *Roll of the Household Expenses of . . .* , ed. John Webb (Camden Society, OS, vols. 59 and 62, 1853-4).

establishment apparently required one hundred pounds of sugar for the winter, while Dame Alice's household contented itself with one pound for the entire year. While the bishop seems to have fed two or three times the number of people Dame Alice did, the discrepancy is certainly striking. The Countess of Lincoln's use of sugar was, apparently about five times as much per person as that of Dame Alice, but even that is not very much by modern standards. Fifty-five pounds of sugar for a year for an average of about two hundred people means about ¼ pound per person per year, or ½ teaspoon per week.

We may, of course, assume that not everyone got much of a taste of the most elegant and sugary dishes; nevertheless, the consumption of sugar in the thirteenth, fourteenth, and fifteenth centuries was nothing in comparison with modern usage. Figures given in newspapers in 1979 estimated the consumption per person in the US that year as 28 pounds of sugar. More recent Canadian figures are even higher. In early medieval English cookery, sugar was a condiment used to bring out or balance various flavours; sweetness was rarely an end in itself, as it gradually became over the next few centuries—notably with the burgeoning of the well-known Elizabethan sweet-tooth. C. Anne Wilson quotes a visitor to England who 'noted the blackness of Queen Elizabeth's teeth as "a defect the English seem subject to, from their too great use of sugar" '.[1]

In the fourteenth century then, and well into the fifteenth century, most foods were neither extravagantly sweetened nor extravagantly spiced. One recipe in BL MS Sloane 468 (S) specifically warns against overdoing the spices: 'do þerto poudre of coloure & of maces & canel & quibibes, but lok it be noȝt to hot'. The fourteenth-century French *Ménagier de Paris* is full of advice for saving spices, suggesting that 'en toutes sausses et potages lians en quoy l'en broie espices et pain, l'en doit premièrement broïer les espices et oster du mortier, car le pain que l'en broie après, requeut ce qui des espices est demouré' (in all sauces and thickened pottages into which one puts ground spices and bread, one should first grind the spices and remove from the mortar, because the

---

[1] *Food and Drink in Britain* (London, 1973), p. 300.

bread which is ground in it afterwards takes up the spices which remain).[1] Nor does it suggest there is anything dubious about re-using spices: it advises that those which were strained out of jellies, spiced wines, and sauces should be mixed with ground mustard seed and vinegar in making up mustard sauce.[2]

3. MANUSCRIPT SOURCES

In making our final selection of the recipes represented in this collection, we used several criteria. First, we included as a matter of course all sizeable collections early enough to be positively or probably identified as written during the fourteenth century. These include the base manuscripts for Parts I, II, and III, and one or two of the variant manuscripts collated for Part IV, although in the latter case we felt we had to use a somewhat later manuscript for our base because it is the only complete manuscript with a minimum of disruption in the order of recipes, as this order can be observed through a comparative study of the whole group. Second, we included for purposes of collation (and sometimes to fill in obvious gaps) groups of recipes included in later fifteenth-century English collections which are copies of earlier versions or translations of known Anglo-Norman recipes; Bodl. MS Rawlinson D 1222 (R), an extensive (278 recipes) culinary manuscript of the mid-fifteenth century which obviously drew on a number of sources, is a notable example of a collection incorporating some recipes of both types.

In addition, we have included a section (Part V) of isolated recipes or small groups of recipes which appear in fourteenth-century manuscripts *or* which represent dishes we know to have been current in the fourteenth century but which did not happen to occur in any of our basic collections, whether or not the manuscripts in which we found them could be dated as before the end of the first quarter of the fifteenth century. And, before the first section of recipes, we have placed a group of menus of fourteenth-century origin from

---

[1] Ed. Jérôme Pichon (Paris, 1896), vol. 2, p. 87 (translated by C. B. H.).

[2] In England, John Russell's fifteenth-century *Boke of Nurture*, probably based on fourteenth-century materials (in Furnivall's *Babees Book*, p. 128), passes on some equally economical advice in suggesting that the spices strained out of the 'ypocras' be saved for use in the kitchen in various sauces.

Durham MS Cosin v. iii. 11 (C). The first of these, which heads f. 1, is a historical menu for a dinner given by Baron Thomas de Spenser for Richard II, no doubt during the last decade of the fourteenth century, and probably some time around 1397, the year in which de Spenser became Earl of Gloucester. The others are suggestions for appropriate menus for different times of the year, which precede the *Forme of Cury* section of this manuscript (described below, under *d*, Part IV). These same menus also precede the *Forme of Cury* recipes in BL MS Cott. Julius D viii (J), on ff. 90^{r-v}, which has been collated with the MS C version. A few also appear in MS Ar, which has been noted where useful.

a. Part I

Except for the generally miscellaneous section which makes up Part V, the groups of recipes have been arranged in roughly chronological order. Thus Part I is based on MS He, the William Herebert manuscript discussed above. While the recipe section is in another (quite similar) hand, the *Explicit doctrina faciendi diversa cibaria* appears to be in Herebert's own hand. This entire collection, with the exception of three recipes skipped towards the end, also appears in MS J, ff. 104^{r}-109^{r}, ending with the scribal signature 'iohannes feckenam'. J, a small octavo parchment volume, is considerably later than Herebert's manuscript, but we have found it impossible to determine exactly how much later. The hand or hands in which the recipes and the immediately preceding treatise are written (it is difficult to say whether the same scribe wrote both) look typical enough of the first half of the fifteenth century, but some of the other contents of the volume may demand a later date. The volume begins with a treatise entitled 'Godefridus super Palladium', which is followed by one on the cultivation of trees by Nicholas Bollard. We have been unable to identify Godefridus, and the *DNB*'s account of Nicholas Bollard is so vague as to make us wonder whether there is any justification at all for the statement 'fl. 1500'. After the Bollard treatise, the manuscript gives various recipes for making coloured waters (inks and tints) and the like, in the midst of which it rather misleadingly inscribes, on f. 87^{v}, 'Explicit de coloribus' and heads 88^{r} 'De arte

coquinae Anglicae'. Nevertheless, the culinary section does
not start until the menus, which begin on 90^r, as noted above.
There are also two other fifteenth-century manuscripts which
have a handful of recipes from the same collection, MSS L
and R.

Our first resource in collating the collection has, of course,
been the two Anglo-Norman sources described above (in Section 2). The first half is a reasonably accurate translation of
the recipes included in MS Ro, while the thirty-third to forty-
sixth inclusive translate the latter half (roughly) of those in
MS A1 so closely that they mirror its scribal errors. Unfortunately, we have not found any Anglo-Norman sources for the
remaining seventeen recipes, three of which appear in the
base manuscript only, although there are indications that
they, too, must have been translated from a French original:
for example, 'cherries' are called *cerise* in No. 54. The difficulties and confusions in some of these recipes may also
testify that the scribe did not understand them very well.

There is one strong indication that the latter series is
actually from two different sources, for after No. 56 a heading is introduced reading 'To maken diuers potages & metes
& sauen veneson of rastichipe. Her þou miht ywiten þe maner
hou þou schalt maken diuers potages & metes & sauen veneson
of rastichipe & don awy.' Since only seven more recipes follow (six in J), none of which has anything to do with salvaging
spoiled venison, it is not surprising that the J scribe omitted
this heading. Those who are curious to know how one was
supposed to salvage the venison will, however, find the answer
in Part II.

b. *Part II*

The base manuscript of Part II is MS D, ff. 86^r–96^v, first
printed by Samuel Pegge, who evidently then owned the
manuscript, as an addendum to his edition of *The Forme of
Cury*[1] under the title of 'Ancient Cookery'. This parchment

[1] London, 1790. Both parts of Pegge's volume were reprinted by Richard Warner in *Antiquitates Culinariae: Tracts on Culinary Affairs of the Old English* (London, 1791), a work further discussed below (under 3d) which contains all the
collections we have used or consulted which have been previously printed, with
the exception of the Anglo-Norman recipes in MS Ro, which, as noted above,
were edited by Paul Meyer in 1893, and a few from L printed by Austin.

volume, written—apparently continuously—in one hand, seems to be a sort of commonplace-book of a man of far-ranging interests, for aside from recipes it contains (among other entries) various mathematical and calendrical treatises, riddling verses, and practical jokes, most of which, apart from the recipes, are in Latin. One of its sections, the 'Massa Computi' of Alexander de Villa Dei, concludes with a date which is certainly approximately correct for the manuscript as a whole:

Anno domini M^{lo}CCC^{mo} Octogesimo primo ip[s]o die felicis & audacti

—i.e., 1381. The feast of SS. Felix and Audactus is August 30.[1]

While there is no one manuscript which parallels the contents of the Douce recipes throughout, there are three which give lengthy groups in the same order and in almost identical wording, interspersed with other material, and others which give some recognizable recipes from this source. One such which we have not collated for this part is the two manuscripts of *The Forme of Cury* (Part IV) which include a group of three recipes almost word-for-word as they appear in MS D. The manuscript which gives the largest number of these recipes is New York Public Library MS Whitney 1 (W). This small vellum culinary volume, which appears to be of the first half of the fifteenth century, includes about a third of the D recipes (ff. 12–14^v), mostly from the earlier part. Bodl. MS Ashmole 1444 (As), pp. 190-2, a fragment of a paper manuscript from the end of the fourteenth century, bound with other, mostly medical, fragments, duplicates much of the first quarter of the collection but has only one recipe from the later section. We have taken our title for this volume from the *incipit* to MS As, which suggests the novelty—in the fourteenth century—of culinary recipes (*cury*) in the English language.

[1] Cf. M. B. Parkes, *English Cursive Book Hands, 1250-1500* (Oxford, 1969), p. 2, which reproduces a segment of an earlier folio of this MS, and the *Summary Catalogue of Western MSS. in the Bodleian Library at Oxford*, 21831. Many of the collections of medieval recipes are to be found in miscellaneous collections like this one; among those consulted for this volume which include recipes among many other sorts of entries are MSS Ro, Al, Ar, and National Library of Wales, Aberystwyth MS Peniarth 394 D (P). Otherwise recipes are most typically to be found in conjunction with herbals and related matters, as is the case with MS L, or medical recipes, as in BL MSS S and S1 (Sloane 374) and Bodl. MS C. C. C. F 291.

Other manuscripts which have some groups of the same family of recipes include BL MS Sloane 1108 (S2), a manuscript written in a cramped Anglicana hand probably in the very early fifteenth century; this is an interesting manuscript, apart from its fragmentary relationship to D, both because it includes a number of recipes which are unusually close to those found in contemporary French sources, such as a dish called 'Sturgyn' made from veal and calves' feet, and because someone has headed f. 22^r, in a hand not that of the scribe of the recipes, 'hony soyte que mally pens'. If it is proper to speak of 'Garter' poems (*Sir Gawain and the Green Knight*, and so forth), then S2 is in some sense a 'Garter' recipe collection. A number of D recipes are also found in MS L, BL MS Sloane 442 (S3), and Peniarth 394 D (P), a fifteenth-century manuscript which contains, among its miscellaneous contents, a recipe collection which is basically *The Forme of Cury* but mixes in groups of recipes from other sources, including MS D.

c. *Part III*

Part III consists of another distinctive, if brief, collection which has as its base manuscript MS S, ff. 80^r-92^r, a vellum octavo volume of the late fourteenth or possibly very early fifteenth century. There is no particular reason to think that this collection pre-dates the prototype of Part IV, but, since the manuscript itself is at least as early as any in the group drawn on for Part IV, it seemed appropriate to place it first. Except for the first four recipes, it is more or less exactly duplicated in BL MS Sloane 374 (S1), which probably dates from the second quarter of the fifteenth century. A few of the recipes are also found in the first of the two recipe sections of MS C, ff. 1-25^v, a section which appears to have been written early in the fifteenth century. While this manuscript group contains some of the inevitable standard fourteenth-century dishes such as 'Viaunde de Cypre' and 'Mawmene'— to the latter eccentrically adding ground figs and raisins—it is interesting in preserving recipes which do not seem to appear elsewhere, such as 'Pyany' (a poultry dish garnished with peonies)[1] and 'Heppee' (rose-hip broth).

---

[1] There is literary evidence for the culinary use of peonies in both *Piers Plowman* and *Pearl*: in the latter, 'pyonys' are among the 'spryngande spycez' of the

d. Part IV

Part IV consists of the most famous and extensive collection of the fourteenth century—the only one, aside from MS D's collection which is here Part II, to have been printed before —*The Forme of Cury*, 'the (proper) method of cookery'. The manuscript which is the only one actually to contain this title, MS A, was printed by Samuel Pegge in 1780, then re-edited by Richard Warner in 1791 without reference to the manuscript, which he wrongly stated had been lost. The title is taken from a headnote in the vellum scroll, which reads:

[The?] forme of cury was compiled of the chef Maister Cokes of kyng Richard the Se[cu]nde kyng of [En]glond aftir the Conquest . the which was acounted þe best and ryallest vyaund[ier] of alle cristen [k]ynges. And it was compiled by assent and auysement of Maisters and [i.e., of] phisik and of philosophie þat dwellid in his court. First it techiþ man for to˙make commune potages and commune mettis for howshold as þey shold be made craftly and holsomely. Aftirwa[rd] it techiþ for to make curious potages & meetes and sotiltees for alle manere of states both h[y]e and lowe. And the techyng of the fourme of makyng of potages & of meetes bot[he] of flessh and of fissh . buth ysette here by noumbre and by ordre . so þis litle table [he]re sewyng wole teche a man with oute taryyng: to fynde what meete þat hym lust for to haue.[1]

Other sources of information suggest that Richard was in-deed a royal 'vyaundier' on a grand scale: Stow's Annals claim that wherever he was, 'his person was guarded by 200 men; he had about him thirteen bishops, besides barons, knights, esquires, and others; insomuch as that the Household came every day to meat 10,000 people'.[2] This may sound suspiciously exaggerated, but actually if one calculates the number of people who would have been provided for on a daily basis according to the figures given for the household

garden where the poem opens (l. 44), and cf. *Piers Plowman* B. V. 311–13: ' "Has tow auȝte in thi purs . any hote spices?" / "I have peper and piones," quod she, "and a pounde of garlike, / A ferthyngworth of fenelseed for fastyngdayes." '

[1] Letters in brackets indicate places where it is difficult or impossible to read all letters. The upper left-hand corner of the MS has been torn (or worn) away; thus the first word is now missing, as are the first letters of 'Englond' and 'kynges', which start, respectively, the second and third lines of the MS. Small rips have been mended with tape, which has darkened and made it very difficult to decipher the words underneath.

[2] Cited in *Household Ordinances*, p. viii.

ordinances of Edward IV, that household also could not have
been much short of 10,000. In the same household ordinances,
we are told of the important duties of the 'Doctoure of Phy-
sique', who must counsel the king and his cooks as to what
dishes will suit the king best, although it is difficult to believe
that medieval medical theories about food would have been
of much help. Theory of the day was much given to sympa-
thetic magic: eggs, for example, were thought to 'augment
sperma and incite copulation'.[1]

The Table of Contents which follows this introductory
note is only partially legible today, but it had apparently not
disintegrated nearly as much in Pegge's time, much less half
a century earlier when Thomas Hearne transcribed the manuscript.[2] It should be noted, however, that the spelling of
recipe-titles within the roll is not always the same as in the
Table of Contents, and Pegge often chose to use the table-
titles rather than those which appear above each recipe. This
led him into several errors, most notably reversing the titles
of recipes 160 and 161 (168 and 169 in this edition) and
giving the last two recipes the same title, although all recipes
are correctly titled within the roll.

After the last recipe—No. 196 in the editions of Pegge
and Warner (our 204)—appears the word '[E]xplicit'. But
there is also a signed memorandum at the foot of the roll
(verso of membrane 4; there are eight membranes in all)
which reads:

Antiquum hoc monumentum oblatum et missum est
majestati vestræ vicesimo septimo die mensis Julij,
anno regno vestri fælicissimi vicesimo viij ab
humilimo vestro subdito, vestræq. majestati
fidelissimo

E^D Stafford
Hæres domus subversæ Buckinghamiens.

That is, Edward, 3rd Baron Stafford, presented the roll to
Queen Elizabeth on 27 July 1586. Hearne's testimony suggests

[1] *The Science of Dining: a Medieval Treatise on the Hygiene of the Table*,
trans. Arthur Way (London, 1936), p. 19; this is a tract attributed to Michael
Scott, who is buried in Melrose Abbey (d. 1250). Among his other invaluable
hints are that cabbage 'banishes intoxication' (p. 27).
[2] This transcript is Bodl. MS Rawlinson D 194.

that in his day the roll was in the possession of Edward Harley, who loaned it to him in 1727; at all events, it was even-
tually purchased by Brander, who presented it to the British
Museum in 1782.

Apparently no one who saw the roll in the eighteenth century knew that there were parallel manuscripts, even though
one of those parallels is a Harley manuscript, and the methods
of work of the early editors were, unfortunately, not as con-
ducive to accuracy as they might have been. While Pegge
knew Hearne had seen the manuscript (see p. xi of his introduction), he apparently did not know of, or did not have
access to, the Hearne transcript, which often has better readings than Pegge's own. Pegge himself must have worked from
another transcript, made by either himself or Brander, for he
did not correct flaws he himself pointed out in his text which
could easily have been rectified if he had had recourse to the
manuscript: see, for example, his notes to recipes 75 and 125
(his numbers 73 and 122). His edition of the manuscript then
in his own possession, now Douce 257, is somewhat more
accurate than that of *The Forme of Cury*.

Warner's edition of a decade later was not based on any
work with manuscripts at all. He simply copied Pegge's text
of *The Forme of Cury* and 'Ancient Cookery', and added, to
round out his volume, the text of MS Ar, which had been
printed by the Society of Antiquaries as an appendix to
Household Ordinances the year before (1790)—erroneously
labelled 'Arundel 344'. That Warner's sources for all his
recipes were these two printed volumes is made obvious by
his invariable reproduction of their typographical and other
errors, including the misnumbering of MS Ar—to which, of
course, he added errors of his own. He evidently did not compare the samples of manuscript facsimile Pegge had reproduced
against the printed texts; if he had looked carefully at the
manuscript version of 'Mawmenny' which appeared in Pegge's
introduction—and which he reprinted in his own edition—
he could have noticed that Pegge (or his printer) had neglected
to transcribe the words 'and grynde hem smale' in the sentence which, in the facsimile and manuscript, reads 'Take the
chese and of flessh of capouns . or of hennes & hakke smal *and
grynde hem smale* in a morter.' While all editors and proof-

readers will sympathize with this classic instance of a phrase dropped presumably because someone's eye skipped from one instance of 'small' to the next, it is distinctly odd that an editor who had no access to the manuscript itself did not check the bit of facsimile available to him. Perhaps Warner was not accustomed to the hands of the period concerned; while he appended some other small items of fourteenth- or fifteenth-century material to the end of his book, all had been previously printed.

For the general reader, Warner's edition is no doubt the easier to read. He expanded the contractions, substituted Arabic for Roman numerals, and put in many parenthetical glosses on the meanings of titles or culinary terms. Unfortunately, the majority of these glosses are simply guesses, often wildly wrong. For example, Warner glosses a dish called 'Corance' as 'currants', although there is nothing faintly resembling a currant in the recipe, and thought that 'ew ardaunt' was 'hot water'—which would have been a very peculiar substance to pour over a pastry castle (see Part IV, No. 197). Warner also added a lengthy introduction on culinary history, but his edition remains of no particular utility to a modern editor.

Pegge's edition and Hearne's transcript are still useful because both men saw the manuscript before it had degenerated to its present condition. We have accepted most of Pegge's readings of words which are no longer legible, especially when these are confirmed by Hearne's independent and earlier transcription. Even in the matter of glossing, both are reasonably helpful since much of the now archaic vocabulary was still in use in the eighteenth century. But neither Hearne (who abandoned his glossary after the tenth recipe) nor Pegge can be entirely trusted. For one thing, it is to be doubted that either had much first-hand experience of kitchen procedures. Hearne, for example, unaccountably glosses the verb *dyce* 'dice, cut into small pieces' as 'dish'. Pegge was more inclined to cite authorities rather than venture wild guesses, but his authorities were rarely earlier than the seventeenth century, and the nature of many dishes which had retained old names had changed drastically by then.

One thing which has never been challenged since these early

editions of *The Forme of Cury* is the manuscript attribution
to the cooks of Richard the Second. For this reason, the
manuscript itself has generally been assigned a date in the
1390s. While this seems a reasonable date for the origin of
the basic compilation, a close examination of this vellum roll
itself makes it quite clear that it did not originate in the fourteenth century. The hand is most likely one of the end of the
first quarter of the fifteenth century. It would thus seem that
this, the only manuscript with the attribution to Richard's
cooks, is—as John Hodgkin had already suggested in 1913
—a late copy of an original which could have been compiled
as early as 1390.[1] And indeed this is only one of a number of
copies. We have consulted seven others in preparing our text
for this edition.

Two of the most closely related versions lack their begin-
nings, so we can never know whether they also contained the
attribution. The copy which is closest to MS A is a remark-
ably similar vellum recipe roll of about the same date, or
somewhat earlier, now in the possession of Dr Curt Bühler of
the Morgan Library, New York. This manuscript is known as
Bühler 36 (B). It now lacks at least one membrane at the
beginning of the roll, and what is left of the first now remaining is in very poor condition. The first few partly-readable
recipes, which begin with the one numbered 17 in MS A, are
partially disintegrated. It is not until after No. 20 that a
really close adherence to MS A can be observed. But from
there on it is very close indeed, following the same numbering, until B skips one recipe. The order of the recipes is the
same except for two reversals (89/90, 168/69), and the spelling and wording are almost identical.

In a number of cases B's readings are clearly superior to
A's, as when in No. 119 B tells us to boil the wheat until it
is tender and 'brokene', while A thinks it ought to be tender
and 'broun'. One does not 'brown' wheat by boiling it: this
is one example, among many, of scribal confusion of *k* and
w (see, e.g., IV 181). But sometimes A had a necessary element which is omitted in B, as is the case in No. 169, 'Sawgeat'. Both are evidently wrong in some cases, as in No. 100,

---

[1] Notes to *A Proper Newe Booke of Cokerie*, ed. Catherine Frances Frere
(Cambridge, 1913), p. 95.

where they tell us to take 'meal' or 'oatmeal' and pick out the stones: a puzzling direction indeed if we did not have another group of manuscripts to make it clear that fruits, probably dates, were intended, rather than oatmeal. Clearly, these two manuscripts were copied from the same original, making their own independent mistakes.

There is one possible indication that the lost original was in better condition when B was copied than when the A version was written. Something was clearly damaged or illegible in that original's version of No. 161, for both the A and B scribes left gaps indicating that there were words they could not read, but the gaps are far more extensive in A. It is, then, rather likely that B is an earlier copy. It is probably not the earliest copy we have, however—only the earliest copy of a particular version which was not itself the 'original' collection. What is possibly the earliest extant manuscript is a partial copy lacking both the beginning and a small part of the end in BL MS Harl. 1605, Part 3 (H). This elegantly decorated parchment manuscript, which is now ff. 98–118ʳ of a bound quarto, probably dates from around 1400; a page from it is reproduced in our frontispiece. That this group of recipes is only a fragment of the original manuscript is evident in the fact that the first page begins with the tail end of a sentence. This sentence can be easily identified as the end of the *Forme of Cury*'s recipe for 'Rosee', No. 53, since it is immediately followed by the title, and recipe, of No. 54, 'Cormary' (a recipe found *only* in the *Forme of Cury* collections). The recipe for 'Rosee' in A ends, 'If þou wilt in stede of almaunde mylke, take swete crem of kyne', and the words which appear just before the title 'Cormary' in MS H are *crem of cyne*.

What follows in H is, in general, the rest of *The Forme of Cury* (unnumbered), in the same order and in similar wording—though not so similar that it could be a copy of the same original from which A and B were copied. For example, A and B constantly direct one to pour the sauce *onoward*, where H suggests you pour it *aboue*. Other minor differences include deletions, possibly made for the sake of format of the pages; in one case, two recipes are amalgamated in the AB version but divided into two in H; H prefers *foules* where A and B give *briddes*. However, these and other similar small deviations are of less importance than the small but significant differences in recipes included: H interpolates, here and there, five recipes which do not appear in A or B. On the other hand, H omits two groups of recipes which are in both A and B, Nos. 116–21 and 198–204, as well as one isolated recipe, No. 138, 'Colde Brewet'.

When we look carefully at the recipes omitted in H, we can see that a good many of them duplicate recipes given elsewhere in A and B. 'Colde Brewet' is the second recipe of that title, although there are some differences between it and the earlier recipe of the same name, No. 135: that is, the later recipe appears to be an elaboration, spelling out the sauce at greater length and directing that meat be added, which may simply have been assumed in the earlier case. Of the group 116–21 in A and B, three are versions of recipes elsewhere in the collection (although never exact duplicates): No. 116, 'Flaumpeyns', anticipates No. 192, 'Flampoyntes'; No. 120, 'Fylettes in galyntyne', is similar to No. 30, of the same title; No. 121, 'Veel in Buknade', recalls No. 19, 'Bukkenade'. Thus, it may well be suspected that these recipes are later additions, added to the prototype of A and B but not in the 'original' from which H also stems.

Further evidence that the source of A and B added recipes which did not belong to the original collection may be found in the second large group omitted in H, Nos. 198–204. Again, three of the recipes repeat ones found in another version elsewhere in the manuscript: Nos. 200, 'Blank maunger', 201, 'Blank desire', and 202, 'Mawmenny', represent recipes that were already given, in slightly different versions, in Nos. 38, 39, and 22. And the source of A and B's Nos. 200–2 is easy to see: these are fairly close copies of the recipes which appear in MS D, Nos. 33, 29, and 30. It has already been remarked above (p. 10) that a remarkable error creeps into the transcription of one of these recipes, but the point remains that all three of them are taken from a different collection and are unnecessary in that they duplicate recipes already in the basic collection represented in H—in so far as H can be checked in these cases: since it lacks its beginning, it cannot have the earlier recipes—as well as A and B; it seems likely that they, and at least some, if not all, of the other recipes to be found in A and B only were not part of the original compilation from which *The Forme of Cury* derives.

While H, then, is copied from a source, probably earlier, which did not have the recipes which can be suspected of being late intrusions into the *Forme of Cury* collection, it is interesting that it has the same reversals in the order of recipes as B, when compared with A. This may again suggest that A often represents its source less well than B. That the source of H was indeed earlier may be implicit in the form of some of its recipe titles, which often seem much closer to what must have been French models. For example, H uses 'bruet' and 'browet' for *Fr. brouet* where A and B invariably give 'brewet'. H is particularly enlightening in some cases where the titles of A and B are so far from their etymological roots as to be puzzling and misleading: for example, No. 184 is a recognizable version of a recipe known in French sources as *hericons* or *herissons*, and in later English manuscripts, such as BL MS Harl. 279, as 'Yrchouns': these are an elaborate variety of sausage made to look like hedgehogs, called 'urchins' in Britain. But one might never know this from the titles given in A and B, which misreadings have corrupted to 'Hert rowce': we thus preferred to use H's 'Hirchones'.

None of this is to say that H represents the original from which the source of A and B derived. That does not seem possible, considering some of the instances in which A and B have obviously better readings. We would suggest, rather, that H represents a second version of the earlier compilation from which A and B stem, and is the earliest example of a 'family' of *Forme of Cury* manuscripts to which belong all other examples we have seen. The fullest of these examples, and closest to A and B as well as to H, are MSS C, ff. 61^v-72^v,[1] and J, ff. 90^v-104^r,[2] which are very obviously copies of the

---

[1] Someone at a later period noted that the recipes in C, ff. 61^r-72^r, corresponded to those in *The Forme of Cury* as published by Pegge and Warner, and added the Pegge numbers to the recipes, in the margins, in what appears to be a nineteenth-century hand. Where this recipe section ends, on f. 72^r, the scribe wrote: 'Nunc scripsi totum per christo da mihi potem'—'Now I have written it all; for Christ's sake give me a drink.'

[2] At the end of the *Forme of Cury* recipes in J, the scribe wrote, 'AMEN. johannes'. But he was evidently not as fatigued as the C scribe, for he continued

same rather confused original. That is, in both C and J large
groups of recipes are transposed to positions other than those
they occupy in the sequence of all other *Forme of Cury*
manuscripts. But the situation is further complicated by the
peculiarities of each manuscript. MS C, for example, not only
has gaps but inserts a group of non-culinary recipes and
charms right after recipe No. 178, which is No. 140 in C.
While their wording and various peculiarities are more or less
the same throughout, and while they share a recipe, 'Vertesaus
broun' (No. 148), which occurs in no other manuscript here,
the two manuscripts have some quite independent errors
which indicate that neither was copied from the other. In
'Crytayne', No. 61, for example, J has a unique classic error
where a scribe's eye has passed from one instance of the word
ȝolkes to the next, omitting all in between.

The ultimate, if not immediate, source of C and J was
most certainly also the source of H and of the *Forme of Cury*
recipes in MS P, pp. 41–90 and 119–20, and very probably of
those in MSS W, ff. 1–12, and Ar, pp. 275–444. The latter
two usually agree with the group HCJP against AB, but unfortunately, we cannot apply our best test cases against either
because they lack the key recipes, which are Nos. 160 and
178: in these two recipes, there are copyist's errors which are
shared by H, C, J, and P. In the first case, A and B read, quite
plausibly, 'Take powdour fort, brede igrated, & safroun, and
cast þerto a gode quantite of buttur. . . .' The others substitute for 'cast þerto' ȝest 'yeast', which would be quite out of
place in this pie filling: no doubt 'cast' or 'kest' was misread
as 'yest'. In 178, 'Tartes of fysshe', H, C, J, and P skip a large
part of a sentence which happens to come between two uses
of the word 'fyssh': again, the classic copyist's error. It would,
then, seem plain, from their common errors, that these manuscripts share a source, which is not that of A and B.

MS W is a fairly careless copy—continually skipping over
phrases or sentences, then adding them later—of what must
have been a good original of the 'H' group, as far as it goes,
but its coverage is capricious. It has no recipes of *The Forme
of Cury* after No. 139, and has skipped over individual

at once, hardly skipping a line, to begin the collection which has been collated
with MS He in Part I of this volume.

recipes and groups of recipes a number of times before that
point. While the recipes of MS P are mostly from *The Forme
of Cury*, much other material is mixed in; and Ar intersperses
groups of *Forme of Cury* recipes, usually in their normal
order, with recipes from other sources, which gradually
prevail and completely take over towards the end of the
collection. C is probably at least as early as H, and may date
from the late fourteenth century; W, as remarked above
(under Section 3*b*), appears to be of the first half of the fifteenth century. The other three manuscripts are also relatively
late, dating from the second quarter of the fifteenth century
or somewhat later. While all of these manuscripts have affini-
ties with H, and with each other, it does not seem possible to
trace any really exact relationships beyond the common
originals of H and the five related manuscripts, except for the
special relationship of C and J. Since this is as far as we can
safely go in tracing family groups, we shall venture a putative
stemma of all groups at this point:

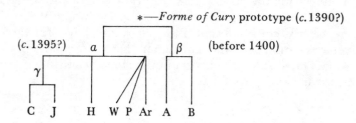

A remarkable fact about the *alpha* group is that each of
the five extra recipes represented in H appears in two or three
of the others, and not always the same two or three, generally
in the H order. This does not necessarily mean that these
recipes belonged in the prototype (*) any more than do those
which appear in A and B only, which we suspect of being
interlopers; but the case for including the five in a complete
edition of *The Forme of Cury* is as good as—in fact better
than—any for including the isolated recipes of the *beta* group.
An example in support of this view is the recipe for 'Malaches',
which, in H, C, J, and P (at a point where W has stopped
giving *Forme of Cury* recipes), precedes the variants 'Malaches
Whyte' and 'Malaches of Pork'. The two variants appear in

A and B (called 'Mylates'): is it not more logical to have a base recipe first? Further, all manuscripts of the *alpha* group, with the sole exception of H (which, it will be recalled, lacks its first third or so), start with a recipe for 'Frumente'; and all but W—which skips over several recipes at this point—give as second recipe 'Blaunche porre'. Considering that the first reference to 'furmente' in MSS A and B says 'make furmente as bifore' (No. 70, 'Furmente with porpays'), it would appear that the *alpha* group represents the prototype of both groups correctly in beginning with 'Frumente'.

We have, therefore, begun *The Forme of Cury* with 'Frumente' and proceeded to include all recipes from both the *alpha* and *beta* groups, even the recipe which appears only in C and J and is the most suspect of all.[1] This means that we could not follow the sequence of numbers familiar to users of the Pegge and Warner editions and the many reference works which use the same numbers; we have therefore added those numbers in parentheses in the table of contents after our own numbers for the appropriate recipes. We have also sometimes chosen to use titles from the *alpha* group where the A titles are clearly confused and misleading, and have, for the convenience of those who have come across such A titles elsewhere, cross-referenced them in the glossary and index section at the back of the volume.

e. Part V

Part V is, as remarked above, a miscellaneous collection of early recipes and others we know to have been current in the fourteenth century, from various sources. The first item is from Bodl. MS Ashmole 1393, a small octavo volume of fragments from a number of different fifteenth-century manuscripts; the fragmentary cookery section appears in ff. 19^v–22^r. Of this, we have included only a group of 'notes', general kitchen hints which certainly apply to medieval cookery in general but are nowhere so clearly set forth as here.

[1] One omission may be considered an exception to this rule. A recipe for 'Elus in sorray' appears in MSS W, P, and Ar, in the same position in relation to *Forme of Cury* recipes in all three. But since these manuscripts are all very much mixtures of *Forme of Cury* material with recipes from entirely different sources, we did not think this constituted sufficient evidence that this recipe was ever included in an independent *Forme of Cury* collection, and have relegated it to a note.

These notes are here followed by two fourteenth-century recipes for 'Formete' (furmenty) and 'Amydoun', written crosswise on f. 72ᵛ of BL MS Royal 8 B iv in a fourteenth-century hand. The writer added the title of another recipe, 'Sank de Sarasyn', but did not continue with the recipe. The 'Amydoun' recipe is very close to one given in Part I from MS He, translating one in MS A1. The title 'Sank de Sarasyn' is close to the spelling for that recipe in MS L, 'Sang saraser'— and MS L has a number of dishes of Anglo-Norman origin. We therefore think these two recipes are probably of very early origin, and their wording does nothing to cast doubt on that view.

The next group is a collection of recipes for common drinks of the period, taken from BL MS Royal 17 A iii, a late fourteenth-century medical collection, through which are scattered these and other, similar, drink recipes. Medical collections often included drinks and confections, and thus the group following drinks—recipes for various confections— also comes from a medical manuscript, BL MS Harl. 2378, of the late fourteenth or early fifteenth century.

Gingerbread, which Chaucerians will recall refreshed Sir Thopas, came in two kinds in the fourteenth century. The most usual type is more a confection than a cake, and is probably the kind called for as a garnish in Part I's 'Viaunde de Cypre' (No. 28). Our recipe for this type is taken from the medical section of MS S, described above (under 3c) as base manuscript for Part III. The more cake-like gingerbread, which has a base of bread crumbs (a recipe which persists in much later versions and is undoubtedly the ancestor of our modern gingerbread), comes here from BL MS Sloane 121, another primarily medical manuscript of the late fourteenth or early fifteenth century. The recipe is collated with the almost identical ones in MSS S1 and As, the latter of which was used for collation with D (Part II), as remarked above (under 3b); the gingerbread recipe comes, characteristically, from the earlier, medical section.

We have included the recipe for 'Stewed colops' from MS R because collops are referred to several times in fourteenth-century literature, including *Piers Plowman*: see the entry in the glossary. And, as has been remarked above, this manuscript, although it dates from the middle of the fifteenth century, includes some recipes of very early origin including the next two printed here. 'Sawge' and 'Mynceleek', both of which translate recipes in the Anglo-Norman MS A1. 'Saugee' and 'Mincebek' are both in the early part of the collection in the latter manuscript, none of which appears in MS He: therefore neither of these recipes will be found in Part I. Later versions, however, occur in *The Forme of Cury* and will be found in Part IV, Nos. 31, 'Pygges in sawse sawge', and 181, 'Nysebek', a recipe which would be unclear in the A and B versions if we did not have the other *Forme of Cury* manuscripts and this older version to correct them.

The recipe for 'Chinche', junket, comes from a fifteenth-century manuscript, Bodl. MS C. C. C. F 291, which was the earliest English source we could find for this dish, one certainly eaten in the fourteenth century. Finally, we have included 'Sturgyn' from MS S2, discussed above (under 3*b*) in relation to its use for collation in Part II, and 'A Disshe mete for sumere' from MS Ar as representing English translations of dishes found in fourteenth-century continental French sources.

4. VARIANTS AND EDITORIAL PRINCIPLES

In choosing which manuscript variants should be used in place of base manuscript readings, we have often had to make editorial decisions for culinary reasons, as in the case of the frumenty recipe mentioned above in which MS A wrongly tells us to boil the wheat until it is *brown*, as against B's more sensible *brokene*. And in choosing base texts for recipes in Part IV which do not appear in MS A, we have preferred H to C and J because it is probably older and certainly closer to A and B in its spellings, and C over J on the grounds that it is older. H is often also more carefully pointed, which can be of great assistance in indicating the meaning of a phrase or clause.

To give all variants for all recipes, especially those in the long and well-documented *Forme of Cury* section, would have been expensive, and extremely tedious for the reader. We have tried to give enough variants to indicate manuscript relationships and have, therefore, given some which are—

while insignificant in meaning—constant and characteristic variants, such as A and B's 'onoward' as against HCJ 'aboue' in Part IV, on first and sometimes second occurrence, but ignored them thereafter. We have tried to give every variant that may conceivably affect meaning, but have completely ignored such differences as '& grynde it' for 'ygrounde' and slight re-arrangements of a sentence in variants where these matters are obviously of no significance. We have occasionally given such relatively insignificant variants as 'in peces' for 'to gobettes', but only in a few instances, and we have not noted at all such minor matters as 'þeruppon' for 'uppon þem' or 'canel & ginger' for 'ginger & canel'.

We have also omitted many routine variant spellings, including them only when they might be useful, as for example, the variants *eurose/ewerose* for 'rose-water'. (Note, by the way, that Pegge's reading of 'curose' for this word in *The Forme of Cury* (No. 179) was simply a misreading.) Among the types of variants we have completely ignored are those of such non-crucial words as *togeder/togedre/togider/togedere*, giving only such spellings as appeared in our base texts. In the glossary section, we have listed many typical examples, but omitted most of the variants which are common and predictable (see headnote to glossary section) and all words which should be easily recognizable to readers of Modern English.

Emendations to the base texts, all of which are indicated in the textual notes, are printed without brackets or italics. Manuscript abbreviations have been silently expanded, so that the reader will find 'wiþ' and 'with', but not 'wíth', for the most usual manuscript form (w^t). In cases where there are several possibilities (-*es, -is, -ys*, for example), we have tried to select the form testified to elsewhere as normal for the base manuscript. Word divisions have been regularized, without resort to the use of hyphens, for words which are sometimes one, sometimes two, in the manuscripts, as 'thereto', 'ysoden'. And we have ignored MS *j* for *i*, spelling the vowel as *i* (or, when our source's usual spelling for the vowel is *y, y*), but transcribed *u* and *v* according to scribal use in the manuscripts. Scribal 3 has been retained except in cases where it clearly represents *z*.

All recipe numbers are editorially added, except in the case of Part IV, the numbering of which is explained above. Punctuation is also purely editorial, although we have been guided as much as possible by manuscript pointing where this was helpful, as it often was in MSS H and A especially. In many cases, however, we should have been glad of more guidance of this sort. For example, No. 120 in *The Forme of Cury*, which appears only in A and B, says 'þanne take rede wyne oþer white grece & raysouns': we would have been happy to have found a point indicating whether this means 'red wine or white, grease . . .' or 'red wine, or white grease . . .', but there was none in either manuscript. In such cases, we had to follow culinary principles to decide on the proper punctuation, and here we decided that grease could never be a substitute for wine and that what was meant was grease *and* either red or white wine.

SELECT BIBLIOGRAPHY

I. GENERAL WORKS

Arnold, Richard. *The Customs of London, otherwise called Chronicle of London*, ed. F. Douce. London, 1811 (reproducing the first edn. of *c.*1504 and generally known as 'Arnold's Chronicle').

Bartholomaeus Anglicus. *On the properties of things: John Trevisa's translation of Bartholomaeus Anglicus De proprietatibus rerum: a critical text*, ed. M. C. Seymour *et al.*, Oxford, 1975.

Bierbaumer, Peter. *De Botanische Wortschatz des Altenglischen*. Grazer Beiträge zur englischen Philologie, Frankfurt-am-Main, 1975. 2 vols.

Boorde, Andrew, *A Compendyous Regyment, or A Dyetary of Helth* (1542), ed. F. J. Furnivall. Oxford, EETS ES 10, 1870.

Brunskill, Elizabeth, 'A Medieval Book of Herbs and Medicine', Part II. *The Northwestern Naturalist*, xxiv (1953), 177–89.

[de Bryene, Dame Alice.] *The Household Book of Dame Alice de Bryene of Acton Hall, Suffolk, September 1412–September 1413*, trans. M. K. Dale, ed. V. B. Redstone. Ipswich, 1931.

Cogan, Thomas. *The Haven of Health: Chiefly Made for the Comfort of Students*. London, 1589.

A Collection of Ordinances and Regulations for the Government of the Royal Household, Made in Divers Reigns, From King Edward III. to King William and Queen Mary; Also Receipts in Ancient Cookery. London (Society of Antiquaries), 1790. (Commonly referred to as 'Household Ordinances'.)

Earle, John. *English Plant Names from the Tenth to the Fifteenth Century*. Oxford, 1880.

Freeman, Margaret B. *Herbs for the Medieval Household, for Cooking, Healing, and Divers Uses*. New York, 1943, repr. 1979.

Furnivall, Frederick J., ed. *The Babees Book, with Aristotle's ABC, The Lytille Childrens Lytil Boke, The Bokes of Nurture of Hugh Rhodes and John Russell, Wynkyn de Worde's Boke of Kervynge, The Booke of Demeanor, The Boke of Curtasye, Seager's Schools of Vertue, etc.* Oxford, EETS OS 32, 1868.

Gerard, John. *The Herball or General Historie of Plantes*. London, 1633 (repr. of 1597 edn.). *Gerard's Herball*, ed. Marcus Woodward (London, 1964), is a convenient but abridged reprint.

Das Hausbuch der Cerruti, trans. Franz Unterkircher. Dortmund, 1979.

Henisch, Bridget Ann. *Fast and Feast: Food in Medieval Society*. University Park (Pennsylvania), 1976.

Henslow, George. *Medical Works of the Fourteenth Century Together with a List of Plants recorded in Contemporary Writings with Their Identifications*. London, 1899.

Liber Albus: The White Book of the City of London, compiled A. D. 1419 by John Carpenter, Common Clerk, Richard Whittington, Mayor, trans. Henry Thomas Riley. London, Roxburghe Club vol. 57, 1841.

Mead, William Edward. *The English Medieval Feast*. London, 1931; repr. New York, 1967.

Monckton, H. A. *A History of English Ale and Beer*. London, 1966.

Oschinsky, Dorothea, ed. *Walter of Henley*. Oxford, 1971.

Perry, Charles. 'Three Medieval Arabic Cookbooks', in *Oxford Symposium on National and Regional Styles of Cookery, Proceedings*, Part 2, 116–23. London, 1981.

Rodinson, Maxime. 'Recherches sur les documents arabes relatifs à la cuisine', *Revue des études islamiques* (1949), 95–165.

Russell, John *see* Furnivall, F. J., ed.

Salzman, Louis Francis. *English Trade in the Middle Ages*. Oxford, 1931.

[Scott, Michael.] *The Science of Dining: a Medieval Treatise on the Hygiene of the Table*, trans. Arthur Way. London, 1936.

Serjeantson, M. S. 'The Vocabulary of Cookery in the Fifteenth Century', in *Essays and Studies by Members of the English Association*, xxiii (1937), 25–37.

Simon, Andre Louis. *The History of the Wine Trade in England*. London, 1906. 3 vols.

[de Swinfield, Richard.] *Roll of the Household Expenses of Richard de Swinfield, Bishop of Hereford, During Part of the Years 1289 and 1290*, ed. John Webb. Camden Society, OS vols. 59 and 62, 1953–4.

Turner, William. *Libellus de re herbaria novis*. London (?), 1551.

Tusser, Thomas. *Good Points of Husbandry* (c.1557), ed. Dorothy Hartley. London, 1931.

Wilson, C. Anne. *Food and Drink in Britain*. London, 1973.

Wright, Thomas, ed. *A Volume of Vocabularies*. London (?), 1957.

II. COOKERY BOOKS

Aebischer, Paul. 'Un manuscrit valaisan du "Viandier" attribué à Taillevent', *Vallesia*, viii (1953), 73–100.

Apicius. *The Roman Cookery Book: a Critical Translation of the Art of Cooking by Apicius, for Use in the Study and Kitchen*, ed. and trans. Barbara Flower and Elizabeth Rosenbaum. London, 1958.

Austin, Thomas, ed. *Two Fifteenth-Century Cookery Books*. London, EETS OS 91, 1888, repr. 1964.

'A Baghdad Cookery Book', trans. A. J. Arberry. *Islamic Culture* xiii (1939), 21–4, 189–214.

La Bataille de Caresme et de Charnage, ed. Grégoire Lozincki. Paris, 1933. (Contains an edition of one of the oldest French culinary treatises.)

Buttes, Henry. *Dyets Dry Dinner*. London, 1599.

Carter, Charles. *The Compleat City and Country Cook: or, Accomplish'd Housewife*. London, 2nd edn., 1736.

[Digby, Kenelme.] *The Closet of the Eminently Learned Sir Kenelme Digbie Kt. Opened . . . Published by his Son's Consent*. London, 1669.

Faccioli, Emilio, ed. *Arte della Cucina: Libri di Ricette Testi Sopra lo Scalco il Trinciante e i Vini dal XIV al XIX Secolo*, Vol. 1. Milan, 1966.

Frati, Ludovico, ed. *Libro di Cucina del Secolo XIV*. Leghorn, 1899, facs. 1979.

Frere, Catherine Frances, ed. *A Proper Newe Booke of Cokerie* (edn. of a C.C.C. Cambridge vol. owned by Matthew Parker and dated to *c.*1572; with notes by John Hodgkin). Cambridge, 1913.

The Good Hus-Wifes Handmaide for the Kitchen. London, 1594.

Grewe, Rudolph, ed. *Libre de Sent Sovi* (14th-century Catalan recipes). Barcelona, 1979.

Hajek, Hans, ed. *Daz bůch von gůter Spise, aus der Würzburg-Münchener Handschrift* (early 14th-century German recipes). Berlin, 1958.

Hodgett, Gerald, A. J., trans. *Stere Hit Well* (Pepysian MS 1047), with intr. by Delia Smith. Cambridge, 1972.

Küchenmeisterei. Nürnberg, 1490; facs. edn. with intr. by Hans Wegener, Leipzig, 1939. Title in original printings generally given as *Kuchemaistrey*: e.g. Augsburg edn. of 1507, facs. of another printing (original date not given), Leipzig, 1978.

Il Libro della Cucina del Sec. XIV. Bologna, Commissione per il testi de lingua, 1968.

Maino de' Maineri. *De saporibus*, ed. Lynn Thorndike, 'A Medieval Sauce-Book', *Speculum*, ix (1934), 183–90.

Markham, Gervase. *The English Hus-Wife*. London, 4th edn., 1631.

Le Ménagier de Paris, composé vers 1393 par un Bourgeois Parisien, ed. Jérôme Pichon. Paris, 1846, 2 vols. The new *Menagier de Paris* ed. Georgine E. Brereton and Janet M. Ferrier (Oxford, 1981) appeared too late to be used in the preparation of the present edition.

Morris, R., ed. *Liber Cure Cocorum* (BL MS Sloane 1986). London, 1882.

Napier, Mrs. Alexander [Robina], ed. *A Noble Boke off Cookry ffor a Prynce Houssolde or eny other estately Houssolde; Reprinted Verbatim from a Rare MS. in the Holkham Collection*. London, 1882.

Newman, Elizabeth Thompson, ed. *A Critical Edition of an Early Portuguese Cookbook*. Chapel Hill, 1964. (Late 15th century.)

Pegge, Samuel, ed. *The Forme of Cury*. London, 1780.

Platina (Bartolomeo Sacchi). *De honesta voluptate*. Venice, 1475; repr. with a trans. by Elizabeth Buermann Andrews. St. Louis, 1967.

Power, Eileen, trans. *The Goodman of Paris* (*Le Ménagier*, abridged). London, 1928.

Roberts, Enid. *Bwyd y Beirdd, 1400–1600*. Cardiff, 1976. English trans. (*Food of the Bards*), 1982.

[Taillevent.] *Le Viandier de Guillaume Tirel dit Taillevent*, ed. Jérôme Pichon and George Vicaire. Paris, 1892.

'A. W.' *A Booke of Cookrye Very necessary for all such as delight therin*. London, 1591; facs. Amsterdam, 1976.

Warner, Richard. *Antiquitates Culinariae: Tracts on Culinary Affairs of the Old English*. London, 1791; facs. London 1981.

Note: Comments in the Glossary section below make occasional reference to *Petits Propos Culinaires*, a periodical published approximately three times a year in London since 1979, containing much serious and informative research on culinary history and related matters.

FOURTEENTH-CENTURY MENUS FROM
MS COSIN V. III. 11 (C)

A. HISTORICAL DOCUMENTS

(1) Thys is the purveanse of þe feste for þe kynge at home f. 1
with þe lord spenser; first for the kynges table. Furmynte
in venesoun, cornude loruȝe, grete flesshe, þe hede of þe
bore, capones of hi gres, swannes rostyd, herones rostyd,
fesantes rostyd, grete tartes, and ii sotelteys.   5
Brawn in gredowse, blaundessorre, pyggys rostyd, conyes
rostyd, curlewes rostyd, bytorys rostyd, venesoun rostyd,
pekokys rostyd, telys rostyd, grete crostude, & brawne
freturys, and i sotelte.
Datys in compaste, vyolette, cranys rostyd, perteryches 10
rostyd, pekokys rostyd endort, qualys rostyd, plouerys
rostyd, grete birdes rostyd, rabatys rostyd, larkys rostyd,
brokon brawne, fretowrys, domedes in paste, quynsys in
past, and ii sotelteys.

(2) Thys is þe porweaunse for the fest for þe kynge at home
for his owne table.
Venesoun with furmynte in potage, borys hedes, grete
flesshe, swan rostyd, capones rostyd of hy grece, pesson,
pyke, and ii sotelltees.   5
Potage callyd blundsorre, potage callyd gele, pyggys
rostyd, crunes rostyd, fesaintis rostyd, herones rostyd,
pekokys rostyd, breme, sartes, broken brawn, conyng
rostyd, & i soteltee.
Potage callyd bruet of almayne, new lombard, venesoun 10
rostyd, egret rostyd, pekokys rostyd, perteryches rostyd,
pegones rostyd, rabetes rostyd, qualys rostyd, larkes
rostyd, a mete callyd payne pufe, perchys, resquyle,
longe freturys, and ii sotelteys.

1. 1 is] his MS   5 ii] to ii MS

B. THE FOLLOWING MENUS ARE GENERAL SUGGESTIONS, NOT HISTORICAL RECORDS

The C version has been collated with J (f. 90ʳ⁻ᵛ), and, in the one menu where there is a close overlap, with Ar.

f. 61 (3) Circa festum Michelis on flesshedays.

Bores hedys enarmyd, frumente with venesoun, þerwith chapons ibake & cheuettes, butores & egredouns. At þe ii cours, swannes & herouns, fesauntes, þerwith tartes
5   bosewes, & drop þerwith to potage. At þe iii cours venesoun rosted, pertrich, wodecok, plouers, & lauerok, þerwith chapelettes, þerwith langettes, peres ifarsyd, with koketris, flampoyntes & daryol, þerwith viaunde real.

(4) In Paschal tempe flesshedays.

þe fyrste cours creteyne to potage & pygges in sauge þerwith, smale felettes indorretes & þerwith cometh smale pertrich ibake & chekenes. þe ii cours bruet saraseyns, þerwith gele & capouns dorres, lechefres & smal
5   rost. þe iii cours, dariol of crem & of refles togedere.

(5) Fleysch days.

Bores hedes enarmyd, bruet of almayne to potage, þerwith telis ybake & wodecokes, fesauntes, & curleus. þe ii cours pertrych, conynges, & malard, þerwith blaundesire, caudel ferre with flampoyntes of crem & tartes. þe iii
5   cours ploueres, lauerokys, & chekenes ifarsed, and þerwith mammane.

(6) On fysch dayes.

þe fyrste cours oystres in graue, pyk & bacound heryng, stokfyssh & merlyng yfryed. þe ii cours porpeys in galentyn, & þerwith congur & samoun fresch endored & rosted

---

3. 1 festum] *add* sancti J;   on flesshedays] *om.* J   5 bosewes]
boseus J   8 viaunde] bran C
    4. 1 tempe] tempere J
    5. 2 bruet] bruel C   3 telis] tellis (*second* l *underdotted,* telis *in margin in different hand*) C, teeles J;   fesauntes] *add* yrostede J   4 malard]
add yrostyd J;   blaundesire] brandesyre C
    6. 2 oystres] oytres C;   heryng] *add* and pyke Ar   3 cours] *add*
elus in graue Ar;   in] and Ar   4 endored &] and dorre Ar

& gurnard, þerwith tartes and flampoyntes. þe iii cours, 5
rosee to potage & crem of almaundes, þerwith sturioun &
welkes, grete eles & lamprouns, dariol, lechefres of frut,
& þerwith nyrsebeke.

(7) On flesch dayes.
     At þe i cours, bores hedes enarmyd, bruet of almayne to
potage, capouns ibake & cheuettes, & þerwith fesauntes
& butorys. þe ii cours, swannes, curles, pigges, veel irosted
& tartes, þerwith blandesyre & morre. Iii cours, conyng, 5
pertrich & wodecok, plouers & lauerokes irosted & þerwith fretour, potwys, sacwys, & yrchons, & þerwith egredoune.

(8) On fysch dayes.
     Perchys in graue & gele, þerwith cheuettes of frut, hakke
ifarsed, rosyn rosthenes, eles ibake, lampreys irosted,
grete luces isoden. þe ii cours, lechefreys, flampoyntes,
dariol, hastelestes of frut & rosted grete bremes, turbot, 5
congur, freysch samoun, sober sauuȝ, cold bruet. þe iii
cours, crustede, fretour of mylk & frutour blaunche,
dariol of almaund, rapey, rosee, & chesan.

(9) Penthecoste fleysch dayes.
     At þe i cours, bores hedes enarmyd, bruce to potage,
capons, beefe, & pestell of porke isode, & torte, þerwith
fesauntes & bytores irosted. þe ii cours, swannes, curlus,
malard & conyng irosted, þerwith corate to potage & þer- 5
with raphiol ibake. þe iii cours, telys, pertrich, wodcokkes,
snytes, & lauerokes irosted with borewys, mulaches of
poork, with connaunce to potage with hastelettes.

5 gurnard] *add* isode J, sothen Ar;   þerwith ... flampoyntes] and bacon elus
and tart Ar   7 eles] *add* irostyd J;   lamprouns] *add* rosted, and
tenches in gele, and therwith Ar   8 nyrsebeke] friture Ar
    7. 6 pertrich] *om.* C   7 yrchons] ychouns CJ
    8. 1 fysch] flessh J   4 lechefreys] lechefeys C
    9. 7 borewys] borrewys J

PART I
DIUERSA CIBARIA

Contents of BL Add. 46919 (He)	Other MS Sources	Page
1. Blanc desire	J, Ro	45
2. Vert desire	J, Ro	45
3. Anesere	J, Ro	45
4. Viaunde despyne	J, Ro	45
5. Kaudel ferre	J, Ro	45
6. Haucegeme	J, Ro	45
7. Maumenee	J, Ro	45
8. Double mortreus	J, Ro	45
9. Poumes amole	J, Ro	46
10. Coudre en tens de nois	J, Ro	46
11. Spinette	J, Ro	46
12. Rosee	J (part), Ro	46
13. Freseyes	J (part), Ro	46
14. Scirresez	J, Ro	46
15. Bruet de Alemayne	J, Ro	46
16. Bruet seec	J, Ro	47
17. Bruet salmene	J, Ro	47
18. Bruet Sarazineys blanc	J, Ro	47
19. Soree	J, Ro	47
20. Dragone	J, Ro	47
21. Pynite	J, Ro	47
22. Dyacre	J, Ro	47
23. Suade	J, Ro	47
24. Rampaunt perre	J, Ro	48
25. Gelee	J, Ro	48
26. Brasee	J, Ro	48
27. Test de Turt	J, Ro	48
28. Viaunde de Cypre	J, Ro	48
29. Ermine	J, Ro	48
30. Sanc dragon	J, Ro	49
31. Hauceleamye	J, Ro	49
32. Murree	J, Ro	49
33. Amydon	J, A1	49
34. Cresterole	J, A1	49
35. Espyne	J, A1, R	50
36. Rosee	J, A1, R	50
37. Fresse	J, A1	50
38. Fuaus	J, A1	50

39. Peyuere egresse	J, A1	51
40. A mete to muche isalt	J, A1, L	51
41. Amydon to holden water	J, A1, L	51
42. Couwe de rouncin	J, A1	51
43. Teste de Turt	J, A1, L	52
44. Suot blanc	J, A1, R, L	52
45. Cuskynoles	J, A1, L	52
46. Emeles	J, A1, L	53
47. Ioute dore	J	53
48. Gentil rost	—	53
49. Qwite plumen	J	54
50. Saumon gentil	J	54
51. Galantine	J	54
52. Seue of lamproun	J	54
53. Nuroles farseys	J	55
54. Mes of chyseberien	J	55
55. Mosserouns florys	—	55
56. Mete of Cypree	J	55
57. Halekaye	J	56
58. Soupe mare	J	56
59. Comeneye	—	57
60. Amidon tried	J	57
61. Woelkeye	J	57
62. Hoistreye	J	57
63. Mule	J	57

Note: The base MS, BL Additional 46919 (He) ff. 19–24^v, is collated throughout with BL Cotton Julius D viii (J) ff. 104–9. Other MSS consulted are BL Royal 12. C. xii (Ro) ff. 11–13, BL Additional 32085 (A1) ff. 118^v–119^v, Bodleian Rawlinson D 1222 (R) ff. 40^v and 42, and Bodleian Laud Misc. 553 (L) f. 5^{r-v}. Readings from these MSS are supplied only where they serve to explain mistranslations and choices of variants. For information on the principal manuscripts, see Introduction, pp. 16–17.

1   Blanc desire. Milke of alemaundes, flour of rys, braun of f. 19
chapoun, gyngere itried, sucre, hwit wyn; vchon of þoes
schulen boillen in a clene possenet, & soþþen idon in þe vessel
hwaryn hit schal beon imad, in a stude wyþouten vulþe; &
poume gernet to strey3en abouen.   5

2   Vert desire. Milke of alemaundes, flour of ris, braun of
chapoun, red wyn, sucre, percelie; þe colour schal beo grene.

3   Anesere. Milke of alemauns, flour of rys, braun of chapoun,
alemaundes qwyte ifried & idon þrin, & alemauns ifried &
ipiht abouen; þe colour schal beo 3olou wyþ saffroun.

4   Viaunde despyne. Milke of alemauns, flour of ris, braun
of chapoun, festicade ane pertie istried abouen, poudree of
clouwes idon þeryn so þat hit 3eue god flauour of þe festicade;
þe colour schal beo 3oelu.

5   Kaudel ferre. Wyn, amnidoun, reysyns wiþoute stones to
don þrin, sucre vort abaten þe streinþe of þe wyn.

6   Haucegeme. Milke of alemauns, flour of rys, veel ipolled,
veel icoruen ase deez & idon þrin, galyngal, canel and sucree;
þe colour schal beon imad wyþ sanc dragoun.

7   Maumenee. Wyn; braun of chapoun ipolled al to poudre,
& soþþen do þryn to boillen wiþ þe wyn; alemauns igrounden
al dru3e & idon þryn, & poudre of clowes idon þryn; alemauns
ifried schulen beon idon þryn, & þer schal gret vlehs beon
igrounden, & sucre fort abaten þe streynþe of þe specerie; þe 5
colour schal beon inde.

8   Double mortreus. Milke of alemauns, ayren, an perti
amydon, galyngal, gynger, ayren harde imad on lutle perties

---

1. 2 gyngere itried sucre] `ginger &´ sugar itryede suger J   4 stude]
stede J
    3. 2 ifried²] blaunches Ro   3 ipiht] iput J, plaunte Ro
    4. 1 Viaunde] Vande He   2 istried] ifryede J, plaunte Ro
    7. 3 dru3e & idon] drye & isoden J, mys leynz Ro   4 beon¹] boen He;
þer schal] om. J;   beon²] shall be J   5 fort abaten] for ta baten (a in
ta from o) He
    8. 2 galyngal] galygal He

& idon þrin, sucre de greles, losenges istryed abouen; þe colour is ȝoelou.

9   Poumes amole. Wyn, ayren, flour of corne itried, appleen igoboned abouen, sucre vort abaten þe streinþe of þe wyn. |

10   Coudre en tens de nois. Milke of alemauns, flour of rys, curneles of nuten ifried, gynger itried, sucre vort abaten þe keneschype; nuten yfried abouen.

11   Spinette. Milke of alemauns, floures of þe þeoueþorne ymedled in þe milke of alemauns, & þat hit habbe god flauour of þe flures, & of amydon; gret vlehs, genger itried, sucur clene vort abaten þe streynþe of þe gynger, & qwyte floures to
5 streyen abouen.

12   Rosee. Milke of alemauns; leues of roseen so þat hit sauoure of þe roseen; kanele, flour of rys oþer of amydon, gret vlehs, poudre of kanele & sucre; þe colour ase roseen, & leues of rosen istried abouen.

13   Freseyes. Streberyen igrounden wyþ milke of alemauns, flour of rys oþur amydon, gret vlehs, poudre of kanele & sucre; þe colur red, & streberien istreyed abouen.

14   Scirresez. Milke of alemauns iþikked wyþ amydon, chiseberien igrounden wiþouten þe stones, a pertie of sucre so þat hit beo wel isauoured of cheseberien, vlehs gret, & cheseberien istreed abouen; þe colour is red.

15   Bruet de Alemayne. Milke of alemauns, itried clouwes de gylofree, quibibes, oyngnones ifried: & schal beon hot of clouwes & of quibibes; þe colour schal beon ȝoelu.

9. 2 igoboned] icoruen J, goboneez Ro
10. 3 keneschype] strengþe J, amerete Ro;   abouen] abuen He, aboue J
12. 2 sauoure] haue sauour J   3-4 ase ... abouen] *om.* J
13. 1-3 Freseyes ... colur] *om.* J (*the beginning of 12 and end of 13 are combined under the title* Rosee *in* J)   2 amydon] anydon He
14. 4 is] shall be J
15. 2 &] hit J

16 Bruet seec. Swete broþ, vergus of grapees, percil ygrounden idon þryn; cloewes, maces, quibibes; in tyme of chekenen
after aster, & þat hit sauoure wel of spices, saffroun ysoden
wiþ þe percil in þe broþ: þe colour ȝoelu.

17 Bruet salmene. Vinegre, galyngal, kanel, poudre of
clouwes of gilofre, muche plente of ayren monie, & sucre gret
plente vorte abaten þe streynþe of þe spicerie; meddlee wyþ
þe speces gyngeree: I þe colour schal beo blake oþur grene.   f. 20

18 Bruet Sarazineys blanc. Milke of cow ilied wyþ ayren &
gyngeer itried gret plentee; in time of appleen, þe colour
qwyt.

19 Soree. Wyn, water, angoyles vorsche & oþur maner vihs;
þin angeylles ifried & þe lyuere iholden, & þe gobouns ipoudred in poudre of kanele; þe colour red.

20 Dragone. Milke of alemauns, flour of rys, braun of chapoun, sucre & kanele; þe colour red of sanc dragoun.

21 Pynite. Wyn, sucre, iboilled togedere; gyngebred & hony,
poudre of gynger & of clouwes; ipiht wiþ pynes gret plentee,
& schal beon adressed in coffyns of flour of chasteyns: þe
colour ȝolou wyþ saffroun.

22 Dyacre. Milke of alemauns, amydon, flour of rys itried,
braun of chapon, poudre of gyngere gret plentee, sucre, qwyt
wyn, archanye greles, losenges ystreyed abouen; þe colour
red ase blod.

23 Suade. Milke of alemauns, amydon, wyþ þe lyure of
floures of þe suade; þe floures schulen beon ywaschen & idon

16. 3 aster] ester J, paschel Ro   4 ȝoelu] shall be ȝelew J
17. 2 clouwes] clouwes & poudre HeJ;   monie] moltz Ro
18. 1 of cow] of corn He, & corn J, de vache Ro
19. 1 Soree] Doree He;   angoyles] eles J;   vihs] fyssh 'þyn ele' J
    21. 2 ipiht] iphyt J;   pynes] þornes HeJ   3 of[1]] of f (*second f underdotted*) He
    22. 2 plentee] plente of J   3 archanye] archamye He;   colour]
add shall be J

in gynger gret plentee, þe floures of þe suade ystreyed
abouen: þe colour schal beon qwyt.

24 Rampaunt perre. Peoren ysoden in water, yþikked wiþ
ayren & wiþ amidon, ystreyed abouen of þe leues; mak of
dowe þe colour ʒoelu of þree lyouns raumpauns in þe dysches.

25 Gelee. Vihs isodeen in win & water & saffron & poudre
of gynger & kanele, galyngal, & beo idon in an vessel ywryen
clanliche; þe colour qwyt.

26 Brasee. Wyn & specerie, kanel; þe vichs ispandled, &
ystreyed wyþinnen þe vessel wiþ þe vische, quibibes, cloues;
f. 20ᵛ & irosted apon a gredyrn, & soþþen iboilled in wyn & | in
specerie; þe colour red.

27 Test de Turt. Foille de pastee bon sarrays, & iplaunted
þrin conynges & volatils, dates ywaschen & isouced in hony,
chese neowe icoruen þryn; clouwes, quibibes, sucre abouen.
Soþþen on legge of fassyng of festigade gret plentee, þe colour
5 of þe farsure red, ʒolou & grene. þat hed schal beon blake
adressed oþe manere of hier of wymmon on an blake dische,
& a monnes visage abouen.

28 Viaunde de Cypre. Milke of alemauns, flour of rys,
poudre of gyngere so þat hit smacche wel of þe gynger, &
þat hit beo istreyed wiþ gyngebred wiþ fasticade; þe colour
ʒoolu.

29 Ermine. Hit schal beon ymad qwit & wel ysauoured of
god poudre of gynger & quibibes & cloues, & þis mete schal
beon perti wiþ vert desire.

---

24. 1 perre] porree He   2-3 ystreyed . . . dowe] plaunte desus des
fueilles secz de paste Ro
   25. 2 ywryen] iwronge J, couert Ro
   26. 1 kanel] of canell J;   þe] with J   3 gredyrn] gredele J;   in¹]
with J
   27. 1 Foille de pastee] fyll þe pasteye with J, fueille de paste Ro;   iplaunted]
iplaunched He, plaunte Ro   5 þat] þe J   6 oþe] in þe J   7 a]
om. He

30 Sanc dragon. Milke of alemauns & flour of rys & god poudre of gyngere & sucre, & hit schal beon icolored wiþ sanc dragon.

31 Hauceleamye. Grape of vine, garette de moutoun; qwen þeos swete þinges beoþ wel ysoden togedre, a lute broþ in þe vergus. Nim poule de mars & hew am & do am to þilke boill- lyng, & qwen abeoþ wel iboilled do god plente of poudre of gynger vorte don awy þe bitternesse of þe grapes; þe colour 5 grene.

32 Murree. Flour of ris oþur of amydon, þe hwuch may best beon ivounden; þenne þoes colours of saundrez schullen beon wel ibrayed in an morter, & soþþen schal beon wel itempred wiþ milke of alemauns & wel ywrongen, & beo idon to poudre of kanel, galingal. Ʒef hit is day of vische, do þerto peoren oþur 5 chistenis oþur saumoun oþur luz oþur perche. Ʒef vlehs day, do þerto vlehs of veel oþur cycchen & so þou schalt habben god mete & real.

33 Anoþour mete þat hatte amydon. |Nim amydon & grind f. 21 in an morter, & make boillen wyþ alemauns, & soþþen nim þe alemaundes ihwyted & saffron & make boillen togederes in water. & soþþen fryen in oylee oþur in grecee, & vnder þe metee þat is ihwyted schulen beon iset alemauns icoloured, 5 & abouen þe mete icoloured schulen beon iset alemauns iwyted & rys & penides.

34 Anoþur mete þat hatte cresterole. Nim flour of corne and ayren & make past, icoloured wyþ saffron þe halue dole

30. 1 sanc] samc He;   flour] *om.* HeRo   2 hit] *om.* He

31. 1 vine] wyn J   2 swete] deus Ro;   a] en Ro;   in þe] ou Ro
3 þilke] þikke J   5 colour] *add* shall be J   6 grene] *first* e *from* o
He (*the same change can be seen in* þoes **32.** 2 grecee **33.** 4 soþþen **43.** 2-3 zeoþen
51. 6 seoþen **53.** 2 seoþ **56.** 11).

32. 1 Murree] Turree J;   hwuch may best] which þanne may J   3 &]
wel & He;   itempred] istempred He, itemperede J, destempre Ro   5 þerto]
þese to J;   oþur] or to J   6 oþur[1,2,3]] oþer to J;   vlehs day] flessh
day do þerto flessh day J   7 cycchen] cyʻcʻchen He, chekenys J, cheueryl
Ro

33. 1 mete] *om.* J   2 boillen] hit buyll J   5 ihwyted] iswyted
He, iwhyʒttede J, blaunche A1;   iset] iset þryn HeJ

34. 2 and] and of HeJ;   make] make a J

þe past, & þe halue dole qwytt; & soþþe rolle on a bord ase
þunne ase parchemin, & rolle rounde al aboutee as a kake; &
5 make ase wel in leynteen ase in oþur tyme, wyþ alemauns
in oile ifried.

35 Anoþur mete þat hatte espyne. Nym þe floures of þeoue-
þorn clanlichee igedered, & mak grinden in an morter al to
poudre, & soþþen tempre wiþ milke of alemauns oþur of cow;
& soþþen do þerto bred oþur amydon vor to lyen, & of ayren;
5 & lye wel wyþ speces & of leues of þe þorne, & strey þron
floures, & soþþen drescee.

36 Anoþur mete þat hatte rosee. Nym a poyne of rose leues
oþer two, & grind in an morter wel, & soþþen wyþ milke of
alemauns tempre, oþur wiþ milke of cow; & do a lutel wastel
bred, & lye wel wiþ speces & ayren icolored wiþ saffroun, &
5 cast a lef oþur two, & soþþen adres.

37 Anoþur mete þat hatte fresse. Nym clanlyche frissiaus &
soþþen grind in an morter, & soþþen nim milke of alemauns
oþer of cou, & tempre wyþ ius of frissiaus; & soþþen do a
lute bred of wastel, & lye wel wiþ speces & ayren & icoloured
5 wiþ saffron, & soþen dresse.

f. 21ᵛ **38** Her hit techeþ hou me schal make fuaus. |Nym clanlichee
and bet wel in an morter al to poudre, & soþþen tempre wiþ
milke of alemauns oþur of cou, & do a lutel of wastel, & lye

5 wel] *om.* J   6 in] & J
    35. 1-2 þeoueþorn] hawthorne R, de aube espine A1   2 mak grinden]
do hit to be grounde J   3 tempre] stempre He, tempre hit J;   oþur of
cow] *om.* R;   cow] corn He, de vache A1   4 þerto] to He;   oþur]
oþur of HeJ   5 lye] lye hit J;   lye . . . þorne] boyl hit þyke R;   strey]
stey He, strew J   5-6 strey þron floures] florysshe hit with grene leues R
    36. 1 poyne] poynt J, handefull R;   of] of of He;   leues] floures R
2 grind] grind hem J;   soþþen] seþe J   3 tempre] stempre He;
cow] corn He, de vache A1   4 bred] *add* or oþer white brede R;   wiþ¹]
om. HeJ;   speces &] *om.* R;   &²] of HeJ   5 cast . . . two] boyl
hit & cast to sugur R
    37. 3 tempre] stempre He, tempre hit J   4 wiþ] *om.* HeJ;   &²] of
HeJ
    38. 1 hit] he J;   Nym] nym hit J   3 wastel] wastell bred J

hit wel wiþ ayren, & seþþen of brineus ifried abouen, & soþþen dres. 5

39 A sauce þat hatte peyuere egresse. Nim þe rote & vache
out þe grapes, & do in an morter wiþ a lute salt, & quest wel
þe grapes; & soþþen vach out þe ius, & do gingere, peyuere in
an morter, & a lute bred, & grind wel togedre al to poudre, &
soþþen tempre wiþ þe ius of þe grapes. 5

40 When a mete is to muche isalt; þat is to suggen, potagee,
to maken remedie in god stat: nym gruel & do in an touuwayl,
& nim þilke touayl wiþ þe gruel & do hit into þilke potage to
þe ground of þe crouhee & so let beon a lute bi þe fur at þe
syde of þe bronde, al þat hit beo a lutel icoled. & soþþen do 5
from þe fur, & hit schal beon god & swete vor to eten.

41 To maken amydon to holden water ase longe ase þou
wolt, wel and veyre. Nym corn clene abouten Seint Iohn &
do hit in a clene vessel, & do veyr water ynoh wiþ þe corne 4
dawes; & vche day beo wel ywaschen. & soþþen ygrounden,
& soþþen iboilled in veyr water, & hit schal stonden in þe 5
water al þat hit beo isoken, & soþþen yhonged in an touwayl
aȝein þe zunne al þat hit beo drue. Soþþen nym hit hout &
do hit in an clene vessel, & hold ase long ase þou wolt, &
wreh wel, & corf to veyre peces.

42 Anoþur mete þat hatte couwe de rouncin. Nym þe veet
& þe eren of swyn & boille heam in god wyn; & qwen abeoþ
wel iboilled, roste heom & nym am out, & corf to veyre mossels. & mince oygnons in god saym, & soþþen do mossels in

4 brineus] breneus J, bramaus A1
  39. 1 peyuere] poyuere He
  40. 1 a] *om.* J   2 in an] hit in J   3 þilke¹] þykke J;   into
þilke] in a þykke J   4 crouhee] crokke J; at] in He   5 þat]
þouȝ J   6 hit] *om.* He
  41. 2 Iohn] *bar over* n He   3 a] *om.* He; veyr] ouer J, bel A1
4 dawes] ix days & ix nyȝt L   5 hit] *om.* He   6 al . . . isoken]
til hit be sunkyn J   7 al] til J; drue] drye J; hit²] *om.* He
8 hold] hold hit J   9 wreh] worch J, couerez le A1; to] hit on J
  42. 1 hatte] me calleþ J   2 of] of a J   3 out] vp J; to]
hit on J   4 do] do þe J

f. 22 þilke broþ, | & soþþen dresse & do god poudre of speces:
6 gynger, kanel, galingal, clowes & saffron; & grind togedere.

43 To maken þilke mete on ʒeolue day of vische þat me
clepeþ teste de Turt. Nim rys itried & wahs am veyre, & soþþen druen, & soþþen grind in an morter al to poudre, & do a
lute amydon wiþinnen. & soþþen nim luce oþur turbet oþur
5 eles, & boill am & soþþe tempre wiþ milke of alemauns & do
wiþinnen speces, saffron & sucre. & make a coffin of past, &
soþþen let scaldeen & soþþen do awey þe fulþ & make to
gobouns; and soþþen nim percil & saugee & of þe broþ, and
mak grinden togedere, & do saffron poudre; & soþþen do
10 into þe ouene.

44 A mete þat hatte suot blanc. Nim chykenen & scald
heom, & hew am to mossels, & do am to zeoþeon; & qwen
abeoþ izeoden, nym þe ʒolc of ey & lye hit wiþ milke of
alemauns. & soþþen nim grapes, & do wiþ salt, & grind in an
5 morter togedere; & also verhe in þe day of vische wiþ lyure
of turbot oþur of oþur vihs, wiþ þe voresayde milke. & gedere
in time of ʒere þilke floures qwen abeoþ inoriced, & drue
heom, & soþþen abeon igrounden wel in an morter; & soþþen
þou miht holden þurh alle ʒer.

45 A mete þat is icleped cuskynoles. Make a past tempred
wiþ ayren, & soþþen nim peoren & applen, figes & reysins,
alemaundes & dates; bet am togedere & do god poudre of

5 do] do of HeJ;   speces] om. J
   43. 1 þilke] þat J;   ʒeolue] ʒol J   2 teste] Ceste J;   itried]
t above underdotted d J   3 druen] drye hem J;   grind] grynd hem J
5 &³] speces & He   6 wiþinnen] þeryn J;   of] om. He   7 let
scaldeen] scalde hem J;   to] om. J, gobonen to He   9 mak grinden]
do grynd hem J   9–10 & . . . ouene] & do al in to bruet J
   44. 2 zeoþeon] add wiþ good beof L   3 ey] add ysoden hard L;
milke] mike He   4 grapes] floures of synycle R, floures of þe rede vyne
L, flrus (frlrus, first r underdotted) de vine sucche A1;   wiþ] with hem J
5 togedere] om. J;   also verhe] ase verhs He, also worch J;   þe] a J
5–6 wiþ . . . vihs] om. J   6–9 & . . . ʒer] om. L   7 of ʒere] om. He
7–8 drue heom] drye þem R, whan þat þey ben drye J, wete heom þat abeon
drue He   8 soþþen¹] so J;   abeon . . . wel] grynde hem hole J
8–9 soþþen . . . ʒer] make pouder of þem to serue oþer tymes R   9 holden]
kepe hem J;   þurh] þur He;   alle] þe J
   45. 1 icleped] callede J;   tempred] stempred He

gode speces wiþinnen. & in leynten make þi past wiþ milke of
alemaundes. & rolle þi past on a bord, & soþþen hew hit on 5
moni perties, & vche an pertie beo of þe leynþe of a paume &
an half & of þreo vyngres of brede. & smeor þy past al of one
dole, & soþþen do þi fassure wiþinnen. | Vchan kake is por- f. 22ᵛ
tiooun. & soþþen veld togedere oþe ʒeolue manere, ase þeos

fugurre is imad: & soþþe boille in veir water, 10

& soþþen rost on an greudil; & soþþen adresse.

46 A fritur þat hatte emeles. Nym sucre, salt, & alemauns
& bred, & grind am togedre; & soþþen do of ayren. & soþþen
nim grece oþur botere oþur oyle, and soþþen nim a dihs, &
smeore heom; & soþþen nym bliue, & cose wiþ sucre drue: &
þis beoþ þin cyueles in leynten ase in oþur time. 5

47 Nou greyþe we ioute dore, of moni muchel ywylned. þe
clene bete & sclarie hokke, iboilled & wel ihakked, in an
crouhhe, clene ywashen. Hakke ioutes gentil & verre; do to
zeoþen over þe fure. Grece of pork hakke, saffron & peopur
greyþe; & so hit doth awey vche goute in þe wombee ouwher 5
þe stomak hath harm. Al hot þat schal beo clene & cler,
hwareuore þe goute hit doth awy.

48 We clepeþ gentil rost, wel con maken & smartliche &
sone & wiþ goustard. In water zeoþeon riht wel þou make, &
soþþe cole wiþinnen. Soþþen þou schalt nimen wiþ þin hon-
den þat enabbe nout of þe velle, & of ayren mysceliche ben
imyed þe seym. Sone let vacchen a molour of bras; greyþen 5
of speces alkyn: de kanel, saffroun verhs of sauour neowe,

5 hew hit] hewed He   6 an] *om.* J   7 of brede] *om.* He
8 Vchan] whan þe J;   Vchan . . . is] in euerych cake his L   9 veld]
flood J;   oþe ʒeolue] on þe ʒol J   10 *figure om.* JL   11 soþþen¹] *om.* J
   46. 1 hatte] is callede J;   emeles] emeles/ciueles(?) He, emeles JA1,
cyueles L   4 cose wiþ] cast in JL   5 cyueles] emeles J;   ase]
as well as J
   47. 1 Nou . . . ywylned] Joute dore J   2 & wel] wel & J   3 to]
þo J   •   4 zeoþen] *add* faire J   5 hit doth awey] do wey He;
ouwher] ouʒwhere where J   6 þe stomak . . . þat] þis naþ harm of
þe stomake aloh þat ne He;   beo] make hit J   7 hwareuore] wherfore
J;   hit doth] don He
   48. 2 wiþ] wiþ & MS

cleowes of gilofre. Also þis grind togedre. Of ayren þe schalt
han gret plente; þenne þe hwyte schal beon ilyed, þe flour
bakinde wiþ þe ȝolkus. þe mes is god to damoyseles.

49 Of qwite plumen þe mes is riche & wel deoree. Nym
plaumen & do out þe stones, & soþþen boill am in watre.
Soþþen drauh out of þe crouhhe & wel hakke heom wiþ
ayren. Meng in an pail, wel istured; seoþþen tak vers seym,
f. 23 peopur, kanel, meddle | wyþ. Qwen hit is yzoden & wel iturnd,
6 þenne is þe mes vorþ ybrouht.

50 Of saumon gentil. Do out þe bones, soþþen in an morter
kast & make hit wel meddelen. Flour & peopur & gilofre; cast
in kanel. Saffron vor to colouren   þurh an horn þou make
passen, seoþþen in water þou make hit boillen, & to gobouns
5 veire hewen. Comin þou kast in, & to þe lord vorþ bringen.

51 Of vn galantine we schulen speken muchel. Mon saiþ þe
laumprey mak scorchen, & soþþen mak hit al tohewen. To þe
fure, mak hit softe boillen, & meddle wiþ speces: peiuere,
kanel. Mak kasten saffron, gilofre, vorta menden hit; & hwyt
5 wyn mak mied wiþ bred, vor þe mete wol lyen þe grece of þe
vische. Make zeoþen; make hit well to meddlen.

52 Nou we schullen suggen al abouten a seue of lamproun.
þe lamproun þe schalt nimen & skalden wel, & don on a
spete, & soþen to þe fure; oygnons þou schalt greyþen &
minsen & soþþen boillen in qwit wyn. Of speces þe schalt
5 nymen peoper, gynger; & kast kanel, gelofree, mie of bred
to lie. Saffren vor to colouren.

49. 1 & wel deoree] *om.* J   3 drauh] draw hem J;   crouhhe] vessell J   4 Meng] menge hem J;   tak] mak HeJ
    50. 2 kast] cast hit J   3 colouren] colouren hit J;   make] make
hit J   4 hit] *om.* He;   &] in J   5 veire] weire He, faire J
    51. 1 vn galantine] unggalantine He;   muchel] muchel is He, *om.* J;   Mon]
he J   2 mak hit] *om.* J   3 wiþ] hit with J   4 kanel]
kanele, *final* e *underdotted* He;   kasten] casten in J;   hit] *om.* He
5 bred] bred meddle wiþ He;   wol] wel He   6 Make] mak hit J;
hit well to] wiþ He
    52. 1 abouten] abouten of J   3 &¹] *om.* J   6 to¹] *om.* HeJ

immetsamimeasmeasumeteумете

53 Nuroles farseys. Ʒe schul taken a uat chapon; þe schalt mynen & seoþen hit. þe vlehs idon, awy poeren, & do to speces & ʒolkus of ayren vor te wel lyen, & soþþen hem in cler seym.

54 Nou ihere gret vessalage of coyntise of inwyt hou þe schalt maken mes of chyseberien: muche comet of gret cointisee. þe ston do awy wyþ al þe tail; after þe schalt maken farsure of verhs þinge & of henne vlehs ibeten in an morter. Ʒolkus harde medle wyþ, & ʒolkus nesche wel to holden, & peopur, kanel, gylofre deore. þe cerise riht wel fassen in an payl cast; do fassure wel abouten. Soþþen do in an dihs of seoluere. Beor þe mes to þe deys tovoren alle men.

55 Mosserouns florys: | in rost ysih hou gentiliche & sone. f. 23ᵛ Veorst þou schalt maken riht wel passen, & soþþen in water cold cast larde cold; make bringen & oneliche hewen; þenne nym sone þe musseruns, lardes coynteliche wiþ larduns. Make as were vor to swerden & soþþen aske a god roste. Nou inoh is þe mes in rost, of ayren do awey þe qwyt. Sone on þe gredil riht veyre floris speces. Nym & caste gilofre & kanel; wiþinnen meddlen.

56 Vor mete of Cypree. Vurst nim of alemauns, & hwyte of heom one pertie, ah hwyte summe hole & þe oþur do to grinden. Soþþen nim þe hole alemauns & corf heom to quartes; soþþen nim fat broþ & swete of porc oþur of vþur vlehs; tempre þin alemauns & soþþen drauh out þi milke & soþþe do hit in an veyre crouhe. Soþþen nim þe braun of chapouns oþur of hennen oþur of porc, & ʒef noed is let hakken, &

53. 1 Nuroles] Ruroles J; Ʒe schul taken] I chul maken He 1-2 þe schalt mynen] *om.* J 2 hit] *om.* He; poeren] purem J 3 wel] *om.* J; hem] lye hit (hit *canc.*) J

54. 4 ibeten] & beten J 5 Ʒolkus] þe ʒolkus He, ʒelkes of eyren J; wyþ] þerwith J; ʒolkus] *om.* J; &²] *om.* J 6 cerise] ceuse J; fassen] ifarsede J 7 do¹] þe J 8 Beor] kerue J; deys tovoren] ʽdys toʼ fore J

55. 3 cold¹] colʽdʼ MS 5 were] werd MS

56. 1 of²] *om.* J; hwyte] whyʒte J 2 ah hwyte] ah wyte He, & whyʒte J; hole] ihole He 2-3 þe ... grinden] summe igrounde J 3 quartes] quarteres J 4 fat] þat He 5 tempre] stempre He 7 noed is] hit nede be J; hakken] hit be hackede J

soþþen do in a morter þat hit beo wel igrounden, & soþþen
nym hit & do hit to þe milke. Soþþen nim blod of cycchen
10 oþur of oþur beste, & soþþen grind hit & do hit to þe vlesche.
Soþþen do þi crouhe to þe vure & seoþ hit wel; & soþþen
nym god poudre of spices: gynger, kanel, maces, quibibes;
& so zeoþ hit wiþ þilke metee. Soþþen nim wyn & sucre &
make me an stronge soupe. Do hit in þilke to zeoþen. Soþþen
15 nym flour of ris & do a quantite þat hit beo wel þikke. Soþþen nim þin alemauns icoruen & frie heom wel in grece; soþþen nim gynger & par yt wel & heuw hit. Soþþen nym þin
alemauns yfried & þi gynger to þe dressur, & so do hit to
þilke mete, & soþþen nym saffron & colore wel þi mete: &
20 ȝef þat to gode men vor god mete & riche.

To maken diuers potages & metes & sauen veneson of rastichipe. Her þou miht ywiten þe maner hou þou schalt maken
f. 24 diuers potages & metes & sauen | veneson of rastischipe &
don awy.

57 To maken a mete þat is icleped halekaye. Nim alemauns
& make heom qwyte, & soþþen braye heom in an morter,
and make god mylke ase god ase þou miht. & soþþen boille
hit & do þrin a lute vynegre; & qwen hit is iboilled do hit in
5 an cloþ þat hit beo drue. & soþþen do hit in an veyr morter,
& do þerto penydes, & a dole of amidon, & of sucre; & qwen
hit is ybrayed, do out half vor to tempren wyþ gingebred, &
þilke halue dole schal beon icolored wyþ saffroun, & þe oþer
halue dele schal beo qwyt. And qwen þus þinges beoþ ysoden,
10 do þe on & þe oþur in an dyhs, & on þe qwyte do þe greyns
of poume gernet oþur reysins yfassed, & soþþen ȝef vorþ.

58 Soupe mare. Mak god milke of alemaundes, & make
oyle of alemauns, & soþþen corf oygnouns & frie heom in

8 in] nn, *corr. to* in He   9 þe] *om.* J   14 in þilke] þikke J
20 þat] þer J;   god mete &] deynte & for J
   Section Heading om. J
   57. 1 is] *om.* He;   icleped] callede J;   halekaye] hale halekaye He
2 heom[1]] hemon He   3 soþþen] so J   4 hit] here He J   7 is]
his He   8 halue dole] almoundes J   11 oþur] *add* of He
   58. 1 Soupe] South J

oyle of alemauns & soþþen do þe roundeles of þe oignons
abouen; & qwen þou hast adressed, streie þeron sucre.

59 To maken comeneye. Make god milke of alemauns & do
hit to boillen, & do þrin comin, & of amidon; & colore hit
wiþ saffron. & soþþen dresse, & strey þron greyns of poume
gernet oþer reysins, ȝef þou nast non oþur sucre.

60 To maken amidon tried. Nim amidon & seoþ hit in god
milke of alemauns, & do þerto sucre; & soþþen let dressen, &
soþþen strye abouen þe greyns of poume gernet.

61 To maken woelkeye. Nym woelkes & scure heom wel
wyþ water & salt, & soþþen let heowen heom on an bord ase
smale ase þou miht; & soþþen let grind hem wel in an morter.
& soþþen zeoþ hit in milke of alemauns oþur of cou, and
deliet wiþ amydon. & colore hit wiþ saffroun, | & do þerin f. 24ᵛ
comyn oþur peopur oþur poudre of spices.   6

62 To maken hoistreye. Nim hostrees & mak am zeoþen,
& soþþen do am out of þe broþ; & wyte þe broþ. & soþþen
heuw am smale on an bord, & braye heom in an morter, &
soþþen do am in þe broþ & do þerto milke of alemauns, & lie
hit wiþ amydon. & let frien oygnons & mynsen heom by am 5
seoluen in oyle; & ȝef þou nast non oyle, let seoþen heom in
god milke of alemaundes. & do þerto a poudre of gode spices,
and colore hit wyþ saffroun.

63 A potage þat me clepeþ mule. Nym potten & let heten in
water, & soþþen let hewen, & grynd am in an morter ase is
tovoren ysaid of hoystres, & do aȝeyn in þe broþ. & do þerto
god milke of alemauns, & lye hit wiþ amidone. & let heten

59. 2 boillen] billen MS   4 oþer] *add* of MS
61. 2 wyþ] in J   3 wel] *om.* J   4 soþþen] *om.* J   5 deliet]
dely et J   6 oþur²] or oþer J
62. 2 & soþþen¹] *om.* J;   & wyte þe broþ] *om.* J
63. 1 clepeþ] calleth J;   heten] heten hem J   1-2 in water] *om.*
He   2 hewen] hewen hem J   3 broþ] bre J

5 chestens, & don awey clanliche þe hole wiþoutee, & do am
þerto al hole; & do þerto comin & peoper & poudre of speces,
& colure wiþ saffren.

Explicit doctrina faciendi diuersa cibaria.

5 awey] *om.* J;   hole] ihole He   7 saffren] saffre He

PART II
DIUERSA SERVISA

Contents of MS Douce 257 (D)	Other MS Sources	Page
1. Furmenty	As, S2	62
2. Pise of Almayne	S2	62
3. Cranys & herons	W	62
4. Pecokys and pertrigchis	As, W	62
5. Mortrellus	As, S2, W	62
6. Caponys in concys	As, W	63
7. Hennys in bruet	As, S2, W	63
8. Harys in ciuee	As, W	63
9. Haris in talbotays	As, W	63
10. Conynggys in grauey	As, S2, W	63
11. Colys	As, S2, W	64
12. Nombles	As, S2, W	64
13. Blanche brewet de Almayne	As, S2, W	64
14. Blomanger	As, S2, W	64
15. Fronchemoyle	As (part), W	65
16. Brynewes	As (part), P, S2, W	65
17. Appulmos	S2, W	65
18. Froys	As, S2, W	65
19. Fruturs	As, S2, W	65
20. Charlet	As, W	66
21. Iussel	As, W	66
22. Gees in hochepot	As, S2, W	66
23. Eyryn in bruet	W	66
24. Craytoun	W	66
25. Mylk rost	As, S2, W	66
26. Cryspys	As, W	67
27. Berandyles	—	67
28. Capons in casselys	—	67
29. Blank de surry	—	67
30. Maumene	—	68
31. Bruet of Almayne	—	68
32. Bruet of Lombardye	S3	68
33. Blomanger	—	68
34. Sandale	—	69
35. Apulmose	—	69
36. Mete gelee	—	69
37. Murrey	—	69
38. Pench of egges	—	69

39. Comyn	—	70
40. Fruturs	—	70
41. Rosee	—	70
42. Pommedorry	—	70
43. Longe de buf	—	70
44. Rew de runsy	—	71
45. Bukkenade	L	71
46. Spine	S2	71
47. Rosee & Fresee & Swau	—	71
48. Mortrellus blanc	—	71
49. Amendement for mete þat ys to salt	L	71
50. Rapy	—	72
51. Egge dows	—	72
52. Mallard in cyuey	—	72
53. Bukkenade	—	72
54. Roo broth	—	72
55. Bruet of sarcynesse	—	72
56. Gely	—	73
57. To kepe venisoun fro restyng	—	73
58. To do awey restyng of venisoun	—	73
59. Poum dorroge	—	73
60. Egerduse	L, S2, W	74
61. Rapy	L, S2	74
62. Fygey	L, S2	74
63. Pommys morles	L, W	74
64. Rys moyle	L, P, W	75
65. Sowpys dorry	As, L, S2, W	75
66. Blomanger of fysch	L, W	75
67. Potage of rys	L, S2, W	75
68. Lampray fresch in galentyne	W	75
69. Salt lomprey in galentyne	W	75
70. Lampreys in bruet	—	76
71. Storchoun	—	76
72. Solys in bruet	—	76
73. Oystryn in bruet	—	76
74. Elys in bruet	W	76
75. Lopister	—	76
76. Porreyne	—	76
77. Chireseye	—	77
78. Blank desure	P	77
79. Graue enforse	—	77
80. Hony douse	—	77
81. Potage fene boiles	—	77
82. Tartys in applis	P	78
83. Rys alkere	—	78
84. Tartys of fysch owt of lente	—	78
85. Morrey	—	78

86. Flownys in lente — 78
87. Rapee — 78
88. Porrey chapeleyn — 79
89. Formenty on a fichssday — 79
90. Blank de syry — 79
91. Pynade — 79
92. Balough broth — 79

Note: The base MS is Bodleian Douce 257 (D) ff. 86-96ᵛ. Other MSS consulted are Bodleian Ashmole 1444 (As) pp. 190-2 and Laud Misc. 553 (L) ff. 5-6ᵛ; British Library Sloane 1108 (S2) ff. 21-24ᵛ and Sloane 442 (S3) f. 12; Aberystwyth Peniarth 394 D (P) pp. 80-1; and New York Whitney 1 (W) ff. 12-14ᵛ. For information on the principal manuscripts, see Introduction, pp. 17-19.

f. 86 *Hic incipiunt diuersa servicia tam de carnibus quam de pissibus.*

1　For to make furmenty. Nym clene wete & bray it in a morter wel, þat þe holys gon al of, & seyt yt til yt þreste; & nym yt vp & lat it kele. And nym fayre fresch broþ & swete mylk of almandys or swete mylk of kyne and temper yt al.
5 & nym þe ʒolkys of eyryn & saffron & do þerto. Boyle it a lityl & set yt adoun, & messe yt forþe wyþ fat venysoun & fresch motoun.

2　For to make pise of Almayne. Nym wyte pisyn & wasch
f. 86ᵛ hem & seþ hem a god | wyle; siþþyn wasch hem in cold watyr vnto þe holys gon of alle, and do hem alle in a pot, & keuer yt wel þat no breþ passe owt, & boyle hem ryʒt wel. & do
5 þereto god mylk of almandys & a party of flowr of rys, & salt & safroun, & messe yt forþe.

3　Cranys & herons schulle be enarmud wyþ lardons of swyne & rostyd & etyn wyþ gyngyuyr.

4　Pecokys and pertrigchis schul ben yperboyld & lardyd & rosted & etyn wyþ gyngeuyr.

5　Mortrellus. Nym hennyn & porke & seþ hem togedere. Nym þe lyre of þe hennyn & þe porke & hakke smal, & grynd hit al to dust, and wyte bred þerewyþ; & temper it wyþ þe selue broþ and wyþ heyryn. And colure it wyþ safroun &
5 boyle it, & disch it, & cast þereon powder of peper & of gyngyuyr & serue it forþe.

Heading Hic . . . pissibus] Here begynnys curye on inglysch bothe of flesche & of fysche As
　　1. 2 seyt] sethe AsS2　　　　　3 kele] *add* but þis most be done ouer nyght S2;　　　3-4 swete . . . or] *om.* S2　　　5 & saffron & do þerto] *om.* D 6 lityl] *add* & salt it AsS2　　　6 &³] oþer with As
　　2. 1 Almayne] maye S2　　　2 siþþyn] siþtyn D, and S2;　　cold] golde D 5 rys] *add* with poudre of gynger S2
　　3. 1-2 lardons of swyne] larder of bakenne W
　　4. 1 & lardyd] *om.* W　　　2 & rostyd] *om.* D
　　5. 1 Mortrellus] mortrews S2, mortereus de chare As　　　2 Nym] & when it is sothen nyme it vp & do of þe skynne of þe hennys (*rest of recipe missing*) As　　　2 Nym þe . . . porke] *om.* S2　　　2 lyre] liuour W; hakke] hakkyþ D　　　5 & disch it] *om.* W　　　5 & of] or of S2

6 Caponys in concys schal be sodyn. Nym þe lyre & brek it smal in a morter, & peper & wyte bred þerwyþ, & temper it wyþ ale, & ley it wyþ þe capoun. Nym hard sodyn eyryn & hew þe wyte smal, & keste þereto, & nym þe ȝolkys al hole & do hem in a dysch; & boyle þe capoun & colowre it wyþ 5 safroun, & salt it, & messe it forþe.

7 Hennys in bruet schullyn be schaldyd & sodyn wyþ porke; & grynd pepyr & comyn, bred & ale, & temper it wyþ þe selue broþ & boyle it, & colowre it wyþ safroun & salt it, & mes it forþe.

8 Harys in ciuee schul be perboyled & lardyd & rostid; & nym onyons & myce hem ryȝt smal & fry hem in wyte gres, & grynd peper, bred, | & ale, and þe onions þereto, and boyll f. 87 it, & do þerto & coloure it wyþ safroun & salt it, & serue it forth. 5

9 Haris in talbotays schul be hewe in gobettys al raw and sodyn with al þe blod. Nym bred, piper & ale & grynd togedere, & temper it wyþ þe selue broth, & boyle it & salt it & serue it forþe.

10 Conynggys in grauey schul be sodyn & hakkyd in gobettys; and grynd gyngyuyr, galyngale & canel, & temper it vp wyþ god almand mylk & boyle it. & nym macys and clowys and kest þerin, & þe conynggis also, & salt hym & serue it forþe.

6. 1 Caponys . . . &] *missing* As;   brek] braie W, brayed As   2 &¹ . . . þerwyþ] *missing* As   3 eyryn] e'y'ryn D, *missing* As   4 & nym] ix of As   5 capoun] counces As   6 it¹] *add* —in ȝolkes (*2 or 3 illeg. letters at edge of page*) As

7. 1 schaldyd &] *om.* W   1-2 wyþ porke &] *om.* As   2 comyn] *om.* AsS2;   & ale] *om.* S2   3 & salt it] *om.* S2   4 mes it forþe] dresse it þe hennys in dysches & messe on þe bruet As

8. 1-2 rostid . . . ryȝt] hakked in gobettes sothen & myced onȝons As   2 in wyte] wyt W   3-4 boyll . . . þerto &] *om.* DW

9. 2 al þe] ale & W

10. 1 sodyn] flayn As;   sodyn . . . gobettys] perboiled and larded and rosted S2   3 macys] *add* quibibes AsS2   4 kest . . . also] dresse it in dysches & kast abouen all of the self powde spices (all, powde *canc.*) As; & þe . . . hym] *om.* S2

11   For to make a colys. Nym hennys & schald hem wel, &
seþ hem after; & nym þe lyre & hak yt smal & bray it wyþ
otyn grotys in a morter, & with wyte bred, & temper it vp
wyþ þe broth. Nym þe grete bonys & grynd hem al to dust, &
5 kest hem al in þe broth & mak it þorw a cloþe, & boyle it &
serue it forþe.

12   For to make nombles. Nym þe nomblys of þe venysoun
& wasch hem clene in water and salt hem, & seþ hem in tweye
waterys. Grynd pepyr, bred & ale & temper it wyþ þe secunde
broþe, & boyle it, & hak þe nomblys & do þeryn & serue it
5 forþe.

13   For to make blanche brewet de Almayne. Nym kedys or
chekenys & hew hem in morsellys & seþ hem in almande mylk
or in kyne mylke. Grynd gyngyuer, galingale, and cast þereto
& boyle it and serue it forþe.

14   For to make blomanger. Nym rys & lese hem & wasch
hem clene, & do þereto god almande mylke & seþ hem tyl
þey al tobrest; & þan lat hem kele. & nym þe lyre of þe hen-
f. 87ᵛ nyn or of capouns & grynd hem smal; kest þere|to wite grese
5 & boyle it. Nym blanchyd almandys & safroun & set hem
aboue in þe dysche & serue yt forþe.

11. 1 hennys] *add* or capons S2;   & schald hem wel] *om.* AsS2   2 lyre]
flesche As;   & hak yt smal] *om.* As   2-3 wyþ otyn grotys] wyt out
grestus W   3 wyte] *om.* W   3-4 & temper . . . broth] *om.* As   4 grete]
om. As, grotus & W   5 hem al in þe] ale & W;   mak . . . cloþe] clence
it thorh an hersyue As, clense it þorough a straynore or ellys þorough an hereseve
S2, drauh hit þeruh a streynoure W;   boyle it] *add* & colowre it with saffron
AsS2W
   12. 1 For . . . venysoun] Nownbols of venyson schal be schauen As   2 hem
& seþ hem] *om.* S2   4 nomblys] *add* small AsS2;   &³] *add* salt it As,
boile and S2
   13. 1 de Almayne] de Alyngyn D, *om.* S2   2 morsellys] *add* al rawe
S2   2-3 in almande . . . mylke] grapes or wyne As   3 galingale]
add & mylk of almondes As   3-4 Grynd . . . boyle it] cast þerto myced
onyons and good poudre S2   4 it¹] *add* salt it As
   14. 1 Nym] *add* a pownd of AsS2   2 god almande mylke] mylk of
two pownd of almondes (*follows* kele *l. 3*) AsS2   3 tobrest] *add* & tak
him down W   3-4 nym . . . þereto] & frye ham browne in As   4 or
of capouns] *om.* S2;   þereto] *add* sugur & W;   wite grese] swynes
grece & sugure of roche S2   5 & safroun] and fry hem in fresshe grece
S2, and frie hem & set hem W   5-6 & boyle . . . dysche] þe mete in
disches & set þe almondes abouen As

15 For to make a fronchemoyle. Nym eyryn wyþ al þe wyte & myse bred & schepys talwe as gret as dysys. Grynd peper and safroun and kast þerto, & do hit in þe schepis wombe. Seþ it wel & dresse it forþe of brode leches þynne.

16 For to make brynewes. Nym þe þarmys of a pygge & wasch hem clene in water & salt, & seþ hem wel; & þan hak hem smale, & grynd pepyr and safroun, bred & ale, & boyle togedere. Nym wytys of eyryn & knede it wyþ flour, & mak smal pelotys & fry hem wyþ wyte grees, & do hem in dysches 5 aboue þat oþere mete & serue yt forþe.

17 For to make appulmos. Nym appelyn & seþ hem, & lat hem kele, & mak hem þorw a cloþe. & on flesch dayes kast þereto god fat broyt of bef & god wyte grees, & sugur & safroun; and god almande mylk on fysch dayes, oyle de olyue & gode powdres; & serue it forþe. 5

18 For to make a froys. Nym veel and seþ yt wel & hak it smal, & grynd bred, peper & safroun and do þereto & frye yt, & presse yt wel vpon a bord, & dresse yt forþe.

19 For to make fruturs. Nym flowre & eyryn & grynd peper & safroun & mak þereto a batour; & par aplyn & kyt hem to brode penys, & kest hem þereyn, & fry hem in þe batour wyþ fresch grees & serue yt forþe.

15. 2 as gret as dysys] and grind all togedur W   2–4 dysys . . . þynne] *missing* As   4 wel . . . þynne] & leche hit forþe W
    16. 1 brynewes] brymes D, bryneuxus S2, drineus W, brinews P;   þarmys of a pygge] bowellys of a gryce S2   3–4 & boyle togedere] *om.* WP 4 wytys of] rawe P;   mak] *add* past þerof & mac As   6 aboue . . . mete] boyle them togedir P;   aboue . . . forþe] boyle þe bryneles (*earlier part of recipe missing*) As, & boile þat and do þeron &c W
    17. 3 fat] fressh S2;   broyt of] broþ of frech W;   god wyte grees] *om.* S2   4 safroun] *add* and good powder (*repeated in l. 5*) W
    18. 1 veel] or ellys porcke, so it be not to fatte S2   2 bred] *om.* W; safroun] *add* and egges W;   yt] *add* in a panne with oyle or fresshe grece or ellys fresshe buttyr, for þat is best, and turne it wele for brennyng to S2 3 wel vpon] in þe panne with S2;   bord] *add* þanne leche it S2;   dresse] leche W
    19. 1 flowre &] *add* yolkes of S2;   grynd peper] *om.* W   2 aplyn] *add* or ellys fyges, but þanne þou most presse þe fyges al abrode S2;   kyt hem] schred hem smal and brod W   2–3 to brode penys] brode As, brode and þynne S2, *om.* W   3 in þe batour wyþ] *om.* As, in a fayre panne with fresshe buttyr or oile or S2   3–4 wyþ fresch grees] *om.* W 4 fresch] white As;   grees] *add* turne hem and take hem vp and cast sugure vpoun hym or ellys poudre of sinamome or of canel S2

20 For to make charlet. Nym porke & seþ it wel & hak yt
f. 88 smal. Nym eyryn wyþ al þe wytys and swyng | hem wel al
togedere, & kast god swete mylke þereto & boyle yt & messe
yt forþe.

21 For to make Iussel. Nym eyryn wyþ al þe wytys & mice
bred; grynd pepyr & safroun and do þereto, and temper yt wyþ
god fresch broth of porke and boyle it wel, & messe yt forþe.

22 For to make gees in hochepot. Nym and schald hem wel,
& hewe hem wel in gobettys al rawe; & seþ hem in her owyn
grees, & cast þerto wyn or ale a cuppe ful; & myce onyons
smal and do þereto & boyle yt & salt yt & messe yt forþe.

23 For to make eyryn in bruet. Nym water & welle yt, &
brek eyryn & kast þeryn, and grynd peper & safroun & temper vp wyþ swete mylk, & boyle it; & hakke chese smal &
cast þeryn, & messe yt forþe.

24 For to make craytoun. Tak checonys & schald hem, &
seþ hem; & grynd gyngeuer oþer pepyr & comyn, and temper
it vp wyþ god mylk & do þe checonys þereyn, & boyle hem
& serue yt forþe.

25 For to make mylk rost. Nym swete mylk & do yt in a
panne. Nym eyryn wyþ al þe wyte & swyng hem wel & cast
þereto & colowre yt wyþ safroun & boyle yt tyl yt wexe
þykke, & þanne seyz yt þorw a culdore, & nym þat leuyþ

20. 1 charlet] *repeated in margin in later hand* D   3 þereto] *add* & do
it in a faire panne As
    21. 3 wel . . . forþe] and hak chese smal & do þerynne &c W
    22. 1 hochepot] ochepot D, hoggepott As;   Nym] *add* a gose and he be
fatte S2;   Nym . . . wel] *om.* As   2-3 her . . . ful] an erthyn potte
and late hym boile in wyne or in goode ale. And lete þe pot be stopped close. And
when þe flesshe is tendre grynde peper and saffron S2   3 a cuppe ful]
om. W   3-4 & myce . . . þereto] *om.* As
    23. 1 welle yt] boil hit ouer þe fuyre W   2 grynd] *add* bred & W
3 swete] *om.* W
    24. 1 & schald hem] *om.* As   2 &¹] *add* sythen do of þe skyn & quar-
ter ham As   3 do . . . þereyn &] *om.* As, & coloure hit safrenne & do
eggus þerynne W;   hem] *add* salt it AsW
    25. 2 Nym] nyn D   3 wyþ] *add* peper and S2   3-4 safroun
. . . seyz] safroun yground and medle it with þe egges. And whan þe mylke is a
lytel hote cast þyne egges and þy spicery þerto and stere it well and late it boile
tyl it crudde, þen take it vp and streyne S2   4 & . . . culdore] set hit
doun & coloure hit W;   seyz] seþ D, streyne S2;   culdore . . . leuyþ]
clothe nyne þat leuys As;   leuyþ] in þe cloþe S2

& presse yt vpon a bord; & wan yt ys cold larde it, & scher yt 5
on schyuerys, & roste yt on a grydern & serue yt forþe.

26   For to make cryspys. Nym flour & wytys of eyryn, sugur
oþer hony, & swyng togedere & mak a batour. Nym wyte
grees & do | yt in a posnet, & cast þe batur þereyn & stury to   f. 88ᵛ
þou haue many; & tak hem vp & messe hem wyþ þe frutours
& serue forþe.   5

27   For to make berandyles. Nym hennys & seþ hem wyþ
god buf, & wan hi ben sodyn nym þe hennyn & do awey þe
bonys & bray smal yn a morter, & temper yt wyþ þe broth &
seyz yt þorw a culdore, & cast þereto powder of gyngeuyr &
sugur & graynys of powmys gernatys, & boyle yt & dresse yt 5
in dysches, & cast aboue clowys gylofres & maces & god powder & serue yt forþe.

28   For to make capons in casselys. Nym caponys & schald
hem. Nym a penne & opyn þe sckyn at þe heuyd & blowe
hem tyl þe sckyn ryse from þe flesche, & do of þe skyn al
hole. & seþ þe lyre of hennyn & ʒolkys of heyryn & god
powder, & make a farsure, & fil ful þe skyn and perboyle yt, 5
& do yt on a spete & rost yt and droppe yt wyþ ʒolkes of
eyryn & god powder rostyng. & nym þe caponys body &
larde yt, & roste it, & nym almaunde mylk and amydoun and
mak a batur, & droppe þe body rostyng, & serue yt forþe.

29   For to make blank de surry, tak braun of caponys oþer
of hennys and þe þyes wyþowte þe skyn, & kerf hem smal als
þou mayst & grynd hem smal in a morter. & tak mylk of
almaundys & do yn þe braune, & grynd hem þanne togedere
& seþ hem togedere. | And tak flour of rys oþer amydoun   f. 89
and lye it þat yt be charchant, and do þereto sugur a god   6
perti and a perty of wyt grees and boyle yt; & wan yt ys
doun in dyschis straw vpon blanke poudere, and do togedere
blank de sury & maumene in a dysch & serue yt forþe.

5–6 scher . . . schyuerys] schredde it þat is to say leche it S2
   26. 1 cryspys] cryppys D;   Nym] tak þe mayn W   3 stury] styr
it fast As   3–5 stury . . . forþe] stere hit whanne þou may tak hit W
   27. 4 seyz] seþ MS
   29. 1 blank de] 'blank' þe MS

30   For to make maumene, tak þe þyys oþer þe flesch of þe
caponys. Seþe hem & kerf hem smal into a morter & tak
mylk of almandys wyþ broth of fresch buf, & do þe flesch in
þe mylk or in þe broth & do yt to þe fyre, & myng yt togedere
5 wyþ flour of rys oþere of wastelys als charchant als þe Blank
de Sure, & wyþ þe ʒolkys of eyryn for to make yt ʒolow, &
safroun. & wan yt ys dressyd in dysches wyþ Blank de Sure,
straw vpon clowys of gelofre & straw vpon powdre of galentyn, & serue yt forþe.

31   For to make bruet of Almayne, tak pertrichys rostyd
and checonys & quaylis rostyd & larkys ywol, & demembre
þe oþer; & mak a god cawdel, & dresse þe flesch in a dysch &
strawe powder of galentyn þervpon. Styk vpon clowys of
5 gelofre & serue yt forþe.

32   For to make bruet of Lombardye, tak chekenys or hennys or oþere flesch, & mak þe colowre als red as any blod; &
tak peper and kanel & gyngyuer bred & grynd hem in a morter, & a porcioun of bred. And mak þat bruet þenne, & do
5 þat flesch in þat broth & mak hem boyle togedere, & stury it
wel. & tak eggys & temper hem wyþ ius of percyle & wryng
hem þorwe a cloþ, & wan þat bruet ys boylyd do þat þereto
& meng þam togedere wyþ fayr grees so þat yt be fat ynow,
& serue yt forþe. |

f. 89ᵛ **33**   For to make blomanger, do ris in water al nyʒt & vp|on
þe morwe wasch hem wel & do hem vpon þe fyre for to þey
breke, & noʒt for to muche; & tak braun of caponis sodyn &
wel ydrawe & smal, & tak almaund mylk & boyle it wel wyþ
5 ris, & wan it is yboylyd do þe flesch þerein so þat it be
charghaunt. & do þereto a god perty of sugure, & wan it ys
dressyd forþ in dischis straw þereon blaunche pouder & strik
þereon almaundys fryed wyt wyte grece & serue yt forþe.

30. 2 Seþe] sede MS
32. 1 chekenys] *add* conynges S3   2 blod] *add* wit alkenet S3
3 kanel . . . bred] *om.* S3   4 bred] *add* do þerto mylke of almondes S3
6 eggys] ʒolkys of eyryn sodyn harde S3   7 boylyd] loylyd D
8 fayr . . . ynow] a lytyl grece or a lytyl bottur claryfyed or þe fatte of porke
& seson it vp wit powder salt & vynegur S3

34   For to make sandale þat is perty to blomanger, tak flesch of caponys & of pork, sodyn. Kerf yt smal into a morter togedere & bray þat wel, & temper it vp wyþ broþ of caponys & of pork þat yt be wel charchaunt als þe crem of almaundys. & grynd egges and safroun or sandres togedere þat it be 5 colourd, & straw vpon powder of galentyn, & strik þereon clowys & maces & serue it forþe.

35   For to make apulmose, tak applys & seþ hem and let hem kele, & after mak hem þorwe a cloþ & do hem in a pot. & kast to þat mylk of almaundys, wyþ god broþ of buf in flesch dayes; do bred ymyed þereto. & þe fisch dayes, do þereto oyle of olyue, & do þereto sugur & coloure it wyth 5 safroun, & strew þeron powder & serue it forþe.

36   For to make mete gelee þat it be wel chariaunt, tak wyte wyn & a perty of water & safroun & gode spicis & flesch of piggys or of hennys, or fresch fisch, & boyle þam togedere; & after, wan yt ys boylyd & cold, | dres yt in f. 90 dischis & serue yt forþe.   5

37   For to make murrey, tak mulbery & bray hem in a morter & wryng hem þorh a cloþ, & do hem in a pot ouer þe fyre; & do þereto bred & wyte gresse, & let yt naȝt boyle non ofter þan onys. & do þereto a god perty of sugur, & ȝif yt be noȝt ynowe ycolowrd brey mulburus; & serue yt forþe.   5

38   For to make a pench of egges, tak water & do it in a panne to þe fyre, & lat yt sethe; & after tak egges & brek hem & cast hem in þe water. & after tak a chese & kerf yt on fowre pertis & kast in þe water, & wanne þe chese and þe eggys ben wel sodyn, tak hem owt of þe water & wasch hem in clene 5 water. & tak wastel breed & temper yt wyþ mylk of a kow, & after do yt ouer þe fyre, & after forsy yt wyþ gyngeuer and wyþ comyn & colowre yt wyþ safroun, & lye yt wyþ eggys. & oyle þe sewe wyþ boter, & kep wel þe chese owt, & dresse þe sewe & do þin eggys þereon al ful, & kerf þy chese in 10

34. 1 is] *om.* MS   4 als] also MS
37. 2 wryng] wþyng MS   3 þereto] *add* fat MS
38. 4 pertis] pertnis MS   10 do þin] dyins(?) *with bar over* y; *perhaps an attempt to copy* do þine *with confusion of* þ/y *and* e/s MS

lytyl schyuis & do hem in þe sewe wyþ eggys, and serue yt
forþe.

39   For to make comyn, tak god almaunde mylk & lat yt
boyle, & do þerein amydoun wyþ flowre of rys, & colowre yt
wyþ safroun; & after dresse yt wyþ greynis of poum garnettes
oþer wyþ reysyns, ȝyf þow hast non oþer. & tak sugur & do
5 þereyn & serue yt forþe.

40   For to make fruturs, tak crommys of wyte bred & þe |
f. 90ᵛ flowris of þe swete appyl tre and ȝolkys of eggys, and bray
hem togedere in a morter, and temper it vp wyþ wyte wyn
and make yt to seþe. & wan yt ys þykke do þereto god spicis
5 of gyngeuer, galyngale, canel, and clowys gelofre, and serue
yt forth.

41   For to make rosee, tak þe flowrys of rosys and wasch
hem wel in water, and after bray hem wel in a morter; & þan
tak almondys and temper hem, & seþ hem. & after tak flesch
of capons or of hennys and hac yt smale, & þan bray hem wel
5 in a morter, & þan do yt in þe rose so þat þe flesch acorde
wyþ þe mylk, & so þat þe mete be charchaunt; & after do yt
to þe fyre to boyle, & do þereto sugur & safroun þat yt be
wel ycolowrd & rosy of leuys of þe forseyde flowrys, & serue
yt forth.

42   For to make pommedorry, tak buff & hewe yt smal al
raw, & cast yt in a morter & grynd yt noȝt to smal. Tak
safroun & grynd þerewyþ. Wan yt ys grounde, tak þe wyte of
þe eyryn, ȝyf yt be noȝt styf; cast into þe buf pouder of
5 pepyr, olde reysyns & reysyns of coronse. Set ouer a panne
wyþ fayr water, & mak pelotys of þe buf; & wan þe water &
þe pelotes ys wel yboylyd, set yt adoun & kele yt. Put yt on
a broche & rost yt, & endorre yt wyþ ȝolkys of eyryn &
serue yt forþe.

43   For to make longe de buf, nym þe tonge of þe rether &
schalde, & schawe yt wel & ryȝt clene, & seth yt; & seþe nym

39. 3 poum] poun MS
41. 8 leuys] *add* & MS
42. 5 reysyns²] *om.* MS   7 yboylyd] *add* & MS

a broche, & larde yt wyþ lardons and wyþ | clowys gelofre, & f. 91
do it rostyng. & drop yt, wel yrostyd, wyþ ʒolkys of eyrin, &
dresse it forþe.

44 For to make rew de runsy. Nym swynys fet & eyr &
make hem clene, & seth hem half wyþ wyn & half wyþ water.
Cast mycyd onyons þereto & god spicis, & wan þey be ysodyn
nym & rosty hem on a grydere. Wan it is yrostyd kest þereto
of þe selue broth ylyed wyþ amydoun and amycyd onyons, 5
& serue yt forth.

45 For to make bukkenade. Nym god fresch flesch, wat
maner so yt be, & hew yt in smale morselys, & seth yt wyþ
gode fresch buf; & cast þereto gode myncyd onyons & gode
spicerye, & alyth wyþ eyryn, & boyle & dresse yt forth.

46 For to make spine. Nym þe flowrys of þe hawþorn clene
gaderyd & bray hem al to dust, & temper hem wyþ almaunde
mylk & aly yt wyþ amydoun & wyþ eyryn wel þykke; &
boyle it & messe yt forth, & flowrys & leuys abouyn on.

47 For to make rosee & fresee & swau: þey schal be ymad
in þe selue maner.

48 Mortrellus blanc. Nym pyggus and hennys & oþer maner
fresch flesch & hew yt in morselys & seth yt in wyth wyn, &
nym gyngyuer & galyngale & gelofre & canel, & bray yt wel
& kest þereto. & alye yt wyþ amydoun oþer wyþ flowr of rys.

49 For to make amendement for mete þat ys to salt, & ouer
mychyl. Nym ote mele & bynd yt in a fayr lynnyn clowt, &

43. 4 yrostyd] yt rostyd MS
44. 2 half¹] alf MS   4 on] in MS   5 ylyed] he lyed MS;
amycyd] anycyd MS
45. 2 maner so yt] it euere L;   & hew . . . morselys] *om.* L;   wyþ] wyþ
wyþ D   4 & boyle] *om.* L
46. 1 þe¹] whyte S2;   hawþorn] haw þhorn D   3 mylk] *add* or
ellys cowe mylke, and grynde brede þerwith S2;   eyryn] egges and swynge
hem S2
47. 1 þey] *om.* MS
48. 1 Mortrellus blanc] *title om.; no gap in* MS   3 nym] *om.* MS
49. 1-2 For . . . mychyl] amendement of salt mete L

f. 91ᵛ lat yt honge | in þe pot so þat yt towche noȝt þe bottym,
& lat yt hongy þereynne a god wyle; & seþe set yt fro þe
5 fyre & let yt kele, & yt schal be fresch ynow wyþoute any
oþer maner licowr ydo þereto.

50   For to make rapy: tak fygys & reysyns & wyn, & grynd
hem togeder; tak and draw hem þorw a cloþ & do þereto
powdere of alkenet oþer of rys. & do þereto a god quantite
of powder of pepir & vyneger, and boyle it togedere, & messe
5 yt & serue yt forth.

51   For to make an egge dows: tak almaundys & mak god
mylk, & temper wyþ god wyneger clene. Tak reysynys &
boyle hem in clene water, & tak þe reysynis & tak hem owt
of þe water & boyle hem wyþ mylk, & ȝyf þow wyl colowre
5 yt wyþ safroun & serue yt forth.

52   For to make a mallard in cyuey, tak a mallard & pul
hym drye, & swyng ouer þe fyre. Draw hym, but lat hym
touche no water; & hew hym in gobettys, & do hym in a pot
of clene water. Boyle hym wel & tak onyons & boyle, & bred
5 & pepyr, & grynd togedere & drawe þorw a cloþ. Temper
wyþ wyn, & boyle yt, & serue yt forþ.

53   For to make a bukkenade, tak veel & boyle it. Tak
ȝolkys of eggys & mak hem þykke. Tak macis & powdre of
gyngyuer & powdere of peper, & boyle yt togedere & messe
yt forth.

54   For to make a roo broth, tak persile & ysop & sauge, &
f. 92 hak yt smal. Boil | it in wyn & in water & a lytyl powdre of
peper & messe yt forth.

55   For to make a bruet of sarcynesse, tak þe lyre of þe
fresch buf & ket it al in pecis, & bred, & fry yt in fresch gres.
Tak it vp & drye it, & do yt in a vessel wyþ wyn & sugur &
powdre of clowys. Boyl yt togedere tyl þe flesch haue drong

---

3 so . . . noȝt] doun to L;   towche] thowche D   4 & . . . wyle] *om.* L;
seþe] seþh D   5 kele]*add* suþþe set hit aȝen to þe fuyr & drawe out þy
clout L   5-6 yt² . . . þereto] þat is goud L

þe lycoure, & tak almande mylk & quibibz, macis & clowys, 5
& boyle hem togedere. Tak þe flesch & do þereto & messe it
forth.

56 For to make a gely, tak hoggys fet oþer pyggys, oþer
erys, oþer pertrichys oþere chiconys, & do hem togedere &
seth hem in a pot; & do in hem flowre of canel and clowys
hole or grounde. Do þereto vineger, & tak & do þe broth in a
clene vessel of al þys, & tak þe flesch and kerf yt in smale 5
morselys & do yt þerein. Tak powder of galyngale & cast
aboue & lat yt kele. Tak bronchys of þe lorere tre & styk
ouer it, & kep yt al so longe as þou wilt & serue yt forth.

57 For to kepe venisoun fro restyng, tak venisoun wan yt
ys newe & cuuer it hastely wyþ fern þat no wynd may come
þereto and wan þou hast ycuuer yt wel led yt hom & do yt
in a soler þat sonne ne wynd may come þerto. & dimembre
it, & do yt in a clene water & lef yt þere half a day, | and f. 92ᵛ
after do yt vpon herdeles for to dre; & wan yt ys drye tak 6
salt, & do after þy venisoun axit, & do yt boyle in water þat
be so salt als water of þe see and moche more. & after lat þe
water be cold, þat it be þynne, & þanne do þy venisoun in þe
water & lat yt be þerein þre daies & þre ny3t; & after tak yt 10
owt of þe water & salt it wyþ dre salt ry3t wel in a barel, &
wan þy barel ys ful cuuer it hastely þat sunne ne wynd come
þereto.

58 For to do awey restyng of venisoun, tak þe venisoun þat
ys rest & do yt in cold water & after mak an hole in þe herþe
& lat yt be þereyn þre dayes & þre ny3t; & after tak yt vp &
frot yt wel wyþ gret salt of poite þere were þe restyng ys. &
after lat yt hange in reyn water al ny3t or more. 5

59 For to make poum dorroge, tak pertrichis wit longe
filettis of pork al raw & hak hem wel smale, and after bray
hem in a morter. & wan þey be wel brayd do þereto god

56. 3 in hem] hem in MS   4 hole] oþer MS
57. 8 be so] yt be oþer so MS
58. 4 frot] spot MS
59. 1 wit] wit wit MS

plente of poudere & ȝolkys of eyryn. & after mak þereof a
5 farsure formed of þe gretnesse of a onyoun, & after do it
boyle in god breth of buf oþer of pork. After lat yt kele, &
after do it on a broche of hasel & do hem to þe fere to roste.
f. 93 & after mak god bature | of floure & egges, on bature wyt &
an oþere ȝelow & do þereto god plente of sugur & tak a
10 feþere or a styk & tak of þe bature & peynte þereon aboue þe
applyn so þat on be wyt & þat oþere ȝelow wel colourd.

*Explicit seruicium de carnibus; hic incipit seruicium de pissi-
bus.*

60 For to make egerduse, tak lucys or tenchis & hak hem
smal in gobettes, & fry hem in oyle de oliue; & syþ nym
vineger & þe þredde perty of sugur & myncyd onyons smal,
& boyle al togedere, & cast þereyn clowys, macys & quibibz
5 & serue yt forþe.

61 For to make rapy. Tak pykes or tenchis or oþere maner
fresch fysch & fry yt wyþ oyle de oliue, & syþ nym þe crustys
of wyt bred & canel & bray it al wel in a mortere, & temper
yt vp wyþ god wyn & cole yt þorw an hersyue, & loke þat
5 yt be al ycoloured of canel; & boyle yt, & cast þerein hole
clowys & macys & quibibz, & do þe fysch in dischis & rape
abouyn, & dresse yt forþe.

62 For to make fygey. Nym figes & boille hem in wyn, and
bray hem in a morter wiþ lied bred. Tempre hit vp wyþ goud
wyn; boille it. Do þerto goud spicere & hole resons. Dresse
hit; florisshe it aboue wiþ pomme garnetes. |

f. 93ᵛ **63** For to make pommys morles. Nym rys & bray hem wel,
& temper hem vp wyþ almaunde mylk & boyle yt. Nym

60. 1 or] and S2   2 de oliue] *om.* LS2W;   syþ nym] seþ hem Tak W;
nym] *add* gyngeuer *canc.* D   4 al togedere] smal L;   macys] of mas W
61. 1 pykes] pyges D, luces S2, luyss L;   or¹] and S2   2 fresch]
om. L;   fysch] *add* and sethe 'it' and sithen S2   3 bred] *add* resons
LS2;   wel . . . mortere] *om.* L   4 loke þat] þat D, let L, loke S2
5 ycoloured] colo D;   hole] *om.* L
62. Nym . . . garnetes] *recipe given as it appears in MS L; recipe in D repeats
No.* **60**

applyn & pare hem & sher hem smal als dicis, & cast hem
þereyn after þe boylyng, & cast sugur wyþal, & colowre yt
wyþ safroun & cast þereto pouder, & serue yt forthe. 5

64 For to make rys moyle. Nym rys & bray hem ryȝt wel
in a mortere, & cast þereto god almaunde mylk & sugur &
salt; & boyle it & serue yt forth.

65 For to make sowpys dorry. Nym onyons & mynce hem
smale & fry hem in oyle dolyf. Nym wyn & boyle yt wyþ þe
onyouns. Toste wyte bred & do yt in dischis, & god almande
mylk also, & do þe wyne with onyons aboue & serue yt forth.

66 For to make blomanger of fysch, tak a pound of rys.
Les hem wel & wasch, & seþ tyl þey breste & lat hem kele; &
do þereto mylk of to pound of almandys. Nym þe perche or
þe lopuster & boyle yt, & kest sugur & salt also þerto, &
serue yt forth. 5

67 For to make potage of rys, tak rys & les hem | and wasch f. 94
hem clene, & seþ hem tyl þey breste, & þan lat hem kele. &
seþ cast þerto almand mylk and colour it wyþ safroun, &
boyle it & messe yt forth.

68 For to make lampray fresch in galentyne schal be latyn
blod atte nauel, and schald yt & rost yt, & ley yt al hole vpon
a plater, & ȝyf hym forth wyþ galentyn þat be mad of galyngale, gyngeuer & canel, & dresse yt forth.

69 For to make salt lomprey in galentyne, yt schal be stoppit ouer nyȝt in lewe water & in braan, & flawe, & sodyn.

63. 3 pare . . . sher] kerue L;   dicis] douste LW;   cast] *om.* W
4 after . . . wyþal] and buyle hit a litel W
64. 1–2 ryȝt . . . god] tempre vp wiþ L   3 & boyle it] *om.* P
65. 2 dolyf] *om.* AsS2W, add or in buttyr S2   3 Toste] two schyues
of As   4 þe . . . onyons] þere D, þerto W
66. 2 Les . . . wasch] *om.* L;   wasch] *add* hem clene W   4 lopu-
ster] *add* or drie haddok tese þerto L, *add* or þe gurnard and meng þerto W;
& salt also] *om.* L
67. 1 tak . . . and] *om.* W;   & les hem] *om.* S2L   3 mylk] *add*
oþer of kyn L   4 boyle] salt L
68. 2 yt³] yd D
69. 2 ouer] a noure of þe W;   lewe] lews D, lue W

& pyl onyons & seþ hem & ley hem al hol by þe lomprey, &
ȝif hem forþe wyþ galentyne makyþ wyþ strong wyneger &
5 wyþ paryng of wyt bred, & boyle it al togedere & serue yt
forþe.

70 For to make lampreys in bruet, þey schulle be schaldyd
& ysode & ybrulyd vpon a gredern, & grynd peper & safroun
& do þerto, & boyle it & do þe lomprey þeryn & serue yt
forth.

71 For to make a storchoun, he schal be schorn in lesys &
stepyd ouer nyȝt, & sodyn longe as flesch; & he schal be etyn
in veneger.

72 For to make solys in bruet, þey schal be fleyn & sodyn
& rostyd vpon a gredern, & grynd peper & safroun, bred &
f. 94ᵛ ale; boyle it wel & do þe | sole in a plater & þe bruet aboue
& serue it forth.

73 For to make oystryn in bruet, þey schul be schallyd &
ysod in clene water. Grynd peper, safroun, bred & ale, &
temper it wyþ broth. Do þe oystryn þerynne & boyle it & salt
it & serue it forth.

74 For to make elys in bruet, þey schul be flayn & ket in
gobettes & sodyn; and grynd peper & safroun, oþer myntys &
persele, & bred & ale, & temper it wyþ þe broth & boyle it &
serue it forth.

75 For to make a lopister, he schal be rostyd in his scalys in
a ouyn oþer by þe feer vnder a panne, & eten wyþ veneger.

76 For to make porreyne, tak prunys fayrist. Wasch hem
wel & clene & frot hem wel in a syue þat þe ius be wel
ywronge, & do it in a pot. & do þereto wyt gres & a perty of
sugur oþer hony, & make hem to boyle togedere, & mak yt
5 þykke wyþ flowr of rys oþer wastel bred, & wan it is sodyn
dresse it into dischis & strew þeron powder & serue it forth.

---

74. 2 oþer myntys] & mise oynons W
75. 2 ouyn] *one letter is erased at the beginning of this word* (nouyn?) MS
76. 2 a] *om.* MS;   þat] for MS;   oþer] *add* of MS

77 For to make chireseye, tak chiryes at þe fest of Seynt
Iohn þe Baptist, & do awey þe stonys. Grynd hem in a morter, & after frot hem wel in a seue so þat þe ius be wel comyn
owt; & do þan in a pot & do þerein feyre gres or boter & bred
of | wastel ymyid, & of sugur a god perty, & a porcioun of f. 95
wyn. & wan it is wel ysodyn & ydressyd in dyschis, stik þerin 6
clowis of gilofre & strew þeron sugur.

78 For to make blank desure, tak þe ȝolkys of egges sodyn
& temper it wyþ mylk of a kow. & do þerto comyn & safroun
& flowre of ris or wastel bred myed, & grynd in a morter &
temper it vp wyþ þe milk; & mak it boyle & do þerto wit of
egges coruyn smal. & tak fat chese & kerf þerto wan þe licour 5
is boylyd, & serue it forth.

79 For to make graue enforse, tak triyd gyngeuer & safroun
& grynd hem in a morter & temper hem vp wyþ almandys, &
do hem to þe fire; & wan it boylyþ wel do þerto ȝolkys of
egges sodyn & fat chese coruyn in gobettis. & wan it is dressid
in dischis, strawe vpon powder of galyngale & serue it forth. 5

80 For to make hony douse, tak god mylk of almandys &
rys, & wasch hem wel in a feyre vessel & in fayre hot water.
& after do hem in a feyre towayl for to drie, & wan þat þey
be drye bray hem wel in a morter al to flowre; & after bet
hem togedere. & afterward tak two pertyis & do þe half in a 5
pot & þat oþer half in a noþer pot, & colowr þat on wyþ þe
safroun & lat þat oþer be wyt. & lat yt boyle tyl it be þykke,
& do þerto a god | perty of sugur, & after dresse yt in two f. 95ᵛ
dischis; & loke þat þou haue almandys boylid in water & in
safroun & in wyn, & after frie hem & set hem vpon þe forseyde 10
mete, & strew þeron sugur þat yt be wel ycolouryt & serue yt
forth.

81 For to make a potage fene boiles, tak wite benes & seþ
hem in water, & bray þe benys in a morter al to noȝt; & lat

77. 5 wastel] wastiel MS
78. 5–6 wan . . . boylyd] than boyle hit togeder P
    80. 2 hot] hoth MS   4 in a] in 'a' MS   10 forseyde] fyre
seþiþ MS

þem seþe in almande mylk & do þerein wyn & hony. & seþ
reysouns in wyn & do þerto & after dresse yt forth.

82 For to make tartys in applis, tak gode applys & gode
spycis & figys & reysons & perys, & wan þey arn wel ybrayd
colour wyþ safroun wel & do yt in a cofyn, & do yt forth to
bake wel.

83 For to make rys alkere, tak figys & reysons, & do awey
þe kernelis; & a god perty of applys, & do awey þe paryng of
þe applis & þe kernelis; & bray hem wel in a morter & temper
hem vp wyþ almande mylk & menge hem wyþ flour of rys
5 þat yt be wel chariand. & strew þervpon powder of galyngale
& serue yt forth.

84 For to make tartys of fysch owt of lente, make þe
cowche of fat chese & gyngeuer & canel & pure creym of
mylk of a kow & of helys ysoden, & grynd hem wel wyþ
f. 96 safroun; & mak þe cowche of canel | & of clowys & of rys &
5 of gode spycys as oþer tartys fallyþ to be.

85 For to make morrey, *require de carnibus vt supra.*

86 For to make flownys in lente, tak god flowr & make a
god past; & tak god mylk of almandys & flowr of rys oþer
of amydoun & boyle hem togedere þat þey be wel chariand.
Wan yt is boylid þykke take yt vp & ley yt on a feyre bord so
5 þat yt be cold, & wan þe cofyns ben makyd tak a perty & do
vpon þe coffyns, & kerf hem in schiueris; & do in hem god
mylk of almandys & figys & datys & kerf yt in fowre pertyis,
& do yt to bake & serue yt forth.

87 For to make rapee, tak þe crustys of wyt bred & reysons
& bray hem wel in a morter, & after temper hem vp wyþ wyn
& wryng hem þorw a cloþ. & do þereto canel, þat yt be al
colouryt of canel, & do þereto hole clowys, macys & quibibz.

82. 3 colour] colouryd D
84. 4 cowche] chowche MS
86. 5 perty] *add* of MS   6 schiueris] schĩue′ris MS;   in hem] him
in MS

þe fysch schal be lucys oþer tenchis fryid, or oþer maner fysch 5
so þat yt be fresch and wel yfryid; & do yt in dischis, & þat
rape vpon, & serue yt forth.

88   For to make a porrey chapeleyn, tak an hundred onyons
oþer an half, & tak oyle de olyf & boyle togedere in a pot; &
tak almande mylk & boyle yt & do þereto. | Tak & make a f. 96ᵛ
þynne paast of dow, & make þerof as it were ryngis. Tak &
fry hem in oyle de olyue or in wyte grees & boil al togedere.

89   For to make formenty on a fichssday, tak þe mylk of þe
hasel notis. Boyl þe wite wyth þe aftermelk til it be dryyd,
& tak & coloure yt wyth safroun; & þe ferst mylk cast þerto
& boyle wel, & serue yt forth.

90   For to make blank de syry, tak almande mylk & flowre
of rys; tak þerto sugur, & boyle þys togedere, & dische yt. &
tak almandys & wet hem in water of sugur, & drye hem in a
panne, & plante hem in þe mete & serue yt forth.

91   For to make a pynade, tak hony and rotys of radich &
grynd yt smal in a morter, & do to þat hony a quantite of
broun sugur. Tak powder of peper & safroun & almandys, &
do al togedere. Boyl hem long & held yt on a wet bord & let
yt kele, & messe yt & do yt forth.   5

92   For to make a balough broth, tak pikys & spred hem
abrod, & helys, ȝif þou hast, fle hem & ket hem in gobettys;
& seþ hem in half wyn & half in water. Tak vp þe pykys &
elys & hold hem hote, & draw þe broth þorwe a cloþe. Do
powder of gyngeuer, peper & galyngale & canel into þe broth 5
& boyle yt, & do yt on þe pykys & on þe elys & serue yt
forth.

Explicit de coquina que est optima medicina.

90. 1 blank de syry] 'Blank de surre' *in margin in a different hand* MS
91. 2 do] *add* yt þer MS   3 sugur] *add* & do þerto MS   4 on]
in MS
92. 1 balough] ballok *erased,* 'Balough Broth' *in margin in a different hand*
MS   3 half¹] alf MS

PART III
UTILIS COQUINARIO

Contents of MS Sloane 468 (S)	Other MS Sources	Page
1. Eles in counfy	—	83
2. Pyany	—	83
3. Pynade	—	83
4. Ruscheues	—	83
5. Crem & botere of almoundes	S1	84
6. Chauden	S1	84
7. Botere of almand melk	S1	84
8. Mortreux of lunges	S1	84
9. Tenche in syuee	S1	84
10. Mete vernis	S1	85
11. A swan	S1, C, As	85
12. Chauden	S1, C	85
13. þe heyroun	S1, As	85
14. Pekokes & partriches	S1, C, As	86
15. þe crane, (botores, curlewes, etc.)	S1, C, As	86
16. Saunc Sarazine	S1	86
17. Dauce egre	S1	86
18. Rapes	S1	86
19. Ro broþe	S1	87
20. Chicones in mose	S1	87
21. Viaunde of Cypre	S1	87
22. Browet of Almayne	S1	87
23. Coynes	S1	87
24. A fresch laumprey	S1	88
25. Mawmene	S1	88
26. Mortreux of fisch	S1, C	88
27. Blawmaunger mole	S1	89
28. Blawmanger	S1	89
29. Blaumaunger gros	S1	89
30. Blamaunger in lenten	S1	89
31. Spynee	S1, C	90
32. Rosye	S1, C	90
33. Syrosye	S1, C	90
34. Primerole	S1, C	90
35. Vyolet	S1, C	91
36. Fawne	S1, C	91
37. Heppee	S1 (part), C	91

Note: The base MS, BL Sloane 468 (S) ff. 81^V–92, has been collated with BL Sloane 374 (S1) ff. 86^V–91^V and with Durham University Library Cosin v. iii. 11 (C) ff. 23^V–25 and Bodleian Ashmole 1444 (As) p. 190 where applicable, but there are few variants in this collection and most of them are insignificant and have, thus, not been noted. For information on the principal manuscripts, see Introduction, p. 19.

Incipit liber utilis coquinario.   f. 81ᵛ

1 For to make eles in counfy. Tak eles & fle hem & cut
hem on thynne gobetes, & frye hem in oyle dolif, & pynes
þerwith; & tak bothe togedere & couche hem in blaunche
poudere, & in ceucre, & couche aboue poudere of gyngere as
þe quantite of þy seruise nedeth. & þan take blaunched 5
almaundes & grynde hem smale & tempre hem with whit
wyn; & streyne hem, & cast hem in to a pot alle togeder.
& tak poudere of clowes & of maces & of quybibes & of
peper, & cast þerto & boyle hem alle in fere, & salt it, &
whan it is dressed florsche it aboue with myced gyngere þat 10
is fayre pared & tryed.

2 To make a pyany. Tak | partriches & pyes þat flen, & f. 82
roste hem þat þey be half ynow. & þan tak þe broth of
chikenes & of fresch beef boyled, & tak bred, & stepe in þe
same broth, & drawe it þorw a streynour. & tak pouder of
gynger & of greyn de parys & of peper, of ech alich & medele 5
hem togedere; & quartre þy partriches & þe pyes & do hem in
a pot, & do alle þy thynges þerto, & boyle alle togedere, &
salte it, & florsche þe disches aboue with floures of pyany &
with þe same frut, & serue it forth manerliche.

3 For to make a pynade. Tak wyn & peres & boyle hem
togedere, & tak tosted bred & grynde hem alle togedere &
draw hem þorw a streynoure, & tak þe thridde part of ceugre
or elles lyf hony | & tak penes & frye hem in fresch gres. & f. 82ᵛ
tak al þis togedere & cast in a pot, & boyle it & force it vp 5
with pouder peper, & salt it; & whan it is dressed florsche it
with hole maces & clowes & with myced gyngere & serue it
forth.

4 Ruscheues. Tak brawn of capounnes & fresch pork & seþ
hem til þey be tendre, & grynde hem in a morter smal; & tak
hole clowes & maces & medele hem wel togedere. & tak
ȝelkes of eyren & floure & mak past þerof, & tak þe lengthe
of þy fyngere.

Heading] Incipit tractus curie S1

5 For to make crem & botere of almoundes. Tak blaunched almaundes & bray hem wel in a morter, & tempre hem with luk water. & draw þerof melk as thikke as þou myȝt, & do it

f. 83 in a newe erthen pot, & do þerto vynegre hett a litel. | Whan
5 þe melk & þe venegre be put togedere perce þe pot benethe þat þe licoure may renne out, & whan it is all ronnen tak þat þat leueth in þe pot & do in a fayre twayle & left it vp & doun; & whan þe licoure is out clene, tak it of þe twayle & it is botere & creem.

6 Chauden for potage. Take þe lyuere & þe lunges of þe ert & þe mederyiu & þe guttes, & score hem with salt & seth hem al togedere, & hew hem smale. & tak bred & peper & grynde togedere, & tempere it vp with þe broth. & coloure it with þe
5 blod, & hew þe chauden & do it þerto, & lye vp with þe ȝelkes of eyren. & if þou do brauens þerto, coloure it with safroun.

f. 83ᵛ **7** Botere of almand melk. Tak þikke | almound melk & boyle it, & as it boyleth cast yn a litel wyn or vynegre, & þan do it on a caneuas & lat þe whey renne out. & þan gadere it vp with þyn hondes & hang it vp a myle wey, & ley it after in
5 cold water, & serue it forth.

8 Mortreux of lunges. Tak good almound melk & tempere it with fresch fisch broth & let kele. & seth þe lunges & þe lyuere, & bray hem wel togedere in a mortere, & do hem into þat melk, & sesoun it with myed bred þat it be charchaunt, &
5 salt it & coloure it with safroun, & florsch it manerlych with poudre of gyngere.

9 A tenche in syuee. Scalde þy tenche & atyre wel & boyle it; & tak þe same broth & myed bred & tempere it togedere,

f. 84 & tak good poudre | of canel & of clowes & do to þe sewe, & coloure it with safroun & salte it & lete hit boile. & tak myced

5. 1 For . . . almoundes] *om.* S1   3-4 melk . . . pot] thykke mylk and do hit in a newe erthen pot and loke that thy mylk be riȝt thykke S1   4 hett a litel] that ychaufed on the fyr S1   5 be put] ensemble S1;   perce] persche S   8 is¹] it S;   it is] *add* bothe S1

6. 1 ert] hert S1   2 mederyiu] myddereue S1

7. 3 caneuas] *add* on brod S1   4 hondes] *add* on an hep S1 5 forth] *add* manerly S1

8. 2 fisch] *om.* S1   3 togedere] *om.* S1

9. 2 broth] tenche S1   4 & lete hit boile] *om.* S

onyounnes & frye hem in oyle dolyf or vynegre or in wyn or   5
in þe same broth, & do hem in þat sewe & sesen it vp with
vynegre or with eysel; & after þat lat it no more boyle.

10   For to make mete vernis. Tak capounnes or hennes or
fresch pork sothen, & tak out þe bones & bray þe flesch wel
in a mortere. & þan stampe vyne leues & croppes & tempre
hem with wyn, & draw it þorw a streynoure & tempere þe
forseyd flesch þerwith. & þan do hem sethe & mak it char-   5
geaunt with flour of rys, & salte it & put þerto poudre of
canel & of greyn de parys & ceucre, & þat colour schal be
vernis. |

11   For to dih3te a swan. Tak & vndo hym & wasch hym, &   f. 84ᵛ
do on a spite & enarme hym fayre & roste hym wel; & dys-
membre hym on þe beste manere & mak a fayre chyne, & þe
sauce þerto schal be mad in þis manere, & it is clept:

12   Chauden. Tak þe issu of þe swan & wasch it wel, &
scoure þe guttes wel with salt, & seth þe issu al togedere til it
be ynow. & þan tak it vp and wasch it wel & hew it smal, &
tak bred & poudere of gyngere & of galyngale & grynde togedere & tempere it with þe broth, & coloure it with þe blood.   5
And when it is ysothe & ygrounde & streyned, salte it, &
boyle it wel togydere in a postnet & sesen it with a litel
vynegre. |

13   þe heyroun schal be di3ht as is þe swan and it come   f. 85
quyk to kechen. þe sauce schal be mad of hym as a chaudoun
of gynger & of galyngale, & þat it be coloured with þe blood
or with brende crustes þat arn tosted.

10. 5 þan] *add* putte hem to the fyr and S1
11. 1 to dih3te a] the S1C;   hym²] hem S   2 enarme] enarne S, an
arme S1, vn arme C   4 mad . . . clept] chaudon, and this ys [ys *om.* C]
the makyng of chaudon S1C, made of chawdon & rosted with crustes & galentyne
& þat it be all blak As
12. 2 issu] *add* guttes *canc.* S1   3 it vp] vp the yssu guttes and al S1C;
wasch it wel &] *om.* C;   smal] *add* guttes & al S1C   5 with þe] *om.*
S1   6 And . . . is] whenne hit S1, *om.* S;   streyned] *add* & SS1C
7 sesen] cessn sen C
13. 2 hym as a] þe cheite of þe heyroun mad als a As   3 of gynger
. . . it be] *om.* S1   3–4 coloured . . . tosted] blak As

14 þe pekokes & partriches schul be parboyled & larded & rosted. þe sauce schal be gynger.

15 þe crane schal be diȝt on a spite riȝt as a wodekok. þe sauce is gyngere. And botores & curlewes schul be diȝt as is þe crane & þe sauce gynger. Cormoraunz schul be scalded & perboyled & larded & rosted. þe sauce is gynger. Pluuers,
5 malardis, teeles, larkes, fynches, buntyngges: alle these schulle be rostyd & seruyd wyth freture and braune; the sauce schal be gyngeuer.

f. 85ᵛ **16** Saunc Sarazine. Tak blaunched almaundes & frye | hem in oyle dolyf & þan bray hem wel in a mortere & tempere hem with thikke almound melk & with wyn & þe thridde part ceugre; & if it be noȝt þikke ynow, lye it with floure of
5 rys or with amodyne & coloure it with alconet, & boyle it. & whan it is dressed florsche it aboue with pumme garnet.

17 A dauce egre. Tak luces or tenches or fresch haddok, & seth hem & frye hem in oyle doliue. & þan tak vynegre & þe thridde pert sugre & onyounnes smal myced, & boyle alle togedere, & maces & clowes & quybibes. & ley þe fisch in
5 disches & hyld þe sew aboue & serue it forth.

18 To make a rapes. Tak figges & reysenes & wasch hem
f. 86 clene in ale. & boyle hem | in a pot with a litel ale ones a walm, & þan grynde hem smale in a mortere & put þerto wyn & draw it vp, & put þerto saundres & salt & poudere of peper
5 & poudre of coloure. & boyle it togedere til it be chargeaunt, for to serue with Blaundesire, bothe in a disch; & do þervpon anys in counfite boþe whit & red.

14. 1 parboyled] boyled S
15. 1 schal be diȝt] Graythe þe crane & do it As   2 is¹] schal be S1;
as is] on þe same maner C   4–6 Pluuers . . . gyngeuer] om. S
5 larkes] om. C   5–6 alle... seruyd] om. As   6 braune] brayne C
7 gyngeuer] add þe plouere ne schall haf bot two & thrytty torne be þe ryght
assys As
16. 1 Saunc] Saune S
17. 2 frye] bray S1   5 forth] add manerly S1
18. 2 a³] & S1   5 boyle] om. S1

19   Ro broþe wel to þe same seruyse. Tak venysoun & wasch
it & culpoun it in a fyngerbroede & perboyle it; & þan tak it
vp & streyne þe broth & do water to þe venysoun, & pike it
clene, & put it into þe broth. & sette it ouer þe feere, & do
þerto salt & percely & ysope & sauerey & poudere of peper, 5
& lat seþe til it be tendre; & do þerto poudre of coloure & of
maces & canel & | quibibes, but lok it be noȝt to hot.   f. 86ᵛ

20   To make chicones in mose. Tak blaunched almaundes &
grynde hem smale & tempere hem with clene watere, & do
hem in a pot & put þerto floure of rys & sugre & salt &
safroun, & boyle hem togedere. & ley þe ȝelkes of harde
sothe eyren in disches, & tak rosted chikenes & tak þe lemes 5
& þe wynges & þe braun, & cut þat oþer del on lengthe, & ley
it in þe disches with yolkes and take the sauche and hilde hit
into the disches & do aboue clowes & serue it forth.

21   To make viaunde of Cypre. Tak þe braun of capounes or
of hennes ysoþe or rosted & bray it in a morter smal as myed
bred, & tak good almound melk lyed with amodyn or with
floure of rys & colour it with safroun & boyle it wel. | &   f. 87
charge it with rosted braun, & sesen it with sugre & salt,   5
& florsche it with maces & quibybes.

22   Browet of Almayne. Tak good almound melk & lye it
with amodyn or with bake floure & coloure it with safroun &
enforce it with poudere of gyngere & of galyngale & canel &
tak pertriches & chikenes rosted & hew hem in quarteres. &
boyle þat forseyd melk, & do it to þe flesch, & sesen it with 5
sugre roset; & tempre floure of rys with almound melk &
boyle it til it be chargeaunt, & grynde þe brawn of capounes
& of hennes smal & charge it þerwith. & coloure it with
saundres or with blod & enforce it with clowes.

23   Coynes. Tak ca|pounes & hennes & rost hem til þey be f. 87ᵛ
browne, & hewe hem yn gobetes & do hem in broth of fresch

19. 1 Ro] To SS1
   20. 7 in] *om.* S   7–8 yolkes . . . aboue] *om.* S   8 forth] *add*
manerly S1
   21. 6 & florsche] *om.* S1
   22. 2 bake] bacon S1   7 til it] *om.* S1

beef & seth hem, & roste hem on a gredyle. & tak þat broth
& lye it with myed bred & enforce it with poudre of peper &
5 of comyn, & coloure it with safroun, & tak harde soþen eyren &
kepe þe ʒelkes hole & hacke smale þe white & do to þe sewe.
& do þe capounes or hennes þerto & boyle hem togedere, and
sesen it with þe ʒelkes of eyren swonge togedere, & florsch it
with þe hole ʒelkes.

24   For to dyʒte a fresch laumprey. Tak & open hym atte
nauele & lete hym a litel blod, & gadere þat blod in a vessel &
do awey þe galle & scorche hym & wasch hym wel. & mak a
f. 88   paste of | dow & put þe launprey þerynne with good spycery;
5 & þan mak a laye with bred & tempre it with wyn or with
vynegre & medele þe blod with al, & put galentyn þerwith al
raw & a tuel aboue. & set it in þe ouene til it bake, & if it be
rosted diʒte hym in þe same manere but þat þou sethe þe
galentyn with oynounes. & if þe laumprey be salt, wasche
10 hym in hoot water & in whete bran, & aftere þat do hym in
hot water al a nyʒt & a morwe scorche hym & seth hym with
oynounes riʒt wel, & mak þe galentyn be hymself: for why,
he schal be serued cold & þe galentyn hot kendlich.

f. 88ᵛ   **25**   To make a mawmene. Tak figges & resynes & wasch | hem
in ale & braye hem wel in a mortere, & do þerto wyn, & braye
þe flesch of hennes or capounes & do þerto. & do good almound melk in a pot, & do þerto þyn thynges, & stere wel
5 togedere & make it for to seþe. & coloure it with blod of a
goot or of a pygg & lok it be sothe & grounde & streyned, &
put þerto poudere of gyngere & of galyngale & clowes &
greyn de parys, & sesen it with sugre & salt it, & do it fro þe
feere.

26   To make mortreux of fisch. Tak plays or fresch meluel
or merlyng & seth it in fayre water, & þan tak awey þe skyn

24. 2 aᵃ] *om.* S   3 mak a] *add* coffyn of S1   4 with] *add*
pouder of S1   5 with³] *add* egre *canc.* S1   7 a] atte S, at the S1
8 hym] hem S   10-11 do . . . hym &] stepe and S1   13 galentyn]
add and sethe yt S1
   25. 2 þerto] to S1   4 thynges] *add* byforseyd S1   6 it]
the blod S1
   26. 2 merlyng] *add* or pike or roge or oþer C;   water] *add* til it be ynowe
S1C

& þe bones & presse þe fisch in a cloth & bray it in a mortere.
& tempre it vp with almond melk, & bray poudere | of gynger f. 89
& sugre togedere & departe þe mortreux on tweyne in two 5
pottes & coloure þat on with safroun & dresch it in disches,
half of þat on & half of þat oþer, & strawe poudere of gyngere
& sugre on þat on & clene sugre on þat oþer & serue it forth.

27 For to make blawmaunger mole. Tak þe braun of
capounnes or of hennes þat ben soþe & hew it & bray it smal
& tempre it vp with almaund melk & do it in a pot, & do
þerto floure of rys & fresch gres & a litel amodyn. & boyle it
al togedere & salt it, & do þerto sugre, & dresch it in disches 5
& sett þeryn greyn of poum gernetes.

28 Blawmanger. Tak þe two del of rys, þe thridde pert of
almoundes; | wasch clene þe rys in leuk water & turne & seth f. 89ᵛ
hem til þay breke & lat it kele, & tak þe melk & do it to þe
rys & boyle hem togedere. & do þerto whit gres & braun of
hennes grounde smale, & stere it wel, & salte it & dresch it in 5
disches. & frye almaundes in fresch gres til þey be browne, &
set hem in þe dissches, & strawe þeron sugre & serue it forth.

29 To make blaumaunger gros. Tak rys & pike hem & wasch
hem & stepe hem & tempere hem with good almound melk,
& do it in a pot & mak it to sethe ones. & þan do it doun &
tak braun of hennes or of capounes, & hew it in gobetes, &
cast þerto & stere it togedere. & do þerto sugre & salt & whit 5
gres & mak it | charchaunt, & dresch it in disches, & set þerin f. 90
fryed almoundes, & straw sugre aboue & serue it forth.

30 To make blamaunger in lenten. Tak almound melk & do
it in a pot, & tak floure of rys aftere þat þe quantite is of þe

---

5 departe] take & dele C   5-7 in two ... half of[1]] þat on halfe in a pot
þat oþer halfe in anoþer pot and colour þat on with safroun and dresse it in dishes
halfe of C, *om.* S1   7 &[1]] *om.* S1   8 clene] clowes & C;   forth]
add manerly S1C
    28. 3 melk] *add* of thyn almandis S1   5 smale] *add* and boile alle
togidere S1   7 sugre] *add* as the manere ys S1
    29. 3 sethe] plawe S1   4 gobetes] *add* as dices S1   7 aboue]
add as the manere ys S1

melk, or hol rys. & take of þe perche or of a luce & hew it as
þou woldest do braun, & if þou fayle þerof tak newe ray &
5 alye it vp, & do þerto sugre & oyl of almoundes, or elles oyle
dolyf þat is newe, or elles þe gres of a brem; & whan it is soþe,
do þe oyle þerto & tak almoundes koruen on foure ifried in
oyle & sette in þe disches whan it is dressed, & strew sugre
aboue manerlych.

31   For to make a spynee þat is a thorne. Tak blosmes of þe
f. 90ᵛ hawþorn | & blosmes of þe swete appeltre & grynde hem to-
gedere in a morter, & tempre hem vp with almound melk &
leye it vp with bred & ȝelkes of eyren, & do þerto wyn. &
5 whan it is sothe wel & thikke do þerto poudere of ginger & of
canel & clowes, & dresch it in disches & straw it aboue sugre.

32   To make a rosye. Tak braun of capounes or of hennes &
hew it smal, & bray it in a morter & do þerto grounde bred &
tempre it vp with almounde melk, & do it into a pot & lye it
with amodyne & colour it with safroun. & do þerto white
5 gres & stere it weel, & tak roses & hewe hem smale & do into
þe pot, & seth it all togedere & ley it with eyre, & do þerto
f. 91 sugre & salt, & dresch it, | & strawe þeron rede rose leues &
serue it forth.

33   To make a syrosye. Tak cheryes & do out þe stones &
grynde hem wel & draw hem þorw a streynoure & do it in a
pot. & do þerto whit gres or swete botere & myed wastel
bred, & cast þerto good wyn & sugre, & salte it & stere it wel
5 togedere, & dresse it in disches; & set þeryn clowe gilofre, &
strew sugre aboue.

34   To make a primerole. Tak prymorole leues & bray hem
in a morter, & tempre hem vp with almound melk or with

---

30. 3 perche] *om.* S1   6 newe] *add* and fresch S1
31. 2 appeltre] plomtre or of oþer tre C   3 melk] *add* ʻor cow milk' C
5–6 do . . . clowes &] *om.* S1
32. 1 or] and S1   4 amodyne] *add* or floure C   5 hewe]
om. C
33. 1 syrosye] cyrisye C   3 wastel] *om.* C   4 sugre] *add* &
whenne yt ys soden S1C
34. 1 primerole] primerose C;   prymorole] primerose C

good cow melk, & charge it with myed bred sethynge, & salte
it. & do þerto sugre & safroun & make it chargeaunt, & dresch
it, & straw þeron prymorole floures aboue & serue it forth. | 5

35 For to make a vyolet. Take vyolet floures & braye hem, f. 91ᵛ
& tak myed wastel bred & do þerto, & tempre it vp with almound melk or with cow melk & do þerto sugre, & mak it
sethe. & salt it & dresch it & primerole togedere, & strewe
vyolet floures aboue riȝt as þou dost on premerole hese 5
floures.

36 To make a fawne. Tak þe leues & blosmes of benes &
bray hem & tempre hem vp with þe broth of fresch bef or
of capounes. & do þerto myed wastel bred þat it be chargeaunt, & salte it; & do þerto sugre & safroun. & dresch it in
disches & sette þeron blosmes of benes & serue it forth. 5

37 For to make an heppee. Tak heppes & pyke out þe
stones & þe regges aboute hem, & wasch | hem, & braye hem. f. 92
& tak þe broth of fresch beef or of capounes & tempre hem
vp withal & seth hem, & salte hem, & do þerto sugre & dresch
it in disches & do þe heppe floures aboue & serue it forth 5
manerliche.

---

3 melk] *add* so that the cow be nouȝt al white of her S1;   bred] *add* and cast
þerto *canc.* C;   sethynge] sethe yt S1   4 dresch] *add* in dysches S1C
5 forth] *add* manerly S1

    35. 1 & bray hem] *om.* S1   2 wastel] *om.* C;   þerto] *add* sugur
and make it to seþe & salte it and dresse it *canc.* C (*passage marked for deletion
by* 'va' *at beginning,* 'cat' *at end, for* vacat)   3 or . . . sugre] *om.* S1;
þerto] *add* 'hony or' C   5-6 riȝt . . . floures] &c. C;   on . . . floures]
of primerole flourez S1

    36. 2 with] *add* almande mylk *canc.* S1;   or] & C   3 wastel] *om.* C
5 of benes] *om.* S1;   forth] *add* manerly S1

    37. 1 heppee] peperyngge S1, pipurynge C   2 & wasch hem] *om.* C;
braye] *recipe section of S1 breaks off with this word*   4 withal] with
ale C   5-6 & . . . manerliche] *om.* C

PART IV
THE FORME OF CURY

Table of Recipes		MS Sources	Page
1.	Frumente	C, J, W, P, Ar	98
2.	Blaunche porre	C, J, P, Ar	98
3. (1)	Grounden benes	A, P, Ar	98
4. (2)	Drawen benes	A, P, Ar	98
5. (3)	Grewel forced	A, P, Ar	98
6. (4)	Caboches in potage	A, C, J, P, Ar	99
7. (5)	Rapes in potage	A, C, J, W, P, Ar	99
8. (6)	Iowtes of flessh	A, C, J, W, P, Ar	99
9. (7)	Chebolace	A, C, J, W, P	99
10. (8)	Gourdes in potage	A, C, J, W, P, Ar	99
11. (9)	Ryse of flessh	A, C, J, W, P, Ar	100
12. (10)	Funges	A, C, J, W, P	100
13. (11)	Bruce	A, C, J, W, P, Ar	100
14. (12)	Corat	A, C, J, W, P, Ar	100
15. (13)	Noumbles	A, C, J, W, P, Ar	100
16. (14)	Roo broth	A, C, J, W, P, Ar	101
17. (15)	Tredure	A, B, C, J, W, P	101
18. (16)	Mounchelet	A, B, C, J, W, P, Ar	101
19. (17)	Bukkenade	A, B, C, J, W, P, Ar	101
20. (18)	Connat	A, B, C, J, W, P	101
21. (19)	Drepe	A, B, C, J, W, P, Ar	102
22. (20)	Mawmenee	A, B, C, J, W, P, Ar	102
23. (21)	Egurdouce	A, B, C, J, W, P, Ar	102
24. (22)	Capouns in councy	A, B, C, J, W, P, Ar	103
25. (23)	Hares in talbotes	A, B, C, J, W, P	103
26. (24)	Hares in papdele	A, B, C, J, W, P, Ar	103
27. (25)	Connynges in cyuee	A, B, C, J, W, P, Ar	103
28. (26)	Connynges in grauey	A, B, C, J, W, P, Ar	104
29. (27)	Chykens in grauey	A, B, C, J, W, P	104
30. (28)	Fylettes in galyntyne	A, B, C, W, P, Ar	104
31. (29)	Pygges in sawse sawge	A, B, C, J, W, P, Ar	104
32. (30)	Sawse madame	A, B, C, J, W, P, Ar	104
33. (31)	Gees in hoggepot	A, B, C, J, W, P, Ar	105
34. (32)	Caruel of pork	A, B, C, J, W, P	105
35. (33)	Chykens in cawdel	A, B, C, J, W, P	105
36. (34)	Chykens in hocchee	A, B, C, J, W, P	105
37. (35)	Fesauntes, pertruches, capouns, and curlewes	A, B, C, J, W, P	106

38.	(36) Blank maunger	A, B, C, J, W, P, Ar	106
39.	(37) Blank dessorre	A, B, C, J, W, P, Ar	106
40.	(38) Morree	A, B, C, J, W, P, Ar	106
41.	(39) Charlet	A, B, C, J, W, P, Ar	107
42.	(40) Charlet yforced	A, B, C, J, W, P, Ar	107
43.	(41) Cawdel ferry	A, B, C, J, W, P, Ar	107
44.	(43) Iusshell	A, B, C, J, W, P, Ar	107
45.	(44) Iusshell enforced	A, B, C, J, P, Ar	107
46.	(45) Mortrews	A, B, C, J, W, P, Ar	107
47.	(46) Mortrews blank	A, B, C, J, W, P	108
48.	(47) Brewet of Almayne	A, B, C, J, W, P, Ar	108
49.	(48) Peiouns ystewed	A, B, C, J, W, P, Ar	108
50.	(49) Losyns	A, B, C, J, W, P	108
51.	(50) Tartlettes	A, B, C, J, W, P	109
52.	(51) Pynnonade	A, B, C, W, P	109
53.	(52) Rosee	A, B, H, C, W, P	109
54.	(53) Cormarye	A, B, H, C, W, P	109
55.	(54) Newe noumbles of deer	A, B, H, C, W, P	110
56.	(55) Loyne of the pork	A, B, H, C	110
57.	(56) Fyletes	A, B, H, C	110
58.	(57) Spynee	A, B, H, C, W, P	110
59.	(58) Chyryse	A, B, H, C, W, P	110
60.	(59) Paynfoundew	A, B, H, C, W, P	110
61.	(60) Crytayne	A, B, H, C, J, W, P, Ar	111
62.	(61) Vinegrate	A, B, H, C, J, W, P, Ar	111
63.	(62) Founet	A, B, H, C, J, W	111
64.	(63) Douce iame	A, B, H, C, J, W, Ar	112
65.	(64) Connynges in cyrip	A, B, H, C, J, W	112
66.	(65) Leche Lumbard	A, B, C, J, Ar	112
67.	(66) Connynges in clere broth	A, B, C, J, Ar	113
68.	(67) Payn ragoun	A, B, C, J, Ar	113
69.	(68) Lete lardes	A, B, Ar	113
70.	(69) Furmente with porpays	A, B, H, C, J, W, Ar	114
71.	(70) Perrey of pesoun	A, B, H, C, J, W, Ar	114
72.	(71) Pesoun of Almayne	A, B, H, J, W, Ar	114
73.	(72) Chyches	A, B, H, J, W, P	114
74.	Lopins	H, J, W, P	114
75.	(73) Frenche iowtes	A, H, J, W, P	115
76.	(74) Makke	A, B, H, J, W, P	115
77.	(75) Aquapatys	A, B, H, J, W, P, Ar	115
78.	(76) Salat	A, B, H, J, W, P	115
79.	(77) Fenkel in soppes	A, B, H, C, J, W, P, Ar	115
80.	(78) Elat	A, B, H, J, W, P	116
81.	(79) Appulmoy	A, B, H, C, J, W, P	116
82.	(80) Slyt soppes	A, B, H, C, J, P, Ar	116
83.	(81) Letelorye	A, B, H, C, J, P	116
84.	(82) Sowpes dorry	A, B, H, C, J, P	116
85.	(83) Rapey	A, B, H, C, J, W, P	116

86.	(84) Sawse Sarzyne	A, B, H, C, J, P	117
87.	(85) Creme of almaundes	A, B, H, C, J, W, P, Ar	117
88.	(86) Grewel of almaundes	A, B, H, C, J, W, P	117
89.	(88) Iowtes of almaund mylke	A, B, H, C, J, W, P, Ar	117
90.	(87) Cawdel of almaund mylk	A, B, H, C, J, W, P	117
91.	(89) Fygey	A, B, H, C, J, W, P, Ar	118
92.	(90) Pochee	A, B, H, C, J, W, P, Ar	118
93.	(91) Brewet of ayren	A, B, H, C, J, W, P, Ar	118
94.	Rauioles	H, C, J, W	118
95.	(92) Makerouns	A, B, H, C, J, P	119
96.	(93) Tostee	A, B, H, C, J, P, Ar	119
97.	(94) Gynggaudy	A, B, H, C, J, P, Ar	119
98.	(95) Erbowle	A, B, H, C, J, W, P	119
99.	(96) Rysmole	A, B, H, C, J, P	119
100.	(97) Vyaunde Cypre	A, B, H, C, J, P, Ar	119
101.	(98) Vyaunde Cypre of samoun	A, B, H, C, J, W, P	120
102.	(99) Vyaund ryal	A, B, H, C, J, W, P, Ar	120
103.	(100) Compost	A, B, H, C, J, P	120
104.	(101) Gele of fyssh	A, B, H, C, J, P, Ar	121
105.	(102) Gele of flessh	A, B, H, C, J, P, Ar	121
106.	(103) Chysanne	A, B, H, C, J, W, P, Ar	121
107.	(104) Congur in sawse	A, B, H, C, J, W, P, Ar	122
108.	(105) Rygh in sawse	A, B, H, C, J	122
109.	(106) Makerel in sawse	A, B, H, C, J, W	122
110.	(107) Pykes in brasey	A, B, H, C, J, W, P, Ar	122
111.	(108) Porpeys in broth	A, B, H, C, J, W	123
112.	(109) Balloc broth	A, B, H, C, J, W, Ar	123
113.	(110) Eles in brewet	A, B, H, C, J, W, P, Ar	123
114.	(111) Cawdel of samoun	A, B, H, C, J, W, P	123
115.	(112) Plays in cyuee	A, B, H, C, J, W, Ar	124
116.	(113) Flaumpeyns	A, B, P	124
117.	(114) Noumbles in lent	A, B	124
118.	(115) Chawdoun for lent	A, B	124
119.	(116) Furmente with porpeys	A, B	125
120.	(117) Fylettes in galyntyne	A, B	125
121.	(118) Veel in buknade	A, B	125
122.	(119) Sooles in cyuee	A, B, H, C, J, W, Ar	125
123.	(120) Tenches in cyuee	A, B, H, C, J, W	126
124.	(121) Oysters in grauey	A, B, H, C, J, W	126
125.	(122) Muskles in brewet	A, B, H, C, J, W, P	126
126.	(123) Oysters in cyuee	A, B, H, C, J, W, P	126
127.	(124) Cawdel of muskels	A, B, H, C, J, W, P, Ar	126
128.	(125) Mortrews of fyssh	A, B, H, J, P, Ar	127
129.	Ryse of fische daye	H, J, W, P	127
130.	(126) Laumpreys in galyntyne	A, B, H, J, W, P	127
131.	(127) Laumprouns in galyntyne	A, B, H, J, W, P, Ar	128
132.	(128) Loseyns in fyssh day	A, B, H, J, W, P	128
133.	(129) Sowpes in galyngale	A, B, H, J, W, P	128

134. (130) Sobre sawse	A, B, H, J, W, P, Ar	128
135. (131) Cold brewet	A, B, H, J, W, P	128
136. (132) Peeres in confyt	A, B, H, J, W, P, Ar	129
137. (133) Egurdouce of fysshe	A, B, H, J, W, P, Ar	129
138. (134) Colde brewet	A, B, Ar	129
139. (135) Peuorat for veel and venysoun	A, B, H, J, W, P, Ar	129
140. (136) Sawse blaunche for capouns ysode	A, B, H, J, P, Ar	130
141. (137) Sawse noyre for capouns yrosted	A, B, H, J, P, Ar	130
142. (138) Galyntyne	A, B, H, J, P, Ar	130
143. (139) Gyngeuer	A, B, H, J, P, Ar	130
144. (140) Verde sawse	A, B, H, J, P, Ar	130
145. (141) Sawse noyre for malard	A, B, H, J, P, Ar	130
146. (142) Gaunceli for gees	A, B, H, J, P, Ar	131
147. (143) Chawdoun for swannes	A, B, H, J, P, Ar	131
148. Vertesaus broun	C, J	131
149. (144) Sawse camelyne	A, B, H, C, J, P	131
150. (145) Lumbard mustard	A, B, H, C, J, P	131
151. (146) Cranes and herouns	A, B, H, C, J, Ar	131
152. (147) Pokok and pertruch	A, B, H, C, J, Ar	132
153. (148) Frytour blaunched	A, B, H, C, J, P	132
154. (149) Frytour of pasternakes, of skirwittes & of apples	A, B, H, C, J, P	132
155. (150) Frytour of mylke	A, B, H, C, J, P	132
156. (151) Frytour of erbes	A, B, H, C, J, P	132
157. Tourteletes in fryture	H, C, J, P, Ar	132
158. (152) Raphioles	A, B, H, C, J, P, Ar	133
159. Malaches	H, C, J, P	133
160. (153) Malaches whyte	A, B, H, C, J, P	133
161. (154) Crustardes of flessh	A, B, H, C, J, P, Ar	133
162. (155) Malaches of pork	A, B, H, C, J, P	134
163. (156) Crustardes of fysshe	A, B, H, C, J, P	134
164. (157) Crustardes of eerbis on fyssh day	A, B, H, C, J, P	134
165. Leche frys of fische daye	H, C, J, P	134
166. (158) Leche frys in lentoun	A, B, H, C, J, P	135
167. (159) Wastels yfarced	A, B, H, C, J, P	135
168. (160) Sawge yfarcet	A, B, H, C, J, P	135
169. (161) Sawgeat	A, B, H, C, J, P	135
170. (162) Cryspes	A, B, H, C, J, P	136
171. (163) Crispels	A, B, H, C, J, P	136
172. (164) Tartee	A, B, H, C, P	136
173. (165) Tart in ymbre day	A, B, H, C, P, Ar	136
174. (166) Tart de Bry	A, B, H, C, P, Ar	137
175. (167) Tart de brymlent	A, B, H, C, P, Ar	137
176. (168) Tartes of flessh	A, B, H, J, P	137

177. (169) Tartletes   A, B, H, C, P   137
178. (170) Tartes of fysshe   A, B, H, J, P   138
179. (171) Sambocade   A, B, H, J, P   138
180. (172) Erbolat   A, B, H, J, P   138
181. (173) Nysebek   A, B, H, J, P   138
182. (174) Farsur to make pomme dorryse and oþere þynges   A, B, H, J, P, Ar   139
183. (175) Cokagrys   A, B, H, J, P, Ar   139
184. (176) Hirchones   A, B, H, J, P, Ar   139
185. (177) Potte wys   A, B, H, C, J, P   140
186. (178) Sac wis   A, B, H, C, J, P   140
187. (179) Ruschewys   A, B, H, C, J, P   140
188. (180) Spynoches yfryed   A, B, H, C, J, P   140
189. (181) Benes yfryed   A, B, H, C, J, P   141
190. (182) Rysshews of fruyt   A, B, H, C, J, P   141
191. (183) Daryols   A, B, H, C, J, P, Ar   141
192. (184) Flampoyntes   A, B, H, C, J, P, Ar   141
193. (185) Chewetes on flesshe day   A, B, H, C, J, P, Ar   141
194. (186) Chewetes on fyssh day   A, B, H, C, J, P   141
195. (187) Hastletes of fruyt   A, B, H, C, J   142
196. (188) Comadore   A, B, H, C, J, P   142
197. (189) Chastletes   A, B, H, C, J, P   142
198. (190) For to make two pecys of flessh to fasten togyder   A, B   143
199. (191) Pur fait ypocras   A, B   143
200. (192) Blank maunger   A, B   143
201. (193) Blank desire   A, B   144
202. (194) Mawmenny   A, B   144
203. (195) Pety peruaunt   A, B   144
204. (196) Payn puff   A, B   145
205.   Clarrey and Braggot   H   145

Since references to *Forme of Cury* recipes are often cited by the numbers assigned by Pegge and Warner, we have supplied their numbers in brackets in this Table of Contents. For information on the principal manuscripts, see Introduction, pp. 20–30, and Appendix B, which includes a table setting out the sequence of recipes in each of the manuscripts.

1   To make frumente. Tak clene whete & braye yt wel in a
morter tyl þe holes gon of; seþe it til it breste in water. Nym
it vp & lat it cole. Tak good broþ & swete mylk of kyn or of
almand & tempere it þerwith. Nym ʒelkys of eyren rawe &
5 saffroun & cast þerto; salt it; lat it nauʒt boyle after þe eyren
ben cast þerinne. Messe it forth with venesoun or with fat
motoun fresch.

2   To make blaunche porre. Tak whyte lekys & perboyle
hem & hewe hem smale with oynouns. Cast it in good broþ &
seþe it vp with smale bryddys. Coloure it with safferoun;
powdur yt with pouder douce.

3   For to make grounden benes. Take benes and dry hem in
a nost or in an ovene. And hulle hem wele, and wyndewe out
þe hulkes, and waisshe hem clene; & do hem to seeþ in gode
broth, & ete hem with bacoun.

4   For to make drawen benes. Take benes and seeþ hem,
and grynde hem in a morter, and drawe hem vp with gode
broth; & do oynouns in the broth grete mynced, & do þerto;
and colour it with safroun, and serue it forth.

5   For to make grewel forced. Take grewel and do to the
fyre with gode flessh and seeþ it wel; take the lire of pork
sodyn and grynd it smal, and drawe the grewel thurgh a straynour to þe porke, and colour it wiþ safroun; and serue forth.

   1. 1 braye] breke *canc.* bre W   2 þe] *add* utter P;   holes] hol
`schall' (*added above line in later hand*) C;   it . . . water] hiit in watur til hiit
breke & þanne wasch hiit clene W;   til it¹] *altered to* til at 'it' *by second hand*
C;   water] whater he (*addition by second hand*) C   3 of kyn or] *om.*
W, *add* or ewe mylk P   4 þerwith Nym] with many W   5 salt it]
add yevyn, þat is, put not to moche salt þeryn P   6 Messe it forth] *om.* W
   2. 1 whyte] the white of P   4 powdur yt with] and cast on P;
powdur yt . . . douce] *om.* J;   pouder douce] pouder marchant Ar
   3. 2 hulle hem wele] hull them at mill P, grynde hom at a mylne Ar
4 broth] *add* fresh or salt P
   4 1 seeþ hem] *om.* P   1–2 Take . . . morter] *Ar's directions link this
clearly to the preceding recipe*: Take benes grounden and breke hom in a morter,
P also reads breke
   5. 1 Take . . . do] Do broth P   2 lire] leue P   3 sodyn]
om. A   4 to þe porke] *om.* A, *add* salt it P

6 Caboches in potage. Take caboches and quarter hem, and seeth hem in gode broth with oynouns ymynced and the whyte of lekes yslyt and ycorue smale. And do þerto safroun & salt, and force it with powdour douce.

7 Rapes in potage. Take rapus and make hem clene, and waissh hem clene; quarter hem; perboile hem, take hem vp. Cast hem in a gode broth and seeþ hem; mynce oynouns and cast þerto safroun and salt, and messe it forth with powdour douce. In the self wise make of pasturnakes and skyrwittes. 5

8 Iowtes of Flessh. Take borage, cool, langdebef, persel, betes, orage, auance, violet, saueray, and fenkel; and whanne þey buth sode, presse hem wel, hakke hem smale; cast hem in gode broth & seeþ hem, and serue hem forth.

9 Chebolace. Take oynouns and erbes and hewe hem small, and do þerto gode broth; and aray it as þou didest caboches. If þey be in fyssh day, make on the same manere with water and oyle, and if it be not in lent, alye it with ʒolkes of eyren; and dresse it forth, and cast þerto powdour douce. 5

10 Gourdes in potage. Take yong gowrdes; pare hem and kerue hem on pecys. Cast hem in gode broth, and do þerto a gode pertye of oynouns mynced. Take pork soden; grynde it and alye it þerwith and wiþ ʒolkes of ayren. Do þerto safroun and salt, and messe it forth with powdour douce. 5

6. 1 quarter hem] kyt them a foure or a fyve P, drawe hem CJ   2 and] in C   3 ycorue] ischredde CJ

7. 1 make] pare CJWP   1-2 and waissh hem clene] in water CJ, wiþ hym welle water W   2 quarter hem] quare hem A, kyt them a thre or foure or a fyve P   3 hem²] add or elles clene watur and oyle on a fyssh day but tho watur moste boyle or the rapes ben put in Ar   4 þerto] add do þerto CJ   4 and salt] om. W   5 self] om. A

8. 1 cool] cowsloppys CJ;   langdebef] add & hokkes CJW (probably error: see use of hakke below)   2 betes] ibet W, letuys P;   auance] om. W   3 hakke hem] & hew hem WP, om. A

9. 1 Chebolace] Chybolade C, Chibolate JW, Gebolat P;   hewe] seþe CJ; small] add and do them to thy gebolet P   2 do ... caboches] do þer- with caboches CJ, om. P   2-3 aray ... day] om. W   3 If ... in] on CJ;   day] add in lent P;   on ... manere] thy sewe P   4 and² ... lent] on a fische day out of lenten W, on þe flesch day out of lentyn CJ

10. 1 Take] tal C   2 on pecys] into smale gobettes P, add and qwar- ter hem and W   3 of] add gode canc. J;   pork] it CJ   4 it] add small P;   and² ... ayren] om. CJW   5 messe it forth] fflorysh hit P;   with] & floresch hiit with W, add florschynge of CJ

11   Ryse of flessh. Take ryse and waisshe hem clene, and do hem in an erthen pot with gode broth and lat hem seeþ wel. Aftirward take almaund mylke and do þerto, and colour it wiþ safroun & salt, & messe forth.

12   Funges. Take funges and pare hem clene, and dyce hem; take leke and shrede hym small, and do hym to seeþ in gode broth. Colour it with safroun, and do þerinne powdour fort.

13   Bruce. Take the whyte of lekes; slytte hem and shrede hem small. Take noumbles of swyne and perboyle hem in broth and wyne. Take hym vp and dresse hym, and do the leke in the broth; seeþ and do the noumbles þerto. Make a
5 lyour of brede, blode, and vynegre and do þerto powdour fort. Seeþ oynouns, mynce hem and do þerto. The self wise make of porpeys.

14   Corat. Take the noumbles of calf, swyne, or of shepe; perboile hem and kerue hem to dyce. Cast hem in gode broth and do þerto erbes, grene chybolles smale yhewe; seeþ it tendre, and lye with 3olkes of eyren. Do þerto verious, safroun,
5 powdour douce and salt, and serue it forth.

15   Noumbles. Take noumbles of deer oþer of a reþer; per- boile hem and kerf hem to dyce. Take the self broth or better, take brede and grynde with the broth, and temper it vp with a gode quantite of vyneger and wyne. Take oynouns and per-
5 boyle hem, and mynce hem smale and do þerto. Colour it with blode, and do þerto powdor fort and salt, and boyle it wele and serue it fort.

11. 2 erthen] yrun W   3 Aftirward] then P;   Aftirward . . . þerto and] þerwith CJ, and W   4 salt] *add* yt CJW
12. 1 hem¹] *add* wel & CJ;   dyce] shred P   2 shrede] sleitt hem & screde CJ, slit them and so shred P, salt him and schrede W   3 fort] *add* seseyn hit with salt P
13. 1 Bruce] Burseu A;   slytte] slype A   2-4 in broth . . . seeþ] *om.* C;   in broth . . . þerto] & do to þe lekes J   3 hym²] *add* small P   4-5 make a lyour of] flowre wiþ W   5-6 powdour . . . þerto] *om.* W   7 porpeys] pigges A
14. 2 kerue . . . dyce] cut them small P   3 erbes] sage and percyl, ysope, saueray Ar;   grene] grynde A
15. 1 a reþer] a bulloc P, oþere beest A   2 kerf . . . dyce] cut them small P;   dyce] peces CJ;   or better] *om.* P   3 with the broth] it þerwyt CJ   4 a . . . of] *om.* P   4-5 and perboyle hem] *om.* P 6 do þerto powder fort] *illeg.* A

16 Roo broth. Take the lire of the boor oþer of the roo, perboile it. Smyte it on smale peces; seeþ it wel half in water and half in wyne. Take brede and bray it wiþ the self broth and drawe blode þerto, and lat it seeth togydre with powdour fort: of gynger oþer of canell and macys, with a grete porcioun 5 of vyneger, with raysouns of corauns.

17 Tredure. Take brede and grate it; make a lyre of rawe ayren, and do þerto safroun and powdour douce, and lye it vp with gode broth, and make it as a cawdel. And do þerto a lytel verious.

18 Mounchelet. Take veel oþer motoun and smyte it to gobettes. Seeþ it in gode broth; cast þerto erbes yhewe gode won, and a quantite of oynouns mynced, powdour fort and safroun, and alye it with ayren and verious: but lat not seeþ after.   5

19 Bukkenade. Take hennes oþer connynges oþer veel oþer oþere flessh & hewe hem to gobettes. Waische it and seþe hit well. Grynde almaundes vnblaunched, and drawe hem vp with þe broth; cast þerinne raysouns of coraunce, sugur, powdour gynger, erbes ystewed in grees, oynouns and salt. If it 5 is to thynne, alye it vp with flour of ryse, oþer with oþere thyng, and colour it with safroun.

20 Connat. Take connes and pare hem. Pyke out the best and do hem in a pot of erthe; do þerto whyte grece, þat he stewe þerinne, and lye hem vp with hony clarified and with

---

16. 1 lire] levir P, lyuere CJ, lyure and a quantite of tho flessh Ar   2 peces] gobetes CJW   3 it] *add* yn a morter P   5 fort . . . macys] pouder of peper, of gynger, of canel CJWP, pouder of pepur and of clowes and of canel Ar   6 of²] & CJ (*same error occurs in CJ for some other recipes*); corauns] *illeg.* A
   18. 2 gode¹] *om.* CJW   2-3 gode won] gode wyne A, *om.* P
3 a quantitie of] *om.* CJWP;   mynced] *add* and let hit seth well P   4 not] it C   4-5 but . . . after] *om.* P   5 after] *Hearne did not transcribe the last word here; it is not visible now in A*
   19. 1 oþer¹] & W;   oþer veel] *om.* CJWP   2 Waische it] *om.* P; seþe] *om.* A   3 vnblaunched] blaunchede J   5 erbes] *om.* W; ystewed in] and fresh P;   oynouns] *add* mynsid small P   6 to] to to A
6-7 flour . . . thyng] amydun Ar;   oþer . . . thyng] *om.* P
   20. 1 connes] coyns J, quoyns C;   pare hem] pare `hem' A   2 whyte] wiþ W;   þat] *add* vnneþe CJW   2-3 whyte . . . stewe] fresh grece & stere them well P

rawe ȝolkes and with a lytell almaund mylke; and do þerinne
5 powdour fort and safroun: and loke þat it be yleesshed.

21 Drepe. Take blaunched almaundes; grynde hem and
temper hem vp with gode broth. Take oynouns, a grete quantite; perboyle hem and frye hem and do þerto. Take smale
bryddes; perboile hem and do þerto, and do þerto pellydore
5 and salt, and a lytel grece.

22 Mawmenee. Take a potell of wyne greke and ii pounde
of sugur; take and claryfye the sugur with a quantite of wyne
& drawe it thurgh a straynour in to a pot of erthe. Take
flour of rys and medle with sum of the wyne & cast togydre.
5 Take pynes with dates and frye hem a litell in grece oþer in
oyle and cast hem togydre. Take clowes & flour of canel hool
and cast þerto. Take powdour gynger, canel, clowes; colour it
with saundres a lytel yf hit be nede. Cast salt þerto, and lat it
seeþ warly with a slowe fyre and not to thyk. Take brawn of
10 capouns yteysed oþer of fesauntes teysed small and cast þerto.

23 Egurdouce. Take connynges or kydde, and smyte hem
on pecys rawe, and fry hem in white grece. Take raysouns of
coraunce and fry hem. Take oynouns, perboile hem and hewe
hem small and fry hem. Take rede wyne and a lytel vynegur,
5 sugur with powdour of peper, of gynger, of canel, salt; and

4 ȝolkes] *add* of eyren CJW   5 fort] strong CJW;   safroun] *add* and
salt P;   and loke . . . yleesshed] *om.* P
    21. 1–2 Take . . . temper] bete blaunched almondes and draw P   2 gode
broth] the same broth P, watur W   2–3 a grete quantite] a good quantite
CJ, small hewyn P   3 hem²] *add* & hewe hem smale CJW;   and do
þerto] *om.* W   4 hem] *add* in good broth P;   pellydore] pouder CJWP
5 salt and] *add* safurn and P, *add* holde it whyȝt & do þerinne CJW
    22. 1 wyne greke] wyne P, wyne crete BW, vinegre CJ   2 take . . .
quantite] wyt a porcioun CJW;   wyne] *add* fyrst clare þe suger CJ   3 erthe]
add with þe remnant of all the wyne P   4 of rys] *canc., add* 'of canel' A;
and . . . togydre] *om.* P   5 pynes with dates] pynes whyȝte CJWP
5–6 in¹ . . . oyle] *om.* P   6 hem . . Take] to hem CJ;   togydre] to W
6–7 Take . . . þerto] *om.* P   8 nede] neþe W   8–9 lat . . . slowe]
kepe hit warme with a sowt P   9 and . . . thyk] *om.* P, saue nod 'to' þik W
9–10 Take . . . þerto] *om.* CJ
    23. 2 on] *add* smale C;   rawe] *om.* P;   in . . . grece] *om.* P
4 and² . . . vynegur] *Ar only*   5 sugur] *add* good won CJW, *add* a good
quantite put all thus yn to an erthyn pot with P, *om.* Ar

cast þerto, and lat it seeþ with a gode quantite of white grece, & serue it forth.

24 Capouns in councy. Take capouns and rost hem right hoot, þat þey be not half ynouh3, and hewe hem to gobettes, and cast hem in a pot; do þerto clene broth. Seeþ hem þat þey be tendre. Take brede and þe self broth and drawe it vp yfere; take strong powdour and safroun and salt and cast þerto. Take ayren and seeþ hem harde; take out the 3olkes and hewe the whyte, take the pot fro þe fyre and cast the whyte þerinne. Messe the dysshes þerwith, and lay the 3olkes aboue hool, and flour it with clowes.

25 Hares in talbotes. Take hares and hewe hem to gobettes and seeþ hem with þe blode vnwaisshed in broth; and whan þey buth ynowh, cast hem in colde water. Pyke and waisshe hem clene. Cole the broth and drawe it thurgh a straynour. Take oþere blode and cast in boylyng water: seeþ it and drawe it thurgh a straynour. Take almaundes vnblaunched, waisshe hem and grynde hem, and temper it vp with the self broth; cast al in a pot. Tak oynouns and perboile hem. Mynce hem small and cast hem in to þis pot. Cast þerinne powdour fort, vyneger & salt.

26 Hares in papdele. Take hares; perboile hem in gode broth. Cole the broth and waisshe the fleyssh; cast a3eyn to-gydre. Take obleys oþer wafrouns in defaute of loseyns, and cowche in dysshes. Take powdour douce and lay on; salt the broth and lay onoward & messe forth.

27 Connynges in cyuee. Take connynges and smyte hem on pecys, and seeþ hem in gode broth; mynce oynouns and seeþ

6 a . . . white] a litel fresh P;   white] om. CJ
    24. 1–2 right . . . be] om. CJW   2 ynouh3] add take them up P
5 strong powdour] powder fort P   6 hem] add & sethe hem W
7 whyte] add smale CJ, add þerinne canc. A   9 aboue hool] hool A, hole
vpon CJW;   flour] florche CJWP
    25. 1 to] in smale CJW   2 þe] `þe´ A   3 ynowh] add take & CJW
4 and drawe it] om. CJWP   7 and¹] & and C   8 Mynce] smyte A
9 to þis] a J
    26. 3 obleys] numblys P;   defaute] þe faute CJ, stede A   3–4 and
. . . dysshes] om. P   4 douce] om. C   4–5 salt the broth] loke þi
broþ be saltyd CJW   5 onoward] þe sew aboue CJ

hem in grece and gode broth; do þerto. Drawe a lyre of brede,
blode, vyneger, and broth; do þerto with powdour fort.

28   Connynges in grauey. Take connynges: smyte hem to
pecys; perboile hem and drawe hem with a gode broth, with
almaundes, blaunched and brayed. Do þerinne sugur, and
powdour gynger, and boyle it and the flessh þerwith; flour
5 it with sugur & with powdour gynger & serue forth.

29   Chykens in grauey. Take chykens, and serue hem in the
same manere, and serue forth.

30   Fylettes in galyntyne. Take fylettes of pork and rost
hem half ynowh; smyte hem on pecys. Drawe a lyour of brede
and blode and broth and vyneger, and do þerinne; seeþ it wele,
and do þerinne powdour of peper & salt & messe it forth.

31   Pygges in sawse sawge. Take pigges yskaldid and quarter
hem, and seeþ hem in water and salt; take hem up and lat hem
kele. Take persel, sawge, and grynde it with brede and 3olkes
of ayren harde ysode; temper it vp with vyneger sumwhat thyk,
5 and lay the pygges in a vessell, and the sewe onoward, and
serue it forth.

32   Sawse madame. Take sawge, persel, ysope and saueray,
quinces and peeres, garlek and grapes, and fylle the gees þerwith; and sowe the hole þat no grece come out, and roost
hem wel, and kepe the grece þat fallith þerof. Take galyntyne
5 and grece and do in a possynet. Whan the gees buth rosted

27. 3 hem] `hem' A;   grece ... broth] gode gres CJ;   and] *add* in *canc.* A;
do þerto] togedir to W;   Drawe] Make CJ   4 fort] *om.* CJ
28. 2 drawe . . . broth] *follows* brayed, *line 3* CJ   4 flour] florche
CJWP
29. 1–2 Take ... forth] þe self manere CJ, in þe selue wise WP
30. 1 in] of A   2 ynowh] *om.* CWP;   Drawe] mak make C
4 powdour of peper] *om.* W;   of peper] *om.* A, fort CWP
31. 1 Take] *add* small P   2 up] *om.* A;   lat hem] ley hem to CW
4 sumwhat thyk] summe swette milke W, *add* tac & J   6 forth] *add* cold
WPAr
32. 1 madame] for goosse *in margin in later hand* C;   saueray] *add* also
good P   2 quinces] coynes W, cornes CJ;   and¹] *add* good CJW
3 sowe the hole] se P;   come] go CJWP   5 and¹] *add* þat CJ, *add* þe
WP

ynowh, take hem of & smyte hem on pecys, and take þat þat
is withinne and do it in a possynet and put þerinne wyne, if it
be to thyk; do þerto powdour of galyngale, powdour douce,
and salt and boyle the sawse, and dresse þe gees in disshes &
lay þe sewe onoward.   10

33 Gees in hoggepot. Take gees and smyte hem on pecys;
cast hem in a pot. Do þerto half wyne and half water, and do
þerto a gode quantite of oynouns and erbes. Set it ouere the
fyre and couere it fast. Make a layour of brede and blode &
lay it þerwith; do þerto powdour fort and serue it fort.   5

34 Caruel of pork. Take the brayn of swyne; perboile it and
grynde it smale, and alay it vp with ʒolkes of ayren. Set it
ouere the fyre with white grece and lat it not seeþ to fast. Do
þerinne safroun & powdour fort and messe it forth: and cast
þerinne powdour douce, and serue it forth.   5

35 Chykens in cawdel. Take chikens and boile hem in gode
broth, and take hem vp; þenne take ʒolkes of ayren rawe &
þe broth and alye it togedre. Do þerto powdour of gynger
and sugur ynowh, safroun and salt. And set it ouere the fyre
withoute boyllyng; and serue the chykens hole oþer ybroke, 5
and lay þe sewe onoward.

36 Chykens in hocchee. Take chykens and scald hem. Take
persel and sawge, with oþere erbes; take garlec & grapes, and
stoppe the chikenus ful, and seeþ hem in gode broth, so þat
þey may esely be boyled þerinne. Messe hem & cast þerto
powdour dowce.   5

6 ynowh] *om.* J;   hem of] *om.* AP;   pecys] gobetes CJ;   þat²] tat A,
om. BCW   7 withinne] thyn P;   possynet and] *mostly illeg.* A
9 and²] *illeg.* A;   dresse] *add* dysches *canc.* B   10 sewe] saus CJWP
    33. 3–4 Set . . . fast] Keuere þi pot & seþe it wel CJ, keuer hit close and when
hit hath sod ynowe P, sethe hem in a pot ouer þe fuyre and seþe hem fast W
4 layour] coloure W   5 fort¹] *add* & salt CJWP
    34. 1 brayn] brawn ABW   1–2 it and grynde it] *om.* P   2 ayren]
add rawe CJ   3 white] *om.* CP;   seeþ to fast] seþe WP, boyle CJ
4 fort] *add* and salt P   5 þerinne] þeron CP
    35. 2 take] ramme AB;   rawe] *om.* A   5 oþer] & CJW
    36. 1 hocchee] broth CJWP;   scald hem] *om.* P   2 with] *add* oute
eny AB;   take] *add* clene CJW   3–4 so . . . þerinne] and when they
be well boyled and sesynd with safurn & salt then P   4 may] moun CJW

37 For to boile fesauntes, pertruches, capouns, and curlewes.
Take gode broth and do þerto the fowle, and do þerto hool
peper and flour of canel, a gode quantite, and lat hem seeþ
þerwith; and messe it forth, and cast þeron powdour dowce.

38 Blank maunger. Take capouns and seeþ hem, þenne take
hem vp; take almaundes blaunched, grynde hem & alay hem
vp with the same broth. Cast the mylk in a pot. Waisshe rys
and do þerto, and lat it seeth; þanne take þe brawn of þe
5 capouns, teere it small and do þerto. Take white grece, sugur
and salt, and cast þerinne. Lat it seeþ; þenne messe it forth
and florissh it with aneys in confyt, rede oþer whyt, and with
almaundes fryed in oyle, and serue it forth.

39 Blank dessorre. Take almaundes blaunched; grynde hem
and temper hem vp with whyte wyne, on fleissh day with
broth; and cast þerinne flour of rys, oþer amydoun, and lye it
þerwith. Take brawn of capouns yground, take sugur and salt,
5 and cast þerto and florissh it with aneys whyte. Take a vessel
yholed and put in safroun, and serue it forth.

40 Morree. Take almaundes blaunched, waisshe hem, grynde
hem, and temper hem vp with rede wyne, and alye hem with
flour of rys. Do þerto pynes yfryed, and colour it with saundres. Do þerto powdour fort and powdour douce and salt;
5 messe it forth and flour it with aneys confyt whyte.

37. 2 the fowle] þi fesauntes &c CJ, feysawnes pertriches &c W   4 forth]
add and sesyn hit with safurn & salt P;   and²] *add* þ *crossed below like abbreviation for* per A;   powdour dowce] *part of another letter between* powdour
and dowce A
38. 3 same] *om.* CJW   4 þe¹,²] *om.* AB;   brawn] braunus CJW
5 teere] tese CJW, myns P;   Take] *add* fayr CJW;   white] *om.* P
6 þenne . . . forth] put hit vpon thy capons P   7 rede oþer whyt] red
WAr, *om.* P;   and with] *om.* CJ, or with P
39. 1 Blank] On fleschday blaun CJ, Braun W   2 whyte] rede *canc.*
with whyte *above* B, *om.* P;   on . . . day] *om.* CJP;   with²] *add* good CJW
3 oþer] and P   4 brawn] braunes W;   yground] *add* smale CJWP
5–6 Take . . . in] coloure hit with P   6 yholed] & hele it CJ   put]
pyt B
40. 1 blaunched] vnblaunched CJWP   2 and temper hem] *om.* W
4 fort] *om.* C;   and¹] or P;   salt] *add* & boyle it CJW   5 flour]
florche CJWP

41 Charlet. Take pork and seeþ it wel. Hewe it smale; cast it in a panne. Breke ayren and do þerto, and swyng it wel to-gyder, do þerto cowe mylke and safroun, and boile it togyder. Salt it & messe it forth.

42 Charlet yforced. Take mylke and seeþ it and swyng þer-with 3olkes of ayren, and do þerto; and powdour of gynger, sugur and safroun, and cast þerto. Take the charlet out of the broth and messe it in dysshes; lay the sewe onoward: flour it with powdour douce, and serue it forth. 5

43 Cawdel ferry. Take flour of payndemayn and gode wyne, and drawe it togydre; do þerto a grete quantite of sugur cypre, or hony claryfied; and do þerto safroun. Boile it, and whan it is boiled, alye it vp with 3olkes of ayren, and do þerto salt, and messe it forth. And lay þeron sugur and powdour gynger. 5

44 Iusshell. Take brede ygrated and ayren and swyng it to-gydre. Do þerto safroun, sawge, and salt, & cast broth þerto, boile it & messe it forth.

45 Iusshell enforced. Take and do þerto as to charlet yforced, and serue it forth.

46 Mortrews. Take hennes and pork and seeþ hem togyder. Take the lyre of hennes and of þe pork and hewe it small, and grinde it al to doust; take brede ygrated and do þerto, and temper it with the self broth, and alye it with 3olkes of ayren;

41. 1 Charlet] Harbet W   2 and do] *om.* CJ   3 do] *add* þeryn J;   boilc it togyder] let hit boyle tyl hit crudde Ar;   it] *add* & gedere it CJW   3-4 and² . . . Salt it] sesyn hit well with salt P
    42. 1 swyng] *add* it wel *canc.* A   2 ayren] *add* rawe CJ   4 flour] florish P   4-5 flour . . . forth] *om.* CJW   5 douce] *add* and sugur BP
    43. 1 gode] *add* and *canc.* B   2 grete] good CJ   3-4 safroun . . . of] *om.* J   5 powdour] *add* or C
    44. 1 ygrated] and grind hit W   2 cast] *add* good J
    45. 1 Take and] *om.* CJW;   to] *add* a C;   yforced] before rehersid P 1-2 yforced . . . forth] *om.* CJW
    46. 2 lyre] liuere CJP   3 al to doust] wel CJ, small P;   and do þerto] *om.* W

5 and cast þeron powdour fort. Boile it and do þerin powdour
of gynger, sugur, safroun and salt, and loke þat it be stondyng;
and flour it with powdour gynger.

47   Mortrews blank. Take pork and hennes and seeþ hem as
to fore. Bray almaundes blaunched, and temper hem vp with
the self broth, and alye the fleissh with the mylke and white
flour of rys; and boile it, & do þerin powdour of gynger,
5 sugur and salt, and look þat it be stondyng.

48   Brewet of Almayne. Take connynges or kiddes, and hewe
hem small on morcels oþer on pecys; perboile hem in good
broth. Drawe an almaunde mylke and do the fleissh þerwith;
cast þerto powdour galyngale & of gynger, with flour of rys,
5 and colour it wiþ alkenet. Boile it, salt it, & messe it forth
with sugur and powdour douce.

49   Peiouns ystewed. Take peiouns and stop hem with garlec
ypylled and with gode erbis ihewe, and do hem in an erthen
pot; cast þerto gode broth and whyte grece, powdour fort,
safroun, verious & salt.

50   Losyns. Take good broth and do in an erthen pot. Take
flour of payndemayn and make þerof past with water, and
make þerof thynne foyles as paper with a roller; drye it harde
and seeþ it in broth. Take chese ruayn grated and lay it in
5 disshes with powdour douce, and lay þeron loseyns isode as
hoole as þou myȝt, and above powdour and chese; and so
twyse or thryse, & serue it forth.

5–6 powdour² . . . sugur] *om.* CJWP   6 and² . . . stondyng] *om.* CJWP;
be] *add, above line* `not' B   7 flour] flurche CJWP   *marg. note*
'+ lacy' *left marg., later hand; same note, sometimes scribbled over or erased,
appears beside recipes 72, 81, 89, 117, 167* A
     47. 1–2 as to fore] togydre CJP, togyder *canc.* as to fore B   3 the³]
om. CJW;   white] *om.* C, wiþ JWP
     48. 1 Almayne] almony A   2 small . . . oþer] *om.* CJ;   in good]
with the same AB   3 Drawe an] Tak C;   the] *om.* B   5 Boile
it] *om.* P
     49. 2 ypylled] *om.* CJ   3 fort] *om.* W
     50. 3 thynne] þanne CJ   4 in broth] *om.* W;   ruayn] rawe W
5 loseyns] þe lof W   6 above] ef sone C, eft sone J, essone W;   and
so] *om.* CJ

51   Tartlettes. Take pork ysode and grynde it small with safroun; medle it with ayren, and raisouns of coraunce, and powdour fort and salt, and make a foile of dowh3 and close the fars þerinne. Cast þe tartletes in a panne with faire water boillyng and salt; take of the clene flessh with oute ayren &   5
boile it in gode broth. Cast þer powdour douce and salt, and messe the tartletes in disshes & helde the sewe þeronne.

52   Pynnonade. Take almaundes iblaunched and drawe hem sumdell thicke with gode broth oþer with water, and set on the fire and seeþ it; cast þerto 3olkes of ayren ydrawe. Take pynes yfryed in oyle oþer in grece, and do þerto white pow-dour douce, sugur and salt, & colour it wiþ alkenet a lytel.   5

53   Rosee. Take thyk mylke;seþe it. Cast þerto sugur, a gode porcioun; pynes, dates ymynced, canel, & powdour gynger; and seeþ it, and alye it with flours of white rosis, and flour of rys. Cole it; salt it & messe it forth. If þou wilt in stede of almaunde mylke, take swete crem of kyne.   5

54   Cormarye. Take colyaundre, caraway smale grounden, powdour of peper and garlec ygrounde, in rede wyne; medle alle þise togyder and salt it. Take loynes of pork rawe and fle of the skyn, and pryk it wel with a knyf, and lay it in the sawse. Roost it whan þou wilt, & kepe þat þat fallith þerfro   5
in the rostyng and seeþ it in a possynet with faire broth, & serue it forth wiþ þe roost anoon.

51. 1 Tartlettes] Tarlettes AB, Torteletys CW, Tortletus J   5 boillyng] *add* saffroun CJ;   clene] selue CJW, same P   6 þer] þerin B 7 helde] ley CJWP

52. 1 iblaunched] *add* grynde hem CW;   hem] *add* vp B   2 and set] seþ hit W   2-3 oþer . . . and] *om.* CP   4 in¹ . . . grece] *om.* P;   white] with CP, *om.* W   5 douce] fort CWP

53. 1 mylke] *add* of almaunds CP;   seþe it] as tofore welled AB, as hit tofore seþ it W, *om.* P   1-2 a gode porcioun] good won CW, a good quantyte P   2 pynes . . . canel] *om.* CWP;   &] of C   3 and seeþ it] *om.* W;   flours of white] floure of whete W   4 Cole it] holde it whyte CWP;   wilt in stede of] lakke C, wolt W   5 mylke] *om.* W;   take] *add* good C;   crem] cremes AB

54. 2 powdour . . . in] *om.* HC   2-3 medle alle þise] temp hem vp HC 3 fle] hylde P   4 pryk] peke CW   5 it whan] þerof what A, þerof what þat B;   fallith þerfro] droppeþ of C   6 in the rostyng] *om.* HC   6 broth] *add* Do þerto poudur of peper & oynouns imeset H 7 wiþ . . . anoon] *om.* H;   anoon] *om.* CWP

55 Newe noumbles of deer. Take noumbles and waishe hem clene with water and salt, and perboile hem in water; take hem vp & dyce hem. Do with hem as with ooþer noumbles.

56 Nota. The loyne of the pork is fro the hippe boon to the hede.

57 Nota. The fyletes buth þo that buth take oute of the pestels.

58 Spynee. Take and make gode thik almaund mylke as to fore, and do þerin flour of hawthorn, & make it as rosee, & serue it forth.

59 Chyryse. Take almaundes, waisshe hem; grynde hem, drawe hem vp with gode broth. Do þerto thridde part of chiryse, þe stones take oute, and grynde hem smale. Make a layour of gode brede & powdour and salt and do þerto; colour
5 it with saundres. Make it so þat it be stondyng, and florissh it with aneys and with chelberyes and strawe þervppon and serue it forth.

60 Paynfoundew. Take brede and frye it in grece oþer in oyle. Take it vp and lay it in rede wyne; grynde it with raisouns. Take hony and do it in a pot, and cast þerinne gleyre of ayren wiþ a litel water, and bete it wele togider

55. 1 noumbles²] *add* of dere HCP   2-3and² . . . dyce hem] *om.* H
3 dyce] dresse *above* dyce B, disch W;   Do with hem] & do þerto C, do þerwiþ W
    56. 1 boon] along HC
    57. 1 þo] two AB;   oute of] on H, of C   2 pestels] *add* of porke
HC
    58. 1 Take and] *om.* HCW;   almaund] *om.* HCW;   mylke] *om.* C
1-2 as to fore] *om.* P   2 flour] flours BHWP;   rosee] a rose AB, rose
W, *add* ys C
    59. 1 Chyryse] Chirise to potage H;   almaundes] *add* vnblaunched ABWP;
waisshe . . . hem²] *om.* HC   2 thridde part] þe rede C   4 layour]
licour W;   gode] *om.* HC;   powdour] pouderes gode H;   and do
þerto] *om.* HC   5 Make it] *om.* ABWP;   so þat it be] *om.* HC
6 with¹] *add* saundres so þat it *canc.*, with *repeated after canc.* A, *add* whit W;
chelberyes] cheseberyes *above* chyselberyes B, cheiȝelberus HW, cheryes C;
and strawe] istiuede HCW, ystrued P
    60. 1-2 in¹ . . . vp] *om.* P   2 lay] do HC   3-8 and¹ . . . oþere]
iclarifiet & do þerto HC   4 of] *add* rawe P

with a sklyse. Set it ouere the fire and boile it, and whan the 5
hatte arisith to goon ouere, take it adoun and kele it; when
hit is almost colde, take of þe wyte wyt a sclyse. And whan
it is þes clarified, do it to the oþere, with sugur and spices;
salt it and loke it be stondyng. Florissh it with white coliaundre
in confyt.   10

61 Crytayne. Take the offall of capouns oþer of oþere
briddes; make hem clene and perboile hem. Take hem vp &
dyce hem; take swete cowe mylke and cast þerinne, and lat it
boile. Take payndemayn and of þe self mylke, and drawe
thurgh a straynowr and cast it in a pot and lat it seeþ. Take 5
ayren ysode; hewe the white and cast þerto, and alye the
sewe with 3olkes of ayren rawe. Colour it with safroun. Take
the 3olkes and fry hem and florissh hem þerwith, and with
powdour douce.

62 Vinegrate. Take smale fylettes of pork and rost hem half,
and smyte hem to gobettes, and do hem in wyne & vyneger
and oynouns ymynced, and stewe it yfere. Do þerto gode
powdours & salt & serue it forth.

63 Founet. Take almaundes vnblaunched; grynde hem and
drawe hem vp with gode broth. Take a lombe or a kidde and
half rost hym, oþer the þridde part; smyte hym in gobetes
and cast hym to the mylke. Take smale briddes yfarsyd and

5 with a sklyse] *om.* P;   sklyse] styke H   5-6 the hatte] hit HCJP,
þat hit W   6-7 when . . . sclyse] *om.* AB   7 wyte] hat WP;
7-8 And . . . oþere] *om.* HC   8 þes] þus B;   sugur and spices] oyle
spyces & good poudurus H, hole spyces good pouder & CW, good spices and
powder P   9 and . . . be] make hit HC;   white] *om.* HCWP.
(*The material in this recipe appears as two separate recipes,* Paunfoundeu *and* For
to claryfy hony, *in* HJC.)
    61. 1 Crytayne] Crotoun AB, Crytayne to potage H;   offall] geblettes P;
oþer] & HCJW   2 briddes] foules HCJW;   make . . . perboile] and
boyle P   5 straynowr] cloth ABW;   cast . . . pot] put the gebelettes
þerto P;   in] *om.* H   6 white] *canc.* (?) A   7 3olkes . . . Take]
om. J;   of ayren] *om.* W;   safroun] *add* and salt P   8 3olkes]
add ysode HCJWP;   hem²] *add* and florisch hem W;   with] *om.* B
    62. 1 Vinegrate] Vynegrace AB;   half] *add* inowe HCJ   3 oynouns]
add & oynons W   4 salt] *add* and salt B
    63. 1 Founet] Founell AB;   vnblaunched] 'vn'blaunched A   4 hym
to the] þerto CJ   briddes] briddes *marg. add., same hand* A;   yfar-
syd] yfasced AB

5 ystyued, and do þerto sugur, powdour of canell and salt.
Take ȝolkes of ayren harde ysode and cleeue a two and
plauntede with flour of canell, and florissh þe sewe above.
Take alkenet fryed and yfoundred in wyne & colour hit
above with a feþer, and messe it forth.

64 Douce iame. Take gode cowe mylke and do it in a pot.
Take persel, sawge, ysope, saueray, and ooþer gode herbes;
hewe hem and do hem in the mylke and seeþ hem. Take
capouns half yrosted and smyte hem on pecys, and do þerto
5 pynes and hony clarified; salt it and colour it with safroun,
& serue it forth.

65 Connynges in cyrip. Take connynges and seeþ hem wel
in good broth. Take wyne greke and do þerto with a porcioun
of vyneger and flour of canel, hoole clowes, quybibes hoole,
and ooþer gode spices, with raisouns coraunce and gyngyuer
5 ypared and ymynced. Take vp the connynges and smyte hem
on pecys and cast hem in to the siryppe, and seeþ hem a litel
in fere, and serue it forth.

66 Leche Lumbard. Take rawe pork and pulle of the skyn,
and pyke out þe synewes, and bray the pork in a morter with
ayron rawe. Do þerto sugur, salt, raysouns coraunce, dates
mynced, and powdour of peper, powdour gylofre; & do it in
5 a bladder, and lat it seeþ til it be ynowhȝ. And whan it is
ynowh, kerf it; leshe it in liknesse of a peskodde; and take
grete raysouns and grynde hem in a morter. Drawe hem vp
wiþ rede wyne. Do þerto mylke of almaundes. Colour it with
saundres & safroun, and do þerto powdour of peper & of

5 powdour of canell] powdur CJW, & god powdur H   7 plauntede]
ypaunced AB, plaunte hit H;   above] aneward W;   8 Take alkenet]
talkenet H;   in wyne & colour hit] and droppe AB, in wyne and gout W
8–9 Take . . . above] *om.* J   9 feþer] ferer W
          64. 1 Douce iame] Doousiane to potage H, Douce iayn W;   gode] *om.* CJ
2 gode] *om.* C   3 hem¹] *add* stiue hem HCJW   4 do þerto] *om.* J;
þerto] *add* whyte B, *add* wiþ HCW
          65. 2 wyne greke] wyne creke B, wyn crete HW, cryk CJ   3 quybibes]
qquiblus C;   hoole²] *om.* CJ   6 to the] ius C   7 in fere]
on the fyre AB
          66. 1 pulle] tak vp CJ   2 pyke out þe] *om.* CJ;   þe] *add* skyn
canc. A;   synewes] senues J   5 til it be] *om.* CJ   6 ynowh]
sode CJ;   leshe it] out CJ

gilofre and boile it. And whan it is iboiled, take powdour of 10
canel and gynger and temper it vp with wyne, and do alle þise
thynges togyder, and loke þat it be rennyng; and lat it not
seeþ after þat it is cast togyder, & serue it forth.

67 Connynges in clere broth. Take connynges and smyte
hem in gobetes, and waissh hem, and do hem in feyre water
and wyne; & seeth hem and skym hem. And whan þey buth
isode, pyke hem clene, and drawe the broth thurgh a straynour, and do the flessh þerwith in a possynet and styue it; 5
and do þerto vyneger and powdour of gynger a grete quantite,
and salt after the last boillyng, and serue it forth.

68 Payn ragoun. Take hony and sugur cipre and clarifie it
togydre, and boile it with esy fyre, and kepe it wel fro brennyng. And whan it hath yboiled a while, take vp a drope
þerof wiþ þy fyngur and do it in a litel water, and loke if it
hong togydre; and take it fro the fyre and do þerto pynes 5
the thriddendele & powdour gyngeuer, and stere it togyder
til it bigynne to thik, and cast it on a wete table; lesh it and
serue it forth with fryed mete, on flessh dayes or on fysshe
dayes.

69 Lete lardes. Take persel, and grynde with a litul cowe
mylke; medle it with ayren and lard ydyced. Take mylke
after þat þou hast to done and myng þerwith, and make þerof
dyuerse colours. If þou wolt haue ȝelow, do þerto safroun
and no persel. If þou wolt haue it whyte, nouþer persell ne 5
safroun, but do þerto amydoun. If þou wilt haue rede, do
þerto saundres. If þou wilt haue pownas, do þerto turnesole.
If þou wilt haue blak, do þerto blode ysode and fryed; and
set on the fyre in as many vessels as þou hast colours þerto,
and seeþ it wel, and lay þise colours in a cloth, first oon, and 10

10 boile it] seþe it wel CJ;   And ... iboiled] *om.* CJ   11-12 and[3] ...
togyder] & cast þerto CJ   13 þat ... forth] *om.* CJ
   67. 2 feyre] *om.* CJ   5 possynet ... it] pot vnneþe ysteued CJ
6 vyneger ... of] pouder vinegre CJ;   gynger] *add* and AB   7 salt]
add it CJ
   68. 1 and[1]] Ar only   2 togydre] in fere CJ   4 wiþ þy fyngur]
om. CJ   5 pynes] *om.* A
   69. 1 grynde] *add* hit vp B;   litul] *om.* A

sithen anoþer vppon hym, and sithen the þridde and the
ferthe, and presse it harde til it be al out clene. And whan it
is al colde, lesh it thynne; put it in a panne and fry it wel, and
serue it forth.

70 Furmente with porpays. Take almaundes blaunched.
Bray hem and drawe hem vp with faire water; make furmente
as bifore and cast þe mylke þerto & messe it with porpays.

71 Perrey of pesoun. Take pesoun and seeþ hem fast, and
couere hem, til þei berst; þenne take hem vp and cole hem
thurgh a cloth. Take oynouns and mynce hem, and seeþ hem
in the same sewe, and oile þerwith; cast þerto sugur, salt and
5 safroun, and seeþ hem wel þerafter, and serue hem forth.

72 Pesoun of Almayne. Take white pesoun; waisshe hem.
Seeþ hem a grete while. Take hem vp and cole hem thurgh a
cloth; waisshe hem in colde water til the hulles go off. Cast
hem in a pot and couere hem þat no breth go out, and boile
5 hem right wel, and cast þerinne gode mylke of almaundes and
a pertye of flour of rys wiþ powdour gynger, safroun, & salt.

73 Chyches. Take chiches and wrye hem in askes al nyȝt
oþer al a day, oþer lay hem in hoot aymers. At morowe
waische hem in clene water, and do hem ouere the fire with
clene water. Seeþ hem vp and do þerto oyle, garlek hole,
5 safroun, powdour fort and salt; seeþ it and messe it forth.

74 Lopins. Take lopins & perboyle hem; do of þo holus
wyt braying, & sethe hem wyt broth of fysche. Do þerto
sugur, salt, saffron, & poudur of ginger, & messe hit forth.

70. 2 faire] om. H   3 bifore] to fore is sayd CJ;   mylke] furmente A
71. 1 pesoun¹] add to potage H;   Take ... fast] Seþe peesen JW, Tethe
peson H;   fast] om. C   2 cole hem] drawe hem H, add drawe hem
CJ
72. 2 vp] om. A   2-3 cole ... cloth] om. HJWAr   4 hem²]
om. A;   breth] broþ WAr   6 flour] colour J
73. 1 Chyches] Chiwes H;   wrye] ley HJW, seth them and ley P;   in]
add lyes of HJWP   1-2 al nyȝt ... aymers] oþer in embre J, all nith or in
hot emere W   2 al ... hem] om. H   5 seeþ it] add wel HJW,
and when hit is well sodyn togedir take hit vp P
74. 1 hem] & perboile hem W   2 braying] brayig H   3 &
messe hit forth] om. H

75   Frenche iowtes. Take and seeþ white pesoun and take
oute þe perrey; & perboile erbis & hewe hem grete, & cast
hem in a pot with the perry. Pulle oynouns & seeþ hem hole
wel in water, & do hem to þe perry with oile & salt; colour it
with safroun & messe it, and cast þeron powdour douce.   5

76   Makke. Take groundon benes and seeþ hem wel; take
hem vp of the water and cast hem in a morter. Grynde hem
al to doust til þei be white as eny mylke. Chawf a litell rede
wyne; cast þeramong in þe gryndyng. Do þerto salt. Leshe it
in disshes, þanne take oynouns and mynce hem smale and   5
seeþ hem in oile til þey be al broun, and florissh the disshes
þerwith, and serue it forth.

77   Aquapatys. Pill garlec and cast it in a pot with water and
oile and seeþ it. Do þerto safroun, salt, and powdour fort and
dresse it forth hoot.

78   Salat. Take persel, sawge, grene garlec, chibolles, oynouns,
leek, borage, myntes, porrettes, fenel, and toun cressis, rew,
rosemarye, purslarye; laue and waische hem clene. Pike hem.
Pluk hem small wiþ þyn honde, and myng hem wel with rawe
oile; lay on vyneger and salt, and serue it forth.   5

79   Fenkel in soppes. Take blades of fenkel; shrede hem not
to smale. Do hem to seeþ in water and oile, and oynouns
mynced þerwith; do þerto safroun and salt and powdour
douce. Serue it forth. Take brede ytosted and lay the sewe
onoward.   5

---

75. 1 iowtes] *add* to potage H;   Take and] *om.* J
   76. 1 groundon] drawen A   3 al to doust] small P;   til] for to H;
eny] *om.* HJW   4 cast] *om.* W   6 seeþ] frye H;   hem] *add*
smal *canc.* W;   al] ryte HJW, H *adds* drye *canc.*
   77. 2 fort] marchant Ar   3 hoot] *om.* HP
   78. 1 grene] *om.* ABP;   oynouns] letys P   2 leek] *add* spinoches
HJW;   myntes] *add* prymros, violettes P   3 rosemarye] *om.* HJWP;
laue] *om.* HJW;   Pike] pele JW   4 Pluk] pulse W;   wiþ þyn
honde] *om.* HJ;   rawe] good P
   79. 1 Fenkel in soppes] Soppes in fenkel BHJW   4 douce] *om.* WAr;
lay] pore PAr, *add* in disches & cast H

80 Elat. Take elena campana and seeþ it in water. Take it vp and grynde it wel in a morter. Temper it vp with ayren, safroun, and salt, and do it ouer the fire, and lat it not boile; cast above powdour douce and serue it forth.

81 Appulmoy. Take apples and seeþ hem in water; drawe hem thurgh a straynour. Take almaunde mylke & hony and flour of rys, safroun and powdour fort and salt, and seeþ it stondyng.

82 Slyt soppes. Take white of lekes and slyt hem, and do hem to seeþ in wyne, oile, and salt. Tost brede and lay in disshes, and cast the sewe aboue, and serue it forth.

83 Letelorye. Take ayren and wryng hem thurgh a stray-nour, and do þerto cowe mylke, with butter and safroun and salt. Seeþ it wel; leshe it, and loke þat it be stondyng, and serue it forth.

84 Sowpes dorry. Take almaundes brayed; drawe hem vp with wyne. Boile it. Cast þervppon safroun and salt. Take brede itosted & cast it in wyne; lay þerof a leyue, and anoþer of þat sewe, and alle togydre. Florissh it with sugur, powdour
5 gynger, and serue it forth.

85 Rapey. Take half fyges and half raisouns; pike hem and waishe hem in water. Skalde hem in wyne, bray hem in a morter, and drawe hem thurgh a straynour. Cast hem in a pot and þerwiþ powdur of peper and ooþer good powdours; alay

---

80. 1 in] *om.* A;   water] *add* drawe h *canc.* B   3 the] an esy P
81. 1 Appulmoy] Appulmoys BH, Amplemose W   2-3 and flour] *om.* C
82. 1 Slyt] Slete AB;   of] *om.* CJ   2 salt] pouder Ar   3 cast] *om.* AB, put P
83. 1 wryng] drawe CJ   2 butter] bottes CJ   3 and salt] *om.* HCJP;   it[2]] *add* in disches H;   loke ... be] make hit HCJ;   stondyng] *add* colour hit wyt saffron HCJP
84. 1 drawe] wringe HCJ   3 & cast it] *om.* AB;   þerof a leyue] alawe þerof H, a cours of þat CJ   4 and] *add* so CJ;   and ... togydre] *om.* P;   Florissh] pouder HCJ   4-5 sugur powdour gynger] pouder & suger C
85. 1 half[1]] *om.* CJ;   half[1] ... raisouns] figys & reson of ich leke moch P   2 in water] clene P   4 and[1]] *add* do pynes HCJW;   powdur] *add* of gynger & J;   ooþer] *add* do *canc.* C

it vp with flour of rys, and colour it with saundres. Salt it, 5
seeþ it, & messe it forth.

86   Sawse Sarzyne. Take heppes and make hem clene. Take
almaundes blaunched; frye hem in oile and bray hem in a
morter with heppes. Drawe it vp with gode rede wyne, and
do þerin sugur ynowhჳ with powdour fort: lat it be stondyng,
and alay it with flour of rys, and colour it with alkenet and 5
messe it forth; and florissh it with pomme garnet. If þou wilt,
in flesshe day, seeþ capouns, and take þe brawn and tese hym
smal, and do þerto, and make the licour of þis broth.

87   Creme of almaundes. Take almaundes blaunched; grynde
hem and drawe hem vp with water thykke. Set hem ouer the
fyre & boile hem. Set hem adoun and spryng hem with vyneger. Cast hem abrode vppon a cloth, and cast vppon hem
sugur; whan it is colde, gadre it togydre and leshe it in disshes. 5

88   Grewel of almaundes. Take almaundes blaunched. Bray
hem with ootmeel, and draw hem vp with water & sethe hyt;
cast þeron safroun & salt, &c.

89   Iowtes of almaund mylke. Take erbes; boile hem, hewe
hem, and grynde hem smale. Take almaundus iblaunchede;
grynde hem and drawe hem vp with water. Set hem on the
fire and seeþ the iowtes with the mylke, and cast þeron sugur
& salt, & serue it forth.   5

90   Cawdel of almaund mylk. Take almaundes blaunched
and drawe hem vp with wyne; do þerto powdour of gynger

5 flour] pouder W
    86. 1 heppes] þe ympes H   4 sugur] poudur H   5 and¹] or CJ,
oþer H   6 If þou wilt] And if hit be P   7 tese] myns P
8 and do þerto] om. HCJ;   licour] lyour HCJ, coloure P;   þis] rys B
    87. 2 and drawe hem] om. H;   with water] om. ABP, add ryth CJ;
thykke] & þike mylke H, and þiuk milk W, om. P   2-3 Set . . . fyre]
sethe hyt HCJ   3 Set] seþ W   4 abrode] in a bord J
    88. 2 ootmeel] oute mele H;   vp with] with vp B;   sethe hyt] om. AB
Title, recipe number, and recipe written in right marg., same hand, following
Creme of almaundes A
    89. 1 boile] perboyle HWP   2 and] or HJW   2-3 Take . . .
hem¹] om. AB   4 seeþ] add on C   4-5 and² . . . salt] om. Ar

and sugur, and colour it with safroun. Boile it, cast a lytle salt
þeron, and serue it forth.

91   Fygey. Take almaundes blaunched; grynde hem and
drawe hem vp with water and wyne, quarter fyges, hole raisouns. Cast þerto powdour gynger and hony clarified; seeþ it
wel & salt it, & serue forth.

92   Pochee. Take ayren and breke hem in scaldyng hoot
water, and whan þei bene sode ynowh take hem vp and take
ȝolkes of ayren rawe & mylke, and swyng hem togydre; and
do þerto powdour gynger, safroun and salt, set it ouere the
5 fire, and lat it not boile. And take ayren isode & cast þe sew
onoward, & serue it forth.

93   Brewet of ayren. Take water and butter, and seeþ hem
yfere with safroun and gobettes of chese; wryng ayren thurgh
a straynour. Whan the water hath soden a while, take þenne
the ayren and swyng hem with verious, and cast þerto; set it
5 ouere the fire, and lat it not boile, and serue it forth.

94   Rauioles. Take wete chese & grynde hit smal, & medle
hit wyt eyren & saffron and a god quantite of buttur. Make a
þin foile of dowe & close hem þerin as turteletes, & cast hem
in boylyng watur, & sethe hem þerin. Take hote buttur mel-
5 tede & chese ygratede, & ley þi ravioles in dissches; & ley þi
hote buttur wyt gratede chese bineþe & aboue, & cast þereon
powdur douce.

90. 3–4 cast . . . þeron] *om.* ABP, cast þerto but litul salt or non CJW
    91. 1–2 and drawe hem] *om.* HJ   2 quarter] a quantite of H;   fyges]
add & take H   3 and] *add* suger couloure hit wiþ safrenne boile hit & W
4 salt . . . forth] colour hit wyt saffron H
    92. 2 ynowh] wel HCJ   3 rawe &] & rawe AB   4 safroun]
sugur HCJ, sugur safrenne WP, sugur or hony and . . . saffroun Ar;   set] seþ W
5–6 sew . . . forth] swete aboue but colour hit wyt saffron H
    93. 1 Take] *add* ayren AB   2 safroun] *add* & salt HCJ;   ayren]
add raw H   4 swyng] wrynge CJ   5 boile] *add* do therto pouder
Ar;   and . . . forth] afterward H
    94. 1 Rauioles] raucoles HCJ;   wete] swete J;   hit] *add* welle & W
2 Make] & tak CJW   3 as] tak CJ   4 hote] hole CJ   5 ravi-
oles] raucoles HCJ;   & ley þi²] let poure CJ   6 gratede] þe CJ, þat W

95 Makerouns. Take and make a thynne foyle of dowh, and kerue it on peces, and cast hym on boillyng water & seeþ it wele. Take chese and grate it, and butter imelte, cast bynethen and aboven as losyns; and serue forth.

96 Tostee. Take wyne and hony and found it togyder and skym it clene, and seeþ it long. Do þerto powdour of gynger, peper and salt. Tost brede and lay the sewe þerto; kerue pecys of gynger and flour it þerwith, and messe it forth.

97 Gynggaudy. Take the poke and the lyuour of haddok, codlyng, and hake, and of ooþer fisshe; perboile hem. Take hem and dyce hem small. Take of the self broth and wyne; make a layour of brede, of galyntyne with gode powdours and salt. Cast þat fysshe þerinne and boile it, & do þerto 5 comyn, & colour it grene.

98 Erbowle. Take bolas and scald hem with wyne, and drawe hem þorow a straynour; do hem in a pot. Clarify hony, and do þerto with powdour fort and flour of rys. Salt it & florissh it with whyte aneys, & serue it forth.

99 Rysmole. Take almaundes blaunched and drawe hem vp with water, and alye it with flour of rys; and do þerto powdour of gynger, sugur and salt, and loke it be stondyng. Messe it and serue it forth.

100 Vyaunde Cypre. Take dates and pike out the stones, and grynde hem smale, and drawe hem thurgh a straynour.

95. 1 Makerouns] Macrows AB;   Take and make] tak CP, make HJ
3 imelte] molt B   4 aboven] add & canc. H;   as] & CJ
  96. 1 found it] stere them P, bete hit well Ar   3 þerto] aboue CJ
3–4 kerue . . . forth] om. Ar   4 flour] florische HCJP
  97. 1 Gynggaudy] Gyngawdry AP, Gigaudre H, Gyngardre CJ;   poke]
powche AB   2–3 Take . . . small] smale canc. J   4 of²] & CJ,
and of H   4–5 make . . . salt] and bred good powders & salt and make a
galantyne P   5 boile] perboyle C   6 comyn] amydoun AB
  98. 2 þorow] with AB;   hony] hem C   4 whyte] om. H
  99. 1 Rysmole] Resmolle AB;   blaunched] add grynde hem CJ
3 loke it be] make hem CJ, do þat hit be H, boyle hit tel hit be P;   be] add
not AB   3–4 Messe . . . forth] om. BH
  100. 1 dates] ootmele A, mele B, melis P, me dates J, damasines H;   pike]
pyl H

Take mede oþer wyne ifounded in sugur, and do þise þerinne;
do þerto powdour and salt, and alay it with flour of rys, and
5 do þat it be stondyng. If þou wilt, on flessh day, take hennes
and pork ysode & grynde hem smale, and do þerto, & messe
it forth.

101 Vyaunde Cypre of Samoun. Take almaundes and bray
hem vnblaunched. Take calwar samoun and seeþ it in water;
draw vp þyn almaundes with the broth. Pyke out the bones
out of the fyssh clene & grynd it small, & cast þy mylk & þat
5 togyder, & alye it with flour of rys. Do þerto powdour fort,
sugur & salt; & colour it with alkenet, and make hyt stondyng, and messe it forth.

102 Vyaund ryal. Take wyne greke oþer red wyne and hony
clarified þerwith. Take flour of rys, pynes, powdour of gynger,
of peper & flour of canel, powdour of clowes, safroun, sugur
cypre, mylberyes oþer saundres, & medle alle þise togider.
5 Boile it and salt it, and loke þat it be stondyng.

103 Compost. Take rote of persel, of pasternak, of rafens,
scrape hem and waische hem clene. Take rapes & caboches,
ypared and icorue. Take an erthen panne with clene water &
set it on the fire; cast alle þise þerinne. Whan þey buth boiled
5 cast þerto peeres, & perboile hem wel. Take alle þise thynges
vp & lat it kele on a faire cloth. Do þerto salt; whan it is colde,
do hit in a vessel; take vyneger & powdour & safroun & do

3 mede oþer] *om.* HCJP;   in] wyþ HCJ   4 þerto] *add* god HCJ;
salt] slat H   5 do þat it be] make hit HCJ, boyle hit tel hit be P
   101. 2 in] *add* lewe A   6 make hyt] do þat hit be W, so hit be P, loke
þat hit be not AB
   102. 1 greke] creke B, cryk CJ, crete HW;   oþer] and oþer W, & gode H;
red] rynysshe AB;   hony] *add* ifryede H   2 pynes] *om.* AB;   gyn-
ger] *add* oþer AB   3 &] *add* canel oþer AB   4 cypre] & salt H,
om. P   5 and² . . . be] make hit HCJ, do þat hit be W, so þat hit be P
   103. 1 of²] *om.* AB;   pasternak] pastronale CJ   2 scrape] sharpe
H, stripe P;   clene] chene H   3 erthen] yren CJ, lytell P   4 set
. . . fire] sethe hyt HCJ;   boiled] perboylet H   5 peeres] porys J;
perboile] boyle H   6 Do þerto] spryng þeron P   7 do hit]
om. AB;   & powdour] *add* of gynger J, *om.* P;   &²] *om.* C;   & safroun]
of saffron & god poudurus H

þerto, & lat alle þise thynges lye þerin al ny3t, oþer al day.
Take wyne greke & hony, clarified togider; take lumbarde
mustard & raisouns coraunce, al hoole, & grynde powdour of 10
canel, powdour douce & aneys hole, & fenell seed. Take alle
þise thynges & cast togyder in a pot of erthe, & take þerof
whan þou wilt & serue forth.

104   Gele of fyssh. Take tenches, pykes, eelys, turbut, and
plays; kerue hem to pecys. Scalde hem & waische hem clene;
drye hem with a cloth. Do hem in a panne; do þerto half
vyneger & half wyne, & seeþ it wel, & take the fysshe & pike
it clene. Cole þe broth thurgh a cloth in to an erthen panne; 5
do þerto powdour of peper and safroun ynowh. Lat it seeþ
& skym it wel. Whan it is ysode, dof þe grees clene; cowche
fisshe on chargours & cole the sewe thorow a cloth onoward,
& serue it forth colde.

105   Gele of flessh. Take swynes feet & snowtes and the
eerys, capouns, connynges, calues fete; & waische hem clene
& do hem to seeþ in the þriddel of wyne & vyneger and water
and make forth as bifore.

106   Chysanne. Take roches, hole tenches, and plays & smyte
hem to gobettes. Fry hem in oyle. Blaunche almaundes; fry
hem & cast þerto raisouns coraunce. Make a lyour of crustes
of brede, of rede wyne & of vyneger, þe þridde part; þerwith
fyges drawen, & do þerto powdour fort and salt; boile it. Lay 5

8 lat . . . day] so let hit ly P;   alle þise thynges] *om.* C, hit J, alle þes B
9 greke] creke B, crek C, cryk J, crete H, *om.* P;   &] or CJ   9–10 lumbarde mustard] *See FC 150*   10 & grynde] tak CJ, *om.* P
    104. 1 and] or P   2 clene] *om.* CJ   5 erthen] *om.* HCJ
5–6 Cole . . . peper] then put to thy broth poudir of pepur, gynger, salt P
8 onoward] *om.* CJ   9 colde] *om.* ABCJ
    105. 1 Gele of flessh] Congur in Sauce (gele of fl . . . *in margin*) J
2 capouns connynges] or capons or conyes or P   3 the þriddel of] *om.* P
4 and . . . bifore] then take up thy mete and cole thy broth thorow a cloth; then
set hit on the fire. Then do þerto pepir, clowes, macys, gynger, saforun or saundirs, sugir and salt, and boyle hit well. Then take of the reme above and let hit ren
thorowe a cloth ynto a faire vessell of yerth; then geve hit another hete and pore
hit ynto dishis. Do þerto hole blanchid almons florishid & hole clowes and when
hit is cold and stondyng serue hit furth P;   forth as] it so as þat C, hit so J
    106. 1 hole] *om.* HP, eles & CJW;   tenches] *om.* H;   and] or P
2 in oyle] *om.* P   2–3 fry hem &] *om.* P   3 a] *om.* AB
4 rede] *om.* P;   þe þridde part] *om.* P

the fisshe in an erthen panne & cast the sewe þerto. Seeþ
oynouns ymynced & cast þerinne; kepe hit and ete it colde.

107   Congur in sawse. Take the congur and scald hym, and
smyte hym in pecys, & seeþ hym. Take persel, mynt, peletur,
rosmarye, & a litul sawge, brede and salt, powdour fort, and a
litel garlec, clowes a lite; take and grynd it wel. Drawe it vp
5   wiþ vyneger þurgh a cloth. Cast the fyssh in a vessel and do
þe sewe onoward, & serue it forth icold.

108   Rygh in sawse. Take rygh3es and make hem clene and
do hem to seeþ. Pyke hem clene and frye hem in oile. Take
almaundes and grynde hem & drawe hem vp wyt water or
wyne; do þerto almaundes blaunched hole, fryed in oile, &
5   raysouns coraunce. Seeþ the lyour, grynde it smale & do þerto
garlec ygrounde & a litel salt & verious, powdour fort &
safroun, & boile it yfere. Lay the fysshe in a vessell and cast
the sewe þerto, and messe it forth colde.

109   Makerel in sawse. Take makerels and smyte hem on
pecys. Cast hem on water and verious; seeþ hem with myntes
and wiþ ooþer erbes. Colour it grene or 3elow & messe it
forth.

110   Pykes in brasey. Take   pykes and vndo hem on þe
wombes and waisshe hem clene, and lay hem on a roost irne.
þenne take gode wyne and powdour gynger & sugur, good

---

6 erthen panne] erhen potte H, yrene panne J, vessell P;   þerto] add kel
canc. C   7 hit] add clene CJ
     107. 2 smyte] drawe (*rest of recipe missing*) P;   hym[1]] add on gobetes or
CJ   3 fort] marchant Ar   4 a lite] om. W, fewe J;   take] om. J;
5 vyneger] and a lytel wyn Ar   6 & ... icold] om. B;   icold] om.
AH
     108. 1 rygh3es] riches H   2 Pyke hem] take hit vp & make hem HCJ
3 almaundes] add iblawnched H;   & ... wyt] in AB;   or] and HCJ
7 Lay] sethe HCJ;   fysshe] flessh J;   in a vessell] om. CJ   8 colde]
om. HCJ
     109. 3 ooþer] om. H
     110. 1 Take] add powder of canell, wyne, venegir, & light bred and stere all
togedir and drawe hit thorowe a straynour; then boyle hit with pouder of peper;
than take P;   þe] add wondes canc. A   2 and[2]] add r canc. A;
roost] for hoot canc. A;   roost irne] rostyng ern & rost hem WAr, gredyren &
rost hem C, gridel & rost hem HJ

wone, & salt, and boile it in an erthen panne; & messe forth
þe pyke & lay the sewe onoward.   5

111   Porpeys in broth. Make as þou madest noumbles of
flessh with oynouns.

112   Balloc broth. Take eelys and hilde hem, and kerue hem
to pecys, and do hem to seeþ in water and wyne so þat it be
a litel ouerstepid. Do þerto sawge and ooþer erbis, with fewe
oynouns ymynced. Whan the eelis buth soden ynowȝ, do
hem in a vessel; take a pyke and kerue it to gobettes and   5
seeþ hym in the same broth. Do þerto powdour gynger,
galyngale, canel and peper; salt it and cast the eelys þerto &
messe it forth.

113   Eles in brewet. Take crustes of brede and wyne and
make a lyour; do þerto oynouns ymynced, powdour gynger
& canel, & a litel water and wyne. Loke þat it be stepid. Do
þerto salt; kerue þin eelis & seeþ hem wel and serue hem forth.

114   Cawdel of samoun. Take the guttes of samoun and
make hem clene; perboile hem a lytell. Take hem vp and dyce
hem. Slyt the white of lekes and kerue hem smale; cole the
broth and do the lekes þerinne with oile, and lat it boile
togyder yfere. Do the samoun ycorue þerin. Make a lyour of   5
almaund mylke & of brede, & cast þerto spices, safroun and
salt; seeþ it wel, and loke þat it be not stondyng.

4 erthen] eyren J.   *Cross in left marg., as also beside recipes 120, 158* A
     111. 1 as þou madest] þe maner of HCW, in þe selue maner J   1-2 noum-
bles of flessh] *See FC 15*
     112. 1 and hilde hem] *om.* HCJ   3 fewe] a lyte HCW
     113. 1 Take] Make a lyour of HCJW;   of brede] *om.* CJ   2 gyn-
ger] fort P   3 canel] *add* & peper H;   Loke] *om.* BHCJ;   be] *add* a
lytel HCJ;   stepid] yholede H, helud CJ   3-4 canel . . . salt] erbes
ynow W   4 kerue . . . forth] couoore þi potte & sethe hem wel HCJ;   eelis]
add on peces and cast þerto pouder and safrenne and salt W.   *A variant
of this recipe follows in WPAr:* Elus in sorry [dorre P]. Tak eles and kerf hem to
peces; do þerto erbes and oynons ymiset, poudir of ginger & of canel, and a litul
of watur and wyne þat þei be lutel ystepud. Do þerto salt; keuer hem fast and seþ
hemme welle (P *adds* saforn *and* Ar saunders *for colour*)
     114. 2 a lytell] *om.* P   3 Slyt] *add* hem *canc.* A, Take HCJ;   and]
add slitte hem HCJ   4 lekes] eles CJ   4-5 with . . . þerin] *om.* CJ;
lat . . . togyder] hony H   5 togyder yfere] in þe fuyre W;   lyour]
licour W   7 not] *add* to BH

115   Plays in cyuee. Take plays and smyte hem to pecys, and fry hem in oyle; drawe a lyour of brede & gode broth & vyneger and do þerto powdour gynger, canel, peper and salt, and colour it with gawdy grene: & loke þat it be not to
5 stondyng.

116   For to make flaumpeyns. Take clene pork and boile it tendre, þenne hewe it small, and bray it smal in a morter. Take fyges and boile hem tendre in smale ale, & bray hem, & tendre chese þerwith; þenne waische hem in water & þenne
5 bray hem alle togider with ayren. þenne take powdour of peper, or els powdour marchaunt, & ayren, and a porcioun of safroun and salt; þenne take blank sugur, eyren & flour, & make a past with a rollere. þenne make þerof smale pelettes & fry hem broun in clene grece, & set hem asyde. þenne
10 make of þat ooþer deel of þat past long coffyns, & do þat comade þerin, and close hem faire with a couertour, & pynche hem smale aboute. þanne kyt aboue foure oþer sex wayes. þanne take euery of þat kuttyng vp & þenne colour it with ȝolkes of ayren, & plaunt hem thick in to þe flaumpeyns
15 aboue þer þou kuttest hem & set hem in an ovene and lat hem bake eselich, and þanne serue hem forth.

117   For to make noumbles in lent. Take the blode of pykes, oþer of congur, and nyme the paunches of pykes, of congur and of grete codelyng, & boile hem tendre & mynce hem smale, & do hem in þat blode. Take crustes of white brede &
5 strayne it thurgh a cloth, þenne take oynouns iboiled and mynced. Take peper and safroun, wyne, vyneger, oþer aysell oþer alegur, & do þerto, & serue forth.

118   For to make chawdoun for lent. Take blode of gur-nardes and congur, & þe paunches of gurnardes, and boile hem tendre & mynce hem smale; and make a lyre of white crustes and oynouns ymynced. Bray it in a morter, & þanne
5 boile it togider til it be stondyng; þenne take vyneger oþer aysell & safroun, & put it þerto, and serue it forth.

115. 2 lyour] licour W   3 powdour ... salt] *om.* H;   salt] cast
þerto CJW   4 with] *om.* C;   to] *om.* J
116. 5 ayren] hard egges P   6 powdour] *om.* B   7 blank]
blank *corr. to* blak, *n underdotted* BP
117. 5 take] *om.* B   6 oþer] *om.* A

119   Furmente with porpeys. Take clene whete and bete it
small in a morter and fanne out clene the doust; þenne
waische it clene, and boile it tyl it be tendre and brokene.
þanne take the secunde mylke of almaundes & do þerto;
boile hem togider til it be stondyng, and take þe first mylke 5
& alye it vp wiþ a penne. Take vp the porpays out of the furmente & leshe hem in a disshe with hoot water, & do safroun
to þe furmente. And if the porpays be salt, seeþ it by hym
self; and serue it forth.

120   Fylettes in galyntyne. Take pork and rost it tyl the
blode be tryed out, & þe broth; take crustes of brede and
bray hem in a morter, & drawe hem thurgh a cloth with þe
broth. þenne take oynouns & leshe hem on brede, & do to
the broth. þanne take pork; leshe it clene with a dressyng 5
knyf and cast it in to þe broth, & lat it boile til it be more
tendre. þanne take þat lyour þerto. þanne take a porcion of
peper and saundres, & do þerto. þanne take persel & ysope &
mynce it smale, and do þerto. þanne take rede wyne oþer
white, grece, & raysouns, & do þerto. & lat it boile a lytel.   10

121   Veel in buknade. Take fayr veel and kyt it in smale
pecys, and boile it tendre in fyne broth oþer in water. þanne
take white brede, oþer wastel, and drawe þerof a white lyour
wiþ fyne broth, and do þe lyour to the veel & do safroun
þerto. þanne take persel & bray it in a morter, & the iuys 5
þerof do þerto; and þanne is þis half ȝelow & half grene.
þanne take a porcioun of wyne & powdour marchaunt, & do
þerto, & lat it boile wele; and do þerto a litel of vyneger, &
serue forth.

122   Sooles in cyuee. Take sooles and hylde hem; seeþ hem
in water. Smyte hem on pecys and take away the fynnes.
Take oynouns iboiled & grynde the fynnes þerwith, and
brede; drawe it vp with the self broth. Do þerto powdour fort,
safroun, & hony claryfied, with salt. Seeþ it alle yfere. Broile 5

119. 3 brokene] broun A
120. 6 þe] *add* pot *canc.* A
121. 3 white¹] *add* wastel *canc.* A   7 take] take take A
122. 5 safroun] *om.* H;   Broile] boyle CJ

the sooles & messe it in dysshes, & lay the sewe aboue &
serue forth.

123 Tenches in cyuee. Take tenches and smyte hem to
pecys; fry hem. Drawe a lyour of raysouns coraunce wiþ
wyne and water; do þerto hool raisouns & powdour of gynger, of clowes, of canel, of peper: do the tenches þerto &
5 seeþ hem with sugur cypre & salt, & messe forth.

124 Oysters in grauey. Schyl oysters and seeþ hem in wyne
and in hare owne broth; cole the broth thurgh a cloth. Take
almaundes blaunched; grynde hem and drawe hem vp with
the self broth, & alye it wiþ flour of rys and do the oysters
5 þerinne. Cast in powdour of gynger, sugur, macys, quibibes &
salt. Seeþ it not to stondyng and serue forth.

125 Muskles in brewet. Take muskels: pyke hem; seeþ hem
with her owne broth. Make a lyour of crustes of brede &
vyneger; do in oynouns mynced, & cast the muskels þerto &
seeþ it. & do þerto powdour fort with a lytel salt & safroun:
5 the same wise make of oysters.

126 Oysters in cyuee. Take oysters; perboile hem in her
own broth. Make a layour of crustes of brede, & drawe it vp
wiþ the broth, and vyneger. Mynce oynouns & do þerto, wiþ
erbes, & cast the oysters þerinne; boile it & do þerto pow-
5 dour fort & salt, & messe it forth.

127 Cawdel of muskels. Take and seeþ muskels; pyke hem
clene, and waisshe hem clene in wyne. Take almaundes & bray

123. 5 cypre] *om.* H
124. 1 Schyl] skale CJ;   seeþ] ley CJ   1-2 in wyne and] *om.*
HCJW   2 the . . . cloth] hit W   3 and drawe hem] *om.* J
4 the self broth] wyne or wiþ ale W   5 sugur] *om.* H   6 to] *om.*
CJ;   stondyng] stronge H, long W   *left marg., later hand* h w (?) A
    125. 1 muskels] *add* & wasche hem CJ;   hem[1] *add* clene CJ   2 her]
the AB;   lyour] licour W;   crustes of] *om.* P;   &] drawen with P
2-4 Make . . . seeþ it] *om.* CJ   3 mynced] *add* & erbis small P
4 fort] *om.* AB   5 the . . . make] þe selue maner W, & so do H,
& do as to CJ
    126. 1 perboile] boyle CJ   2 Make] tak CJ;   layour] licour W
5 fort] *add* and saforn P
    127. 1 pyke] pil H   2 clene] *om.* H, wel CJW;   bray] boile W

hem. Take somme of the muskels and grynde hem, & some
hewe smale; drawe the muskels yground with the self broth.
Wryng the almaundes with faire water. Do alle þise togider; 5
do þerto verious and vyneger. Take whyte of lekes & perboile
hem wel; wryng oute the water and hewe hem smale. Cast
oile þerto, with oynouns perboiled & mynced smale; do þerto
powdour fort, safroun & salt a lytel. Seeþ it, not to stondyng,
& messe it forth.   10

128   Mortrews of fyssh. Take codlyng, haddok, oþer hake,
and lyuours with the rawnes, and seeþ it wel in water. Pyke
out þe bones. Grynde smale the fysshe; drawe a lyour of
almaundes & brede with the self broth, & do þe fysshe grounden þerto, and seeþ it and do þerto powdour fort, safroun 5
and salt; and make it stondyng.

129   Ryse of fische daye. Blaunche almaundes & grynde
hem, & drawe hem vp wyt watur. Wesche þi ryse clene, & do
þerto sugur roche and salt: let hyt be stondyng. Frye almaundes browne, & floriche hyt þerwyt, or wyt sugur.

130   Laumpreys in galyntyne. Take laumpreys and sle hem
with vyneger oþer with white wyne & salt. Scalde hem in
water. Slyt hem a litel at þe nauell, & rest a litel at þe nauel.
Take out the guttes at the ende. Kepe wele the blode. Put the
laumprey on a spyt; roost hym & kepe wel the grece. Grynde 5
raysouns of coraunce; drawe hym vp with vyneger, wyne, and
crustes of brede. Do þerto powdour of gynger, of galyngale,
flour of canel, powdur of clowes; & do þerto raisouns of

---

5 Wryng . . . water] *om., material added above:* almaunds iblaunched (ibrayede
J) & drawe hem wyt watur HCJ   9 a lytel. Seeþ it] sethe hyt a lyte
HJW, then boyle P;   not to stondyng] *om.* P;   to] to to A
    128. 1 Take . . . hake] Take gurnard or codlyng P;   codlyng] colde lynge H
3 drawe] mak J   5 safroun] *om.* J   6 make it stonding] dres
hit as mortrews; cast þeron powder of gynger P
    129. 1 almaundes] add & blanch hem W   3 roche] *om.* P   4 or]
and P;   wyt] add oþer W
    130. 2 vyneger . . . white] *om.* HJW;   oþer . . . wyne] *om.* P   3 nauell]
add take out the *canc.* A, eyne HJWP;   & rest] kut hem P;   & . . . nauel]
ende B, *om.* P   3-4 & rest . . . ende] *om.* HJW   4 ende] eyen P
5 spyt] small broche P   6 drawe . . . vyneger] *H inserts later lines of*
galyngale . . . coraunce *then repeats* drawe *and continues as in AB; no indication
of cancellation*   7-8 powdour . . . þerto] *om.* J

coraunce hoole, with þe blode & þe grece. Seeþ it & salt it:
10 boile it not to stondyng. Take vp the laumprey; do hym in a
chargeour, & lay þe sewe onoward & serue hym forth.

131   Laumprouns in galyntyne. Take laumprouns and scalde
hem; seeþ hem. Meng powdour galyngale and some of the
broth togyder & boile it, & do þerto powdour of gynger &
salt. Take the laumprouns & boile hem, & lay hem in dysshes,
5 & lay þe sewe aboue & serue fort.

132   Loseyns in fyssh day. Take almaundes vnblaunched
and waische hem clene & grynde hem; drawe hem vp with
water. Seeþ þe mylke & alye it vp with loseyns. Cast þerto
safroun, sugur, & salt, & messe it forth with colyaundre in
5 confyt rede, & serue it forth.

133   Sowpes in galyngale. Take powdour of galyngale, wyne,
sugur and salt; and boile it yfere. Take brede ytosted, and lay
the sewe onoward, and serue it forth.

134   Sobre sawse. Take raysouns; grynde hem with crustes
of brede, and drawe it vp with wyne. Do þerto gode powdours
and salt, and seeþ it. Fry roches, looches, sooles, oþer ooþer
gode fyssh; cast þe sewe aboue, & serue it forth.

135   Cold brewet. Take creme of almaundes; drye it in a
cloth, and whan it is dryed do it in a vessel. Do þerto salt,
sugur and powdour of gynger, and the iuys of fenel and wyne,

10 vp] *om.* B;   vp the laumprey] þe lampray of þo spyte HJW
    131. 2 galyngale] of galentyne HJAr   3 powdour of] good W;
gynger] *add* sawndirs sugir and salt with a fewe reysens of corans P, *add* and of
canel Ar
    132. 2 waische hem clene] *om.* W;   & grynde hem] *om.* AB;   vp] *add*
as þykke mylk HJWP   3 þe mylke] hit J
    133. 1 galyngale¹] galyntyne ABHJW;   wyne] with ABP   2 sugur]
add reysons P;   salt] *add* then take crustes of bred and drawe hit with wyne P;
it] *add* togedir ouer þe fire P;   lay] *add* hit yn vessel and put P   3 the
sewe] hit in þe sewe W
    134. 2 gode powdours] gynger, canell, sawndirs, sugir P   3 salt] *add*
& wyne H;   roches] `roches´ (*in margin, marked for insertion*) loches (*given
twice*) J;   oþer] & HJ
    135. 1 Take] *add* god HJ   2 is] *add* drawe *canc.* H   3 and¹]
add white AB, wyt HJ, hele hit wiþ whit W;   iuys] geust J;   wyne] vine W

and lat it wel stonde by þo fenel; & messe, & dresse it forth.

136 Peeres in confyt. Take peeres and pare hem clene. Take gode rede wyne & mulberies, oþer saundres, and seeþ þe peeres þerin, & whan þei buth ysode take hem vp. Make a syryp of wyne greke, oþer vernage, with blaunche powdur, oþer white sugur and powdour gynger, & do the peres þerin. 5 Seeþ it a lytel & messe it forth.

137 Egurdouce of fysshe. Take loches or roches oþer tenches oþer solys; smyte hem on pecys. Fry hem in oyle. Take half wyne, half vyneger, and sugur, & make a siryp; do þerto oynouns icorue, raisouns coraunce, and grete raysouns. Do þerto hole spices, gode powdours and salt; messe þe fyssh & 5 lay þe sewe above and serue forth.

138 Colde brewet. Take almaundes and grynde hem. Take þe tweydel of wyne oþer the þriddell of vyneger; drawe vp the almaundes þerwith. Take anys, sugur, and braunches of fenel grene, a fewe, & drawe hem vp togyder with þe mylke. Take powdour of canell, of gynger, clowes & maces hoole. 5 Take kydde oþer chikens oþer flessh, & choppe hem small and seeþ hem. Take al þis flessh, whan it is soden, & lay it in a clene vessel, & boile þe sewe & cast þerto salt. þenne cast al þis in þe pot with flessh, &c.

139 Peruorat for veel and venysoun. Take brede & fry it in grece; drawe it vp with broth and vyneger. Take þerto powdour of peper & salt, and sette it on the fyre. Boile it and messe it forth.

4 wel . . . by] kepe þe coloure of P;   by þo fenel] lay full AB
  136. 1 peeres] wardons Ar   1-2 Take gode] take gode take gode
(*twice, first time canc.*) A   4 greke] creke BJ, crete HAr;   vernage]
add or other gode swete wyne Ar   5 white] wyt HJP, wyþ whit W
gynger] *add* & resons of corans P
  137. 1 or roches] *om.* AB;   oþer tenches] *om.* J   3 make] *om.* J
4 icorue] ymenset HJ   5 hole spices] clowes and maces Ar;   salt]
add boyle but a litel P
  139. 2 Take] cast J   3 peper] *add* and of clowes Ar;   and . . .
fyre] *om.* PAr   4 forth] *add* upon venson or vele rosted P

140 Sawse blaunche for capouns ysode. Take almaundes blaunched and grynde hem al to doust; temper hit vp with verious and powdour of gyngyuer, and messe it forth.

141 Sawse noyre for capouns yrosted. Take þe lyuer of capouns and roost it wel. Take anyse and greynes de parys, gynger, canel, & a lytull crust of brede, and grinde it smale, and grynde it vp with verious and wiþ grece of capouns.
5 Boyle it and serue it forth.

142 Galyntyne. Take crustes of brede and grynde hem smale. Do þerto powdour of galyngale, of canel, of gyngyuer, and salt it; tempre it vp with vyneger, and drawe it vp þurgh a straynour, & messe it forth.

143 Gyngeuer. Take payndemayn and pare it clene, and funde it in vyneger. Grynde it and temper it vp wiþ vynegur and with powdour gynger and salt. Drawe it thurgh a stray-nour, and serue forth.

144 Verde sawse. Take persel, mynt, garlek, a litul serpell and sawge; a litul canel, gynger, piper, wyne, brede, vyneger & salt; grynde it smal with safroun, & messe it forth.

145 Sawse noyre for malard. Take brede and blode iboiled, and grynde it and drawe it thurgh a cloth with vyneger; do þerto powdour of gynger and of peper, & þe grece of the maulard. Salt it; boile it wel and serue it forth.

---

140. 3 gyngyuer] *add* and of canell Ar   *left marg., later hand* For my lord A

141. 2 wel] *add* and grynd hit with oynons P;   Take . . . parys] *om.* P; greynes de parys] grounde parys J, parys H   4 grynde it] temper hit HJ 5 Boyle it] *om.* P

142. 2 gyngyuer] *add* sugir P   3 vyneger] verius J;   vp] 'vp' *canc.* A, *om.* B   4 straynour] cloþ HJ

143. 1 payndemayn] faire white bred PAr   2 funde] stepe PAr 2-3 Grynde . . . salt] *om.* P   3 gynger] *add* and of canell Ar   3- 4 straynour] *add* put þerto poudir of gynger P

144. 1 a litul serpell] peletus and costmaryn Ar;   serpell] cerfoyl J 1-2 garlek . . . and] *om.* P   2 litul] *add* mageran HJ;   wyne] *om.* HJPAr;   brede] brown brede P   3 with safroun] *om.* HJPAr

145. 1 blode] broth J   3 grece] lyuere HJ   4 boile it wel] *om.* J (*recipe added to bottom margin*).

146 Gaunceli for gees. Take garlec and grinde it smale, safroun and flour þerwith, & salt; temper it vp with cowe mylke, and seeþ it wel, and serue it forth.

147 Chawdoun for swannes. Take þe lyuer and þe offall of the swannes, & do it to seeþ in gode broth; take it vp. Pyke out þe bonys; take & hewe the flessh smale. Make a lyour of crustes of brede & of þe blode of þe swan ysoden, & do þerto powdour of gynger, of clowes, & of piper, & a litul wyne & 5 salt, & seeþ it, & cast þe flessh þerto ihewed; & messe it forth with þe swan irostede.

148 Vertesaus broun. Tak percely, a good quantite, & a litel peletre, & mynte, sauge, dytayne, grene garlyk; wasche hem, grynde smal, & bred þerwyt. Tempere it wyt verius or wyt sorel & serue it forth.

149 Sawse camelyne. Take raysouns of coraunce & kyrnels of notys & crustes of brede & powdour of gynger, clowes, flour of canel; bray it wel togyder and do þerto salt. Temper it vp with vyneger, and serue it forth.

150 Lumbard mustard. Take mustard seed and waisshe it, & drye it in an ovene. Grynde it drye; sarse it thurgh a sarse. Clarifie hony with wyne & vyneger, & stere it wel togedre and make it thikke ynowȝ; & whan þou wilt spende þerof make it thynne with wyne.
5

151 Nota. Cranes and herouns shul be armed with lardes of swyne, and eten with gynger.

146. 1 Gaunceli] Cawdel AB   3 wel] *om.* J
    147. 2 Pyke] take AB   3 out] vp J   5 of gynger] *om.* AB;
a litul wyne] of wyne A, saundirs vynegir P   7 with . . . irostede] *om.* P
irostede] *om.* AB
    148. 1 a²] *om.* C   3 grynde] *add* hem J
    149. 3 flour] pouder P;   it wel] hem CJ;   togyder] *add* yn a morter P;
do þerto salt] do it þerto, salt it A, do hit þerto salt B
    150. 1 it] *add* clene CJ   2 Grynde] bete P;   drye . . . sarse²] sarce
hit HCJ   3 togedre] in fere J   4 spende] take P   5 thynne]
thykk B;   wyne] *add* and vynegir P
    151. 1 herouns] *add* þey CJ;   armed] ilardet HCJ;   lardes] fat HCJ

152   Nota. Pokok and pertruch shul be perboiled, lardid and rosted, and eten with gyngeuer.

153   Frytour blaunched. Take almaundes blaunched, and grynde hem al to doust withouten eny lycour. Do þerto poudour of gyngeuer, sugur, and salt; do þise in a thynne foile. Close it þerinne fast, and frye it in oile; clarifie hony with
5 wyne, & bake it þerwith.

154   Frytour of pasternakes, of skirwittes, & of apples. Take skyrwittes and pasternakes and apples, & perboile hem. Make a batour of flour and ayren; cast þerto ale & ȝest, safroun & salt. Wete hem in þe batour and frye hem in oile or in grece;
5 do þerto almaund mylke, & serue it forth.

155   Frytour of mylke. Take cruddes and presse out þe wheyȝe clene; do þerto sum whyte of ayren. Fry hem as to fore, & lay on sugur, and messe forth.

156   Frytour of erbes. Take gode erbys; grynde hem and medle hem with flour and water, & a lytel ȝest, and salt, and frye hem in oyle. And ete hem with clere hony.

157   Tourteletes in fryture. Take figus & grynde hem smal; do þerin saffron & powdur fort. Close hem in foyles of dowe, & frye hem in oyle. Claryfye hony & flamme hem þerwyt; ete hem hote or colde.

    152. 1 pertruch] *add* þey CJ   1–2 perboiled ... rosted] ilardet HCJ; gyngeuer] *add* & pyionus wyt þo same sauce H, *add* þe same wyse J
    153. 2 doust] durst C;   withouten eny lycour] *om.* P;   eny] *om.* CJ 2–3 withouten ... salt] *om.* A
    154. 3 cast ... &[1]] & ale CJ;   & ȝest] *om.* AB   4 Wete] wynde H, swyng CJ
    155. 2 clene] *om.* AB;   ayren] *add* floure este saforn and salt P 2–3 as to fore] do þerto AB, yn oyle or yn grese P
    156. 1 hem] *add* smal HCJ   2 hem] *om.* B;   & ... ȝest] *om.* J; ȝest] iouste H, ius C   3 hem[1]] *add* wyt ter hony HCJ;   And ... hony] ley þeron sugir and serue hit furth P;   clere] ter HCJ
    157. 1 in] *add* hony CJ   2 foyles of dowe] small foyles P 3 claryfye] clarifyet H   3–4 Claryfye ... colde] þen bawme them with clarified hony and serue them furth P

158 Raphioles. Take swyne lyuours and seeþ hem wel, take
brede & grate it; and take ʒolkes of ayren, & make hit sowple,
and do þerto a lytull of lard caruoun lyche a dee, chese gratyd,
& white grece, poudour douce & of gynger, & wynde it to
balles as grete as apples. Take þe calle of þe swyne & cast 5
euere by hymself þerin. Make a crust in a trape, & lay þe
balles þerin, & bake it; and whan þey buth ynowʒ, put þerin
a layour of ayren with powdour fort and safroun and serue it
forth.

159 Malaches. Take blode of swyne, floure, & larde idysed,
salt & mele; do hit togedre. Bake hyt in a trappe wyt wyte
gres.

160 Malaches whyte. Take ayren and wryng hem thurgh a
cloth. Take powdour fort, brede igrated, & safroun, & cast
þerto a gode quantite of buttur with a litull salt. Medle all
yfere. Make a foyle in a trap & bake it wel þerinne, and
serue it forth.   5

161 Crustardes of flessh. Take peiouns, chykens, and smale
briddes; smyte hem in gobettes. & sethe hem alle ifere in god
broþ & in gres wiþ veriows. Do þerto safroun & poudur fort.
Make a crust in a trap, and pynche it, & cowche þe flessh þerinne; & cast þerinne raisouns coraunce, powdour douce and 5
salt. Breke ayren and wryng hem thurgh a cloth & swyng þe

158. 1 Raphioles] Rasyols AB   1–2 take brede] *om.* HCJP
2 ayren] *add* rawe P   3 a¹ . . . dee] lytel gobetes of larde idiset HCJ;   lard]
add bred *canc.* H   4 gynger] safron & salt P;   wynde] viade C, make J
5 cast] ech *canc.* A   5–6 & . . . þerin] eueruche by selues HCJ;   cast
euere] wynde euereche B   6 crust in a] *om.* CJ;   trape] cap H, paste P
7 balles] ball AB;   ynowʒ] ibake HCJ;   put] pou H, do pouder C, poure J
8 layour] lyour J;   fort] *om.* HCJP
    159. 1 Malaches] Mulaches H, Mylachis P   2 mele do] then medil P;
trappe] tarppe C
    160. 1 Malaches whyte] Whyte mylates A, Mylates whyte B, Mulaches wythe
H, Milachis white P;   wryng] swyng CJ, strayne P   2 safroun] & ʒest
HCJ   2–3 cast þerto] *om.* J   3 buttur] vyneger A;   a litull
salt] *om.* H
    161. 1 chykens] *om., space left for 15–20 letters* A;   and] or P
2 gobettes] peces CJP   2–3 sethe . . . gres] *om., space left for 10–15
letters* A, in grece B   3 broþ] brroy H;   & poudur fort] *om.* AB
6 Breke] take HCJP;   wryng] drawe HCJ;   cloth] straynoure H

sewe of þe stewe þerwith, and helde it vppon the flessh. Couere
it & bake it wel, and serue hit forth.

162 Malaches of pork. Hewe pork al to pecys and medle it
with ayren & chese igrated. Do þerto powdour fort, safroun
& pynes with salt. Make a crust in a trap; bake it wel þerinne,
and serue it forth.

163 Crustardes of fysshe. Take loches, laumprouns, and
eelis; smyte hem on pecys, and stewe hem wiþ almaund mylke
and verious. Frye the loches in oile. Make a foyle and lay þe
fissh þerinne; cast þeron powdour fort, powdour douce, with
5 raysouns coraunce & prunes damysyns. Take galyntyn and þe
sewe þerinne and swyng it togyder, and cast in the trape, &
bake it and serue it forth.

164 Crustardes of eerbis on fyssh day. Take gode eerbys
and grynde hem smale with wallenotes pyked clene, a grete
porcioun. Lye it vp almost wiþ as myche verious as water;
seeþ it wel with powdour and safroun withoute salt. Make a
5 crust in a trap and do þe fyssh þerinne, vnstewed, wiþ a litel
oile & gode powdour. Whan it is half ybake, do þe sewe þerto
& bake it vp. If þou wilt make it clere of fyssh, seeþ ayren
harde & take out þe ȝolkes & grinde hem with gode powdours,
and alye it vp with þo sewe and serue it forth.

165 Leche frys of fische daye. Take god chese & dyse hit;
medel þerwyt ȝolkes of eyren rawe. Cast þerto poudur of

7 of þe stewe] *om.* CJ; stewe] *om., space left for 8-9 letters* AB; helde]
poure H, pouder CJ; it] *add* togedre HCJ; vppon] þervppon B;
Couere] kerue J 8 wel] *add* in a trappe HCJ
  162. 1 Malaches] Mylates AB, Mulaches H; pork[1]] poke H; Hewe]
Tak & hewe C; al to pecys] as to pyes HCJ 3 with] *add* saffron
(*repeated; also appears in line above*) H
  163. 2 stewe] sethe HCJ 3 Make a foyle] as to fore AB, *add* as to
fore HCJ, make a paste as ys afore P 4 powdour douce] *om.* J; douce]
om. C, *add* saforn & salt P 5 prunes] *om.* HCJ; damysyns] *om.* P;
galyntyn] galyngale P 6 þerinne] *om.* CJ, of þe stewe H; swyng]
wringe HCJ 7 bake it] *add* wel HCJ
  164. 1 on fyssh day] *om.* H; gode] *om.* J 3 almost wiþ as
myche] wyt hasse milkel H 5 þe] *om.* B; fyssh] fleche H
7 fyssh] fleche H 8 ȝolkes] *add* of eyren H 9 þo sewe] gode
stewes AB
  165. 1 fische daye] chese CJP 2 rawe] *om.* CJ

gynger, sugur and salt. Make a cophyn of þe heghte of þi lyte
fingur, and do þi fars þerin & bake hyt as tartes. Set þerin
flowre of canel & clowes.   5

166 Leche frys in lentoun. Drawe a thik almaunde mylke
wiþ water. Take dates and pyke hem clene with apples and
peeres, & mynce hem with prunes damysyns; take out þe
stones out of þe prunes, & kerue the prunes a two. Do þerto
raisouns coraunce, sugur, flour of canel, hoole macys and 5
clowes, gode powdours & salt; colour hem vp with saundres.
Meng þise with oile. Make a coffyn as þou didest bifore & do
þis fars þerin, & bake it wel, and serue it forth.

167 Wastels yfarced. Take a wastel and holke out þe
crummes. Take ayren & shepis talow & þe crummes of þe
wastell, powdour fort & salt, with safroun and raisouns
coraunce; & medle alle þise yfere, & do it in þe wastell. Close
it & bynde it fast togidre, and seeþ it wel.   5

168 Sawge yfarcet. Take pork and seeþ it wel, and grinde it
smal, and medle it wiþ ayren & brede ygrated. Do þerto powdour fort and safroun wiþ pynes & salt. Take & close litull
balles in foiles of sawge; wete it with a batour of ayren & fry
it, & serue it forth.   5

169 Sawgeat. Take sawge; grynde it and temper it vp with
ayren. Take a sausege & kerf hym to gobetes, and cast it in a
possynet, and do þerwiþ grece & frye it. Whan it is fryed
ynow3, cast þerto sawge with ayren; make it not to harde.

3 sugur] *om.* CJ;   heghte] lengh P   3-4 of . . . fingur] half an vnche
dep CJ   4 Set þerin] so þat þer be in C, seþe þeryn J   5 clowes]
add with reysons of corans small ygrounde P
   166. 1 Leche frys] Lesshes fryed AB;   Drawe] Take and drawe HCJ
4 out of . . . two] & take pynes hole hem & cleue hem itoo HCJ   5 cor-
aunce] *om.* AB   7 þise] rys H;   þou . . . bifore] tofore HCJ
8 þerin] *add* with þe thyk almoun mylk P
   167. 1 holke] hole HCJ   2 shepis talow] sewet of an ox P;   þe²]
add same AB   4 coraunce] *add* sugir P
   168. 1-2 it smal . . . Do] *om.* CJ   4 sawge] *add* fast bownd P
4-5 wete . . . fry it] so seth hit P
   169. 2 a sausege] *om.* B;   sausege] sawcyste A, sauciche C, sawsygill P;
gobetes] go gobetes H   3 þerwiþ grece] þerto wyte gres HCJ
4 ynow3] wel HCJ

5 Cast þerto powdour douce & messe it forth. If it be in ymbre
day, take sauge, buttur, & ayren, and lat it stonde wel by þe
sauge, & serue it forth.

170   Cryspes. Take flour of payndemayn and medle it with
white of eyren. Set wyte grece ouer the fyre in a chawfour
and do the batour þerto queyntlich, þurgh þy fyngours, or
thurgh a skymmour. And lat it a litul quayle so þat þer be
5 hooles þerinne. And if þou wilt, colour it wiþ alkenet yfoundyt. Take hem vp & cast þerinne sugur, and serue hem forth.

171   Crispels. Take and make a foile of gode past as thynne
as paper; kerue it out wyt a saucer & frye it in oile, oþer in
grece; and þe remnaunt, take hony clarified and flamme
þerwith. Alye hem vp and serue hem forth.

172   Tartee. Take pork ysode; hewe it & bray it. Do þerto
ayren, raisouns corauns, sugur and powdour of gynger, powdour douce, and smale briddes þeramong, & white grece.
Take prunes, safroun, & salt; and make a crust in a trap, & do
5 þe fars þerin; & bake it wel & serue it forth.

173   Tart in ymbre day. Take and perboile oynouns & erbis
& presse out þe water & hewe hem smale. Take grene chese
& bray it in a morter, and temper it vp with ayren. Do þerto
butter, safroun & salt, & raisouns corauns, & a litel sugur
5 with powdour douce, & bake it in a trap, & serue it forth.

5 douce] saforn & salt P   5-7 If . . . forth] *om.* CJ   7 sauge]
sause A, same B, P *combines this with the next recipe.*
    170. 1 Cryspes] *title om.* P;   flour of payndemayn] fyne floure P
2 white . . . wyte] white A, *om.* B;   wyte] it wyt CJ;   wyte grece] buttir P
3-4 queyntlich . . . quayle] and se hit haue holys made with thy fynger and bake
hit a lytell while P   3-5 or . . . þerinne] & bake hyt a lytel HCJ
4 quayle] *add* a litell A   5-6 yfoundyt . . . &] *om.* P   6 þerinne]
þeron BCJ, *om.* H
    171. 1 Take and] *om.* HCJ   2 wyt a saucer] *om.* AB   3 grece]
þe grece A;   þe] *add* alle C;   hony] heny H;   and²] a C;   flamme] *add*
hem BHC   4 Alye . . . forth] *om.* P, *missing* J
    172. 2 ayren] *om.* H;   corauns] *om.* AP;   sugur] *add* poudur fort H
3 white] wyt C   4 prunes] pynes C   5 þe] þer A
    173. 1 Take and] *om.* H;   erbis] sauge and parsel Ar   2 grene]
om. AB, fat PAr;   chese] brede AB   *left marg.* my—lord lacy (?),
scribbled over A

174 Tart de Bry. Take a crust ynche depe in a trap. Take ʒolkes of ayren rawe & chese ruayn & medle it & þe ʒolkes togyder. Do þerto powdour gynger, sugur, safroun, and salt. Do it in a trap; bake it & serue it forth.

175 Tart de brymlent. Take fyges & raysouns, & waisshe hem in wyne, and grinde hem smale with apples & peres clene ypiked. Take hem vp and cast hem in a pot wiþ wyne and sugur. Take calwar samoun ysode, oþer codlyng oþer haddok, & bray hem smal, & do þerto white powdours & hoole spices & salt, & 5 seeþ it. And whanne it is sode ynowʒ, take it vp and do it in a vessel, and lat it kele. Make a coffyn an ynche depe & do þe fars þerin. Plaunt it above with prunes damysyns: take þe stones out; and wiþ dates quartered and piked clene. And couere the coffyn, and bake it wel, and serue it forth. 10

176 Tartes of flessh. Take pork ysode and grynde it smale. Take harde eyren isode & ygrounde, and do þerto with chese ygrounde. Take gode powdours and hool spices, sugur, safroun and salt, & do þerto. Make a coffyn as tofore sayde & do þis þerinne, & plaunt it with smale briddes istyued & connynges, 5 & hewe hem to smale gobettes, & bake it as tofore, & serue it forth.

177 Tartletes. Take veel ysode and grinde it smale. Take harde eyren isode and yground, & do þerto with prunes hoole, dates icorue, pynes and raisouns coraunce, hoole spices &

174. 1 Take[1]] make BH, take and make P; depe] depe depe (twice; second canc.) A; in a trap] om. H 2 ruayn] of bry diset HCP 3 powdour] add of of, first one canc. C; sugur] om. C 4 it[2]] add wel C
175. 1 hem] add clene H 2 with] take C 3 Take hem vp] & grynde hem smale (repeated above) H 4 calwar] om. P; oþer[1]] om. C; oþer[2]] & C 5 white] god HCP 6 And . . . do it] om. C; sode] om. H 7 depe] thyk P 8 above] boue A; prunes] add and AB, pynes C; damysyns] om. P 9-10 And . . . coffyn] om. P 10 bake] make C
176. 2 Take] tarde A; & ygrounde] om. H 3 powdours] poudour B 4 as . . . sayde] of an ynch thik P 5 & connynges] om. P 6 & hewe hem] ihewe HCJ; hem to smale] hit smale to B
177. 1 veel] porke HC, om. P; ysode] ysop P; grinde] hewe HC 1-2 Take . . . yground] & menge hit wyt ʒolkes of eyren rawe HCP 2 with prunes hoole] om. C

powdour, sugur & salt; and make a litell coffyn and do þis
5 fars þerinne. Couer it & bake it & serue it forth.

178 Tartes of fysshe. Take eelys and samoun and smyte
hem on pecys, & stewe it in almaund mylke and verious.
Drawe vp an almaund mylk wiþ þe sewe. Pyke out þe bones
clene of þe fyssh, and saue þe myddell pece hoole of þe eelys,
5 & grinde þat ooþer fissh smale; and do þerto powdour, sugur
& salt and grated brede, & fors þe eelys þerwith þere as þe
bonys were. Medle þat ooþerdele of þe fars & þe mylke togider, & colour it with saundres. Make a crust in a trap as
bifore, and bake it þerin, and serue it forth.

179 Sambocade. Take and make a crust in a trap & take
cruddes and wryng out þe wheyȝe and drawe hem þurgh a
straynour and put hit in þe crust. Do þerto sugur the þridde
part, & somdel whyte of ayren, & shake þerin blomes of elren;
5 & bake it vp with eurose, & messe it forth.

180 Erbolat. Take persel, myntes, sauerey & sauge, tansey,
veruayn, clarry, rewe, ditayn, fenel, southrenwode; hewe hem
& grinde hem smale. Medle hem vp with ayren. Do buttur in
a trap, & do þe fars þerto, & bake it & messe forth.

181 Nysebek. Take þe þridde part of sowre dowe, and flour
þerto, & bete it togeder tyl it be as towh as eny lyme. Cast
þerto salt & do it in a disshe holke in þe bothom, and let it

---

4 powdour] gode poudurus HC, saforn P   5 Couer it] om. A, kerve hit P
   178. 4-5 clene . . . ooþer] of þe HJ   5 smale] om. H;   powdour]
gode poudrus HJ   6 fors] fars H;   þere as] wiþ J   7 were]
add take out H, om. J   9 þerin] add and bake hit þerinne B
   179. 1 Take and make] make H, take J;   in . . . take] of a crape J
2 cruddes] add of mylke HJ;   wryng] presse H, þrust J, threst P   3 hit
in þe crust] in þe straynour crustes AB   3-4 the . . . somdel] a good quantyte P   4 þerin] the sede of þe P;   blomes] blausedes HJ, blowys P;
elren] oler H, eler J, eldirn P   5 eurose] ewerose JP, efrose H
   180. 1 sauerey] om. HJ;   tansey] om. HJ   2 veruayn] ferbayn B,
vereuoy H, fetherfoy P;   rewe] om. J;   southrenwode] om. H;   hewe]
whash P   3 & grinde hem] om. HJ
   181. 1 Nysebek] not clear in A, Nirsebek HJ;   þe . . . of] om. P;
dowe] dokkes AB   2 tyl] for to H;   towh . . . eny] `as tog-' (in mar-
gin) J   3 holke] iholede HP;   holke . . . bothom] ibuyllede wiþ þe
bature J

out wiþ þy fyngur queyntliche in a chawfer wiþ oile, & frye
it wel. And whan it is ynowh3, take it out and cast þeron 5
sugur, &c.

182 Farsur to make pomme dorryse and oþere þynges. Take
þe lire of pork rawe, and grynde it smale. Medle it vp wiþ
eyren & powdre fort, safroun and salt; and do þerto raisouns
of coraunce. Make balles þerof, and wete it wele in white of
ayren, & do it to seeþ in boillyng water. Take hem vp and put 5
hem on a spyt. Rost hem wel, and take persel ygrounde and
wryng it vp with ayren & a perty of flour, and lat erne aboute
þe spyt. And if þou wilt, take for persel, safroun; and serue it
forth.

183 Cokagrys. Take and make þe self fars, but do þerto
pynes and sugur. Take an hold rostr cok; pulle hym & hylde
hym al togyder saue þe legges. Take a pigg and hilde hym fro
þe myddes dounward; fylle him ful of þe fars, & sowe hym
fast togeder. Do hym in a panne & seeþ hym wel, and whan 5
þei bene isode: do hem on a spyt & rost it wele. Colour it
with 3olkes of ayren and safroun. Lay þeron foyles of gold
and of siluer, and serue hit forth.

184 Hirchones. Take þe mawe of þe grete swyne, and fyfe
oþer sex of pigges mawes. Fyll hem full of þe self fars & sowe
hem fast. Perboile hem; take hem vp, & make smale prikkes
of gode past, and frye hem. Take þese prickes yfryed & set hem
þicke in þe mawes on þe fars, made after an vrchoun withoute 5

4 out] *om.* J   5 And . . . out] tac hit vp J
    182. 1 Farsur] For AB   2 lire] lyuer P;   rawe] *om.* H
3 eyren &] *om.* ABP   4 balles] *add* þer B;   wete] wynde H;   wele]
om. J   6 persel ygrounde] þe yoyse of persely P   7 a perty of]
om. HJ;   erne] 3erne B   8 And . . . wilt] or HJ;   And . . . safroun]
om. P
    183. 1 Cokagrys] Cotagres A, Cotagrys B, Coketris H, Cokatrys JP;   Take
and] *om.* HJ   2 hold rostr] hole rowsted A, olde (*canc.*) hole rowsted B,
hold rosti H, olde J   2-3 pulle . . . saue] scald hym & kut of the body by
P;   & hylde . . . hilde hym] *om.* H   3 fro] fror H   3-4 and
hilde . . . dounward] skaldid and kut of þe body vndir þe shuldirs then P
4 myddes] mydsyde H
    184. 1 Hirchones] Hert rowce AB, Vrchons J, hyrchounys P   1-6 Hir-
chones . . . legges] *missing* C   2 mawes] *om.* HJ   3 hem vp &
make] *om.* J;   prikkes] prews AB, pernis P   4 Take . . . yfryed] *om.*
P;   þese] rys & HJ;   prickes] prews AB;   set] seeþ AB;   hem²]
om. B   5 in] and B   5-6 on . . . legges] *om.* HJ

legges. Put hem on a spyt & roost hem, & colour hem with safroun, & messe hem forth.

185   Potte wys. Take pottes of erþe lytell, of half a quart, and fyll hem full of fars of pomme dorryes. Oþer make with þyn honde, oþer in a moolde, pottes of þe self fars. Put hem in water and seeþ hem vp wel. And whan þey buth ynowh3,
5   breke þe pottes & do þe fars on þe spyt & rost hem wel. And whan þei buth yrosted colour hem as pomme dorryes. Make lytel bouwes of gode past; frye hem wel in grece, & make þerof eerys to pottes, & colour it. And make rosys of gode past & frye hem, & put þe steles in þe hole þer þe spyt was,
10   & colour it with whyte oþer rede & serue it forth.

186   Sac wis. Take smale sachellis of canuas and fille hem full of þe same fars, & seeþ hem; and whan þey buth ynow3, take of the canuas, rost hem & colour hem, &c.

187   Ruschewys. Take pork; seeþ it and grynde it smale wiþ soden ayren. Do þerto gode powdours and hole spices and salt with sugur. Make þerof smale balles and cast hem in a batour of ayren, & wete hem in flour, and frye hem in grece
5   as frytours: and serue hem forth.

188   Spynoches yfryed. Take spynoches; perboile hem in seþyng water. Take hem vp and presse out þe water and hew hem in two. Frye hem in oile & do þerto powdour douce, & serue forth.

6 hem²] *add* as to fore B   6–7 with safroun] *om.* HCJ, as is aforesaid P
  185. 1 Potte wys] Potews ABP, Putowys C, Potewys J;   of half a quart] *om.* P   2–3 Oþer ... fars] *om.* HCJP   3–4 Put ... water] *om.* P
4 ynowh3] soden wel CJ   5 pottes] *add* of erþe AB   6 yrosted] inowe HCJ   7 lytel bouwes of] of litull prewes AB;   hem] *add* oþer rost hem AB   7–8 make ... pottes] festen hem þeron wyt smale broches contely (quyntleche CJ) HCJ   8 it] *add* in fere HCJ;   make] mabe H
9 steles] stalkes J;   spyt] spyces H   10 with ... rede] *om.* P
  186.1 Sac wis] Sachus AB, Sakkys CJ, Sacheus P;   sachellis] sakkys CJ
2 same] selue CJ
  187. 1 Ruschewys] Bursews AB, Herun sewes H;   seeþ it] *add* and pyke hyt H   2 powdours] *add* reysons of corans P   3 sugur] *add* saforn P   4 wete] wynde CJ;   wete hem in] *om.* P   5 as frytours] *om.* P;   forth] *add* wyt pouder troch (*poss.* croch) CJ
  188. 2 presse] *add* hem *canc.* A;   out] out of A;   hew] *om.* A
3 in two] on peces CJ;   oile] *add* clene AB;   & do] cast HCJ;   douce] *add* & salt HCJP

189 Benes yfryed. Take benes and seeþ hem almost til þey bersten. Take and wryng out þe water clene. Do þerto oynouns ysode and ymynced, and garlec þerwith; frye hem in oile oþer in grece, & do þerto powdour douce, & serue it forth.   5

190 Rysshews of fruyt. Take fyges and raisouns; pyke hem and waisshe hem in wyne. Grynde hem wiþ apples and peeres ypared and ypiked clene. Do þerto gode powdours and hole spices; make balles þerof, frye in oile, and serue hem forth.

191 Daryols. Take creme of cowe mylke, oþer of almaundes; do þerto ayren with sugur, safroun and salt. Medle it yfere. Do it in a coffyn of ii ynche depe; bake it wel and serue it forth.

192 Flampoyntes. Take fat pork ysode. Pyke it clene; grynde it smale. Grynde chese & do þerto wiþ sugur & gode powdours. Make a coffyn of an ynche depe, and do þis fars þerin. Make a thynne foile of gode past & kerue out þeroff smale poyntes, frye hem & put hem in þe fars, & bake it vp &c. 5

193 Chewetes on flesshe day. Take þe lire of pork and kerue it al to pecys, and hennes þerwith, and do it in a panne and frye it; & make a coffyn as to a pye smale & do þerinne, & do þervppon ʒolkes of ayren harde, powdour of gynger and salt. Couere it & fry it in grece, oþer bake it wel, & serue forth.   5

194 Chewetes on fyssh day. Take turbut, haddok, codlyng, and hake, and seeþ it. Grynde it smale & do þerto dates ygrounden, raysouns, pynes, gode powdours and salt. Make a

189. 2 wryng] swyng CJ;   clene] *om.* HCJ   4 grece] *add* & salt HCJP

190. 1 pyke hem] *om.* P   3 clene] *om.* CJP

191. 1 oþer] *om.* P   3 ii] an CJP;   wel] *om.* HCJ

192. 1 Flampoyntes] Flaumpeyns ABH   4 thynne foile] foyl þenne C, foyle þanne J;   kerue] *add* it C   5 & put hem] *om.* ABCJ;   þe] *om.* AB;   vp] wel H   *P follows this with an alternate recipe*

193. 2 al to pecys] as to pyes HCJ, as to a py P;   hennes] hony CJ 3 it] *add* do it C;   pye] "pye" A   5 Couere] kerue CJ;   in grece] *om.* P;   oþer . . . forth] *om.* HCJ

194. 1 turbut] buttur CJ   2 and[1]] or HP;   hake] hakke hem CJ 3 pynes] prunes CJP;   powdours] *add* saforn P

coffyn as to fore saide; close þis þerin and frye it in oile, oþer
5 stue it in sugur & in wyne, oþer bake it, & serue forth.

195 Hastletes of fruyt. Take fyges iquarterid, raysouns
hool, dates and almaundes hoole, and ryne hem on a spyt and
roost hem; and endore hem as pomme dorryes, & serue hem
forth.

196 Comadore. Take fyges and raisouns. Pyke hem and
waisshe hem clene, skalde hem in wyne; grynde hem right
smale. Cast sugur in þe self wyne and founde it togyder.
Drawe it vp thurgh a straynour, & alye vp þe fruyt þerwith.
5 Take gode peerys and apples; pare hem and take þe best.
Grynde hem smale and cast þerto. Set a pot on þe fuyre wiþ
oyle & cast alle þise þynges þerinne, and stere it warliche
and kepe it wel fro brennyng; & whan it is fyned, cast þerto
powdours of gynger, of canel, of galyngale, hool clowes,
10 flour of canel, & macys hoole. Cast þerto pynes, a litel fryed
in oile & salt. And whan it is ynowȝ fyned, take it vp anon
and do it in a vessel, & lat it kele. And whan it is colde, kerue
out with a knyf smale pecys of þe gretnesse & of þe length
of a litel fyngur, & close it fast in gode past, & frye hem in
15 oile & serue forth.

197 Chastletes. Take and make a foyle of gode past with a
rollere of a foot brode, & lynger by cumpas. Make iiii coffyns
of þe self past vppon þe rollere þe gretnesse of þe smale of

4 saide] om. HCJ   5 stue it] stif hit H, stef CJ;   stue it in] add
gynger AB;   &¹] oþer A;   oþer . . . forth] om. HCJ
    195. 2 hoole] om. HCJ;   and ryne] and ryse B, do hem on a þrede &
broche HCJ   3 and . . . dorryes] om. HCJ
    196. 1-2 Pyke . . . clene] om. P;   and waisshe hem] om. HCJ
2 right] om. HCJ   3 Cast . . . togyder] om. P;   founde] menge J
5 hem] add clene CJ;   best] past CJ   7 oyle] add clarified P;
þynges] om. HCJ;   warliche] om. HCJ   8 kepe] hepe H;   brennyng]
add with good sugir P;   fyned] ifoundede HCJ, fryed P   10 flour of
canel] om. HCJ;   canel] add hole canel P   10-11 a . . . salt] om. P
11 in] in in B;   ynowȝ] om. HCJ;   fyned] ifryede HP   13 knyf]
kyne corr. to kyfne H, knyȝt C   13-14 of² . . . length of] as myche as HCJ
14 fast] om. C;   gode] add towh BP   15 oile] add harde BHJP
    197. 1 Take and make] make HJ, take CP   2 lynger] rounde HCJP;
cumpas] add euery way P   3 þe smale of] om. HCJ

þyn arme of vi ynche dep; make þe gretust in þe myddell.
Fasten þe foile in þe mouth vpwarde, & fasten þe oþere foure 5
in euery syde. Kerue out keyntlich kyrnels above, in þe
manere of bataillyng, and drye hem harde in an ovene oþer in
þe sunne. In the myddel coffyn do a fars of pork with gode
poudour & ayren rawe wiþ salt, & colour it with safroun; and
do in anoþer creme of almaundes, and helde it why3t. In 10
anoþer, creme of cowe mylke with ayren; colour it red with
saundres. þerof anoþer maner: fars of fyges, of raysouns, of
apples, of peeres, & holde it broun. þerof anoþer manere: do
fars as to frytours blaunched, and colour it with grene; put
þis to þe ovene & bake it wel, & serue it forth with ew ardaunt. 15

198   For to make two pecys of flessh to fasten togyder.
Take a pece of fressh flessh and do it in a pot for to seeþ; or
take a pece of fressh flessh and kerue hit al to gobetes: do it
in a pot to seeþ, & take þe wose of comfery & put it in þe
pot to þe flessh & it shal fasten anon, & so serue it forth.   5

199   Pur fait ypocras. Troys vnces de canell & iii vnces de
gyngeuer; spykenard de Spayn, le pays dun denerer; garyngale,
clowes gylofre, poeure long, noie3 mugade3, ma3io3ame,
cardemonii, de chescun i quarter donce; grayne de paradys,
flour de queynel, de chescun dm. vnce; de toutes soit fait 5
powdour &c.

200   For to make blank maunger. Put rys in water al a ny3t,
and at morowe waisshe hem clene. Afterward put hem to þe

4 þyn arme] þn harme H;   vi] vii C, seuene J;   dep] depnesse AB
4–6 make . . . above] mak þe fysch [fyrist H, fyft P] coffyn a litul gretter & ix
vnche dep tak þe gretteste & amydde [H *breaks off here*] þe foyl wyt þe foure
oþer fast hym on eueryeh syde quentylych HCJP   6 þe] þoo A
7–8 oþer . . . sunne] *om.* CJ   8 coffyn] *om.* CJ   9 poudour]
pork A, *add* sugir safurn P   10 it why3t] *om.* AB   11 with ayren]
om. P;   red] *om.* AB   12 þerof] In B;   þerof . . . maner] do
in anoþer CJP   13 þerof] in B;   þerof . . . do] do in anoþer CJP
14 with] *om.* BCJ   15 to] in B
     198. 1 two] ii A
     199. 1 fait] fayre B;   canell] queynel B   2 de Spayn] *om.* B
4 grayne] *add* & AB   [To make Ypocras: Three ounces of cinnamon and
three ounces of ginger; spikenard of Spain, a pennysworth; galingale, cloves, long
pepper, nutmeg, marjoram, cardamom, of each a quarter of an ounce; grain of
paradise, flour of cinnamon, of each half an ounce; of all, powder is to be made,
etc.]

fyre fort þat þey berst, & not to myche. Sithen take brawn of
capouns, or of hennes, soden, & drawe it smale. After take
5 mylke of almaundes and put in to þe ryys & boile it. And
whan it is yboiled, put in þe brawn & alye it þerwith þat it be
wel chargeaunt, and menge it fynelich wel þat it sit not to þe
pot. And whan it is ynowhȝ & chargeaunt do þerto sugur
gode part, put þerin almandes fryed in white grece, & dresse
10 it forth.

201 For to make blank desire. Take brawn of hennes, or of
capouns, ysoden withoute þe skyn, & hewe hem as smale as
þou may & grinde hem in a morter. After, take gode mylke
of almaundes & put þe brawn þerin, & stere it wel togyder &
5 do hem to seeþ, & take flour of rys & amydoun & alay it so
þat it be chargeaunt, & do þerto suger, a god perty, & a perty
of white grece. And when it is put in dysches, strawe vppon
it blaunche powdour, and þenne put in blank desire and
mawmenye in disshes togider, and serue forth.

202 For to make mawmenny. Take þe chese and of flessh
of capouns or of hennes & hakke smal, and grynde hem smale
in a morter. Take mylke of almaundes with þe broth of
freissh beef oþer freissh flessh, & put the flessh in þe mylke
5 oþer in the broth, and set hem to þe fyre; & alye hem with
flour of ryse or gastbon, or amydoun, as chargeaunt as þe
blanke desire, & with ȝolkes of ayren and safroun for to make
hit ȝelow. And when it is dressit in dysshes with blank desire,
styk aboue clowes de gilofre, & strawe powdour of galyngale
10 aboue, and serue it forth.

203 The pety peruaunt. Take male marow hole parade, and
kerue it rawe; powdour of gynger, sugur, ȝolkes of ayren,
dates mynced, raisouns of coraunce, salt, a lytel, & loke þat
þou make þy past with ȝolkes of ayren 7 þat no water come
5 þerto; and fourme þy coffyn and make vp þy past.

200. 3 þat þey] om. B   7 menge] mung A   8 ynowhȝ] add
boyled B   9 in white grece] & white grece fryed of pork freysche, &
salt; & whan hit is ydressed in dysches, strawe þeron sugur & styk þerin almaundes
yfryed in whyte grece B
    201. 6 be] add wel B
    202. 6 or²] of B
    203. 1 male] om. B

204 Payn puff. Eodem modo flat payn puf, but make it more tendre þe past, and loke þe past be rounde of þe payn puf as a coffyn & a pye.

205 Clarrey and Braggot. Take . . . ounces kanel & galinga, greyns de paris, and a lytel peper, & make poudur, & temper hit wyt god wyte wyne & þe þrid perte hony & ryne hit þorow a cloþ. In þe same manere of ale, but take viii galones of god stale ale to on galon of hony ipurede clene, & boyle 5 iii galonus of ale wyt þo hony. Or hit bygyne to boyle, do in þi spicery; set hyt fro þo fyre & styre hit soft & let hit cole, & ryne hit þorow a wyde bultyng cloþ. Do hit in a clene vessel to þo ale, & do gode berme aboue, & hange in a cloute þe spyceri in þe ale & kouore hit wel, & wene hit is fourtene 10 nyte holde, drynke þereof. Amen.

204. 1 Payn puff] And þe pety paruaunt B;   Eodem . . . puf] 'Payn puff is made in the same way'.   2 loke] *add* þat B
    205. 1 Clarrey . . . Take] *missing* MS

PART V
GOUD KOKERY

Table of Recipes	MS Sources	Page
1. Culinary notes	Ashmole 1939	148
2. Formete	Royal 8 B iv	148
3. Amydoun	Royal 8 B iv	148
4. Potus clarreti	Royal 17 A iii	148
5. Potus ypocras	Royal 17 A iii	148
6. A pype of clarrey	Royal 17 A iii	149
7. Aqua vite	Royal 17 A iii	149
8. Brakott	Royal 17 A iii	149
9. Mede	Royal 17 A iii	150
10. Fyn meade & poynaunt	Royal 17 A iii	150
11. To clarifie suger	Harl. 2378	150
12. Anneys in counfyte	Harl. 2378	151
13. Suger plate	Harl. 2378	152
14. Penydes	Harl. 2378	152
15. Ymages in suger	Harl. 2378	153
16. Blawnce pouder	Harl. 2378	153
17. Pymente	Harl. 2378	154
18. Gyngerbred	Sloane 468, collated with Ashmole 1444 (pp. 185-6) and Sloane 374 (f. 59ᵛ)	154
19. Gingerbrede	Sloane 121	154
20. Stewed colops	Rawl. D 1222	155
21. Sawge	Rawl. D 1222	155
22. Mynceleek	Rawl. D 1222	155
23. Chinche	Oxford, CCC F 291	155
24. Sturgyn	Sloane 1108	155
25. A disshe mete for somere	Arundel 334	156

Ashmole 1393

f. 19ᵛ For goud kokery & sotilteis & goud sawces

f. 21 **1**   Item, nota: þat all comyn reisons & resons of corans be
clene pikid & cast into water wiþ a litel hete till þat þey bolt
rounde. Item, cast salt in all þynge. Item, all oynons mysid,
boile hem in clene water or þat þey go to eny werce, saue in
f. 21ᵛ aloes. . | . . Item, nota: þat all þynge þat is fried, cast on
6 sugur aboue or hit be set forþe.

Royal 8. B. iv

f. 72ᵛ **2**   For to maken formete. Tak whete and pyk it faire & stamp
it in a morter, and spreing it with water, and stomp it al to
holye. Wasch it faire and do it in a pot. Boille it wel til it
breste; set it adoun. Tak cwe melk and pley it til it be þekke.
5 Tak & lye it up with ʒelkes of eiren. Coloure it with saffren.
Stere it wel.

3   For to make amydoun. Tak whete and step it ix daies, &
eueri dai chaunge þe water. And bruse it wel in a morter riʒt
smal. Tempre it. Seþ it with muchel water and seye it þourh
an herseue, & let it stonden and kelen. Poure out þe water.
5 Ley it on a cloþ. Turn it til it be drye.

Royal 17. A. iii

f. 97ᵛ **4**   Potus clarreti pro domino. Take of canel i lb. | as it
f. 98 comeþ out of þe bale; of gyngyuer, xii unce in þe same maner;
iii quarter of a lb. of pepir; ii unce of longe peper; ii unce &
a half of greynes; iii unce & a half of clowis; ii unce & a half
5 of galyngale; ii unce of carewey; ii unce of macis; ii unce of
notemugges; ii unce of coliaundir; a quarter of a pynte of
aqua ardaunt; with iii galouns of hony: rescett for xx galouns
of clarrey.

5   Potus ypocras. Take a half lb. of canel tried; of gyngyuer
tried, a half lb.; of greynes, iii unce; of longe peper, iii unce;

1. 1 be] *om.* MS   5 aloes] *stuffed rolls of beef, for which a recipe*
appears on previous page of MS. Five recipes and a note related to the last inter-
vene here
    2. 2 it¹] 'it' MS.
    3. 2 riʒt] rit MS

of clowis, ii unce; of notemugges, ii unce & a half; of carewey,
ii unce; of spikenard, a half unce; of galyngale, ii unce; of
sugir, ii lb. Si deficiat sugir, take a potel of hony. 5

6 For to diȝte a pype of clarrey. Take and drawe þi wiyn
fiyn into a pype þat is clene | & lete it not be ful by vii or f. 98ᵛ
viii vnchis. & þanne take iii lb. of gyngyuer, iiii lb. of canel,
1 quarter of greynes, a half unce of notemugges, & half a
quarter of clowis, i unce of spikenard, i unce of longe peper. 5
Do alle þese togider in at a bunge; þanne take a staf and cleue
it on foure with a kniif into þe myddil, þat þe wiyn & þe
poudir may renne þoru þe staf til þe poudir be broken
þoruout þe vessel. If þe vessel be strong inouȝ, lete rolle him
wel. & þanne lete take vi galouns of hony wel clarified, þanne 10
do it into þe pype a ȝelk warm, & hete it þerwiþ. þanne take
& fille up þi pype & stoppe him faste, & on þe fourþe day it
is fiyn. For to colouren, take an unce of safren & rolle it
þerwiþ.

7 Aqua vite: þat is to seie, water of liif. Fille þi viol ful of f. 99ᵛ
lyes of strong wiyn, & putte þerto þese poudris: poudir of
canel, of clowes, of gyngyuer, of notemugges, of galyngale,
of quibibis, of greyn de parys, of longe peper, of blake peper:
alle þese in powdir. Careawey, cirmunteyn, comyn, fenel, 5
smallage, persile, sauge, myntis, ruwe, calamynte, origanum:
and a half unce or moore or lasse, as þee likiþ. Pownd hem a
litil, for it will be þe betir, & put hem to þese poudris. þanne
sette þi glas on þe fier, sett on the houel, & kepe it wel þat
þe hete come not o it; & sette þervndir a viol, & kepe þe 10
watir.

8 Ad faciendum brakott. Take xiiii galouns of good fyn f. 123
ale þat þe grout þerof be twies meischid, & put it into a
stonen vessel. & lete it stonde iii daies or iiii, til it be stale.
Afterward take a quart of fyn wort, half a quart of lyf hony;
& sette it ouer þe fier, & lete it seþe, & skyme it wel til it be 5
cleer. & þut þerto a penyworþ of poudir of peper & i penyworþ of poudir of clowis, & seþe hem wel togidere til it boile.

6. 11 into] *add* it into it into *canc.* MS
7. 6 origanum] *abbrev. follows,* au *with squiggle over* u—*perhaps* aveir de
pois?
8. 1 brakott] brhkptt MS

Take it doun & lete it kele, & poure out þe clere þerof into
þe forseid vessel, & þe groundis þerof put it into a bagge, into
10 þe forseid pot, & stoppe it wel wiþ a lynnen clooþ þat noon
eir come out; & put þerto newe berm, & stoppe it iii dayes or
iiii eer þou drinke þerof. Put aqua ardente it among.

f. 123ᵛ 9 To make mede. Take hony combis & put hem into a greet
vessel & ley þereynne grete stickis, & ley þe weiȝt þeron til it
be runne out as myche as it wole; & þis is callid liif hony. &
þanne take þat forseid combis & seþe hem in clene water, &
5 boile hem wel. After presse out þerof as myche as þou may
& caste it into anoþer vessel into hoot water, & seþe it wel &
scome it wel, & do þerto a quarte of liif hony. & þanne lete
it stonde a fewe dayes wel stoppid, & þis is good drinke.

10 To make fyn meade & poynaunt. Take xx galouns of þe
forseid pomys soden in iii galouns of fyn wort, & i galoun
of liif hony & seþe hem wel & scome hem wel til þei be cleer
inowȝ; & put þerto iii penyworþ of poudir of pepir & i peny-
5 worþ of poudir of clowis & lete it boile wel togydere. &
whanne it is coold put it into þe vessel into þe tunnynge up
f. 124 of þe forseid mede; put it þerto, & close it wel | as it is aboue
seid.

Harley 2378

f. 155 11 To clarifie suger. Take a quarte of fayre water & put it
in a panne, & þerto þe whyte of iii egges; and take a brusche
made of birchen bowes and bete þe water and þe egges
togyddyr tyl it be resolued & kast a grete scome abouen. þan
5 put away þi birchen and put þerto ii pound of suger and
medel all togyddyr. And þan sette it ouer þe fyre on a furnes,
& whan it begynnyth to boyle wythdrawe þi fyr and lat it
noght ryse. And so claryfye it wyth esy fyr. And whan it
waxes fayr and clere in þe myddell, take it fro þe fyre and
10 cole it þurgh a fayr streynour, and in þe colyng holde þi
brusche before þe panne syde for comynge downe of þe scome

12 Put aqua ardente] but avente MS
    10. 1-2 þe forseid pomys soden] *evidently refers to a recipe the scribe has
    omitted*
    11. 4 it] þe *canc.* 'it' MS

into þe streynour. And wyth þat suger þou may make all
maner confectyons.

12 To mak anneys in counfyte. Take ii unc of fayre anneys
& put þem in a panne & drye þem on the fyr, euermore
steryng þem wyth ȝowre hand, till þei ben drye. Put þem þan
owte of þe panne into a cornes and take up þi suger in a
ladell þe montynance of a unc and sett it on þe fyr. & ster þi 5
suger wyth a spatyle of tree, & whan it begynneth to boyle
take a lityll vp of þe | suger betwene þi fyngers & þi þombe, f. 155ᵛ
& whan it begyneth any thyng to streme þan it is sothyn
inowe. þan sett it fro þe fyre & stere it a lytyll wyth þi
spatyll, and put þin anneys þan to þe panne to þe suger, and 10
euermore stere in þe panne wyth þi flatte hand sadly, euermore on þe bothum, tyl þei parten. Bot loke þou ster þem &
smertyly for cleuyng togedyr. & þan sette þe panne ouer þe
forneys ageyn, euermore steryng wyth þi hand, & wyth þat
oþer hand euermore tourne þe panne for cause of more hete 15
on þe othyr syde tyl þei ben hote & drye. But loke þat it mel
noȝt be þe bothyn. And al so as ȝe see þat it ges ageyn in þe
bothym, sette it fro þe fourneys and euermore stere wyth
ȝoure hand, and put on þe fourneys ageyn tyl it be hote &
drye. And in þis manere schull ȝe wyrke it vp til it be as grete 20
as a peys, and þe gretter þat it waxes þe more suger it takys,
and put in ȝoure panne at ilke a decoccioun. And ȝif ȝe see
þat ȝoure anneys wax rowgh and ragged, gyf ȝoure suger a
lower decoccioun, for þe hye decoccioun of þe suger makys
it rowgh and ragged. And ȝif it be made of potte suger, gyf 25
hym iiii decocciouns more abouen, and at ilk a decoccioun ii
vnc of suger: and it be more or lesse, it is no forse. And whan
it is wroght vp at þe latter ende, drye it ouer þe fyre, steryng
euermore | wyth þi hand, and whan it is hote and drye sette f. 156
it fro þe fyre and stere it fro þe fyre wyth þi hand sadly att 30
þe panne bothym til þei ben colde, for þan will þei noght
chaunge þer colour. And þan put þem in cofyns, for ȝif
ȝe put þem hote in cofyns þei will change þer colour. And in
þis maner schull ȝe make careawey, colyandre, fenell, and all
maner round confecciouns, and gyngeuer in counfyte; but 35
þi gynger sud be cote leke a dyce in smale peses, fowr sqware,

and gyf þi gynger a litill hyar decoccioun þan þou gyffes þe
oþer sedys.

f. 157 **13**   To make suger plate. Take a lb. of fayr clarefyde suger
and put it in a panne and sette it on a furneys, & gar it sethe.
f. 157ᵛ And asay þi suger betwene | þi fyngers and þi thombe, and if
it parte fro þi fynger and þi thombe þan it is inow sothen, if
5 it be potte suger. And if it be fyner suger, it will haue a litell
lower decoccioun. And sete it þan fro the fyr on a stole, &
þan stere it euermore with a spature till it tourne owte of hys
browne colour into a ȝelow colour, and þan sette it on þe
fyre ageyn þe mountynance of a Aue Maria, whill euermore
10 steryng wyth þe spatur, and sette it of ageyne, but lat it
noght wax ouer styfe for cause of powrynge. And loke þou
haue redy beforne a fair litel marbill stone and a litell flour
of ryse in a bagge, shakyng ouer þe marbill stone till it be
ouerhilled, and þan powre þi suger þeron as þin as it may
15 renne, for þe þinner þe platen þe fairer it is. If þou willt, put
þerin any diuerse flours, þat is to say roses leues, violet leues,
gilofre leues, or any oþer flour leues, kut þem small and put
þem in whan þe suger comes firste fro þe fyre. And if þou
wilt mak fyne suger plate, put þerto att þe first sethyng ii
20 unces of rose water, and if ȝe will make rede plate, put þerto
i unce of fyne tournesole clene waschen at þe fyrst sethynge.

14   To mak penydes. Tak a lb. suger þat is noght clarefyed
but euen colde wyth water wythowten þe white of a egge for
if it were clarefyed wyth þe white of a egge it wold be clammy.
f. 158 And þan put it in a panne & sette | it on þe fyre and gar it
5 boyle, and whan it is sothen inow asay betwyx þi fyngers and
þi thombe and if it wax styfe and perte lightly fro þi fynger
þan it is inow: but loke þou stere it but lityl wyth þi spatur
in hys decoccioun, for it will benyme hys drawyng. And whan
it is so sothen loke þou haue redy a marbyll stone. Anoynte
10 it wyth swetemete oyle as thyne as it may be anoynted and
þan pour þi suger þeron euen as it comes fro þe fyre sethyng.
Cast it on þe stone wythouten any sterynge, and whan it is a
litel colde medel hem togedyr wyth bothe ȝoure handes and
draw it on a hoke of eren til it be fair and white. And þan

14. 1 a lb.] a i lb. MS   6 lightly] lighly MS   8 benyme]
bemyme MS

haue redy a faire clothe on a borde, and cast on þe clothe a 15
litell floure of ryse, and þan throw owte þi penedes in þe
thyknes of a thombe wyth þi handes as longe as þei will reche,
and þan kut þem wyth a peyre scherys on þe clothe, ilk a pese
as mychell as a smale ynche, and þan put þem in a cofyn and
put þem in a warme place, and þan þe warmenesse schall put 20
away þe towghnesse: but loke ȝe make þem noȝt in no
moyste weder nor in no reyne.

15 To make ymages in suger. And if ȝe will make any f. 161ᵛ
ymages or any oþer þing in suger þat is casten in moldys,
sethe þem in þe same manere þat þe plate is, and poure it
into þe moldes in þe same manere þat þe plate is pouryde,
but loketh ȝoure mold be anoyntyd before wyth a litell oyle 5
of almaundes. Whan þei are oute of þe moylde ȝe mow gylde
þem or colour þem as ȝe will. Ȝif ȝe will gilde þem or siluer
þem, noynte þem wyth gleyre of a egge and gilde þem or
siluer þem, and if ȝe will make þem rede take a litell pouder
of brasyll and boyle it a litell whyle wyth a litell gum araby, 10
and þan anoynt it all abowte and make it rede. And ȝif ȝe
will make it grene, take ynde wawdeas ii penyweyȝte, | ii f. 162
penyweyte of saffron, þe water of þe gleyr of ii egges, and
stampe all wele togeder and anoynte it wyth all. And if ȝe
will make it lightly grene, put more saffron þerto. And in þis 15
maner mow ȝe caste alle manere froytes also, and colour it
wyth þe same colour as diuerse as ȝe will, and þer þat þe
blossom of þat per or appell schull stand put þerto a clowe,
& þer þe stalke schall stand makes þat of kanell.

16 To mak blawnce pouder. Tak a fair morter and make it
hote on þe fyre, noȝt ouer hote; and make þi pestell hote in
þe same manere, but loke it be clene. And put in þi morter
a half lb. suger and ii unc gynger, wele paryd, and stampe
euermore smertly wyth þi pestell till it begynne to flye leke 5
mele. And whan it begynnys so to flye, stampe it no more
but euermore grynde it wyth ȝoure pestell be þe bothum,
and whan ȝe will wyte whan it is inow take þerof a lytell on
ȝoure tounge, & if it krase betwyxx ȝoure tethe þan it is
noȝt inow, and whan it crase noȝt þan it is inow.   10

16. 1 morter] moter MS   7 euermore] eumore MS

f. 164ᵛ **17** To mak pymente. Take i galloun rede wyne or white, for summe loue it red and summe whyte. Put þerto ii lb. of hony and wyrke it vp in þe same maner þat þe clarrey is wroȝte. Take þe rote of enula campana dry, ii unc, and galyngale, 5 longe peper, notemuges, greynes, clowes: of eche, i quarter of a unc. Rosemaryn, baye leuys, ysope, mynte, sauge, vi penywey ȝte drye; and make pouder, and put þerto.

Sloane 468

f. 80 **18** For to make gyngerbred. Tak & put half a quart hony in a bras panne & boyle it wel ouer þe fer, & stere it with a potstyk of tre þat it sit noght to, & lat seth til it be thikke as wex. & þanne tak a dischful of fayre water & drop þeryn of 5 þe hony, & if it fare as wex tak it doun & wete a gret treen vessel wel with water, & þan por in þe hony. & tak a pound of pouder gyngere & a quartroun of an vnce of pouder peper & medele hem wel with þe hony & lat kele. & whan it is cold tak a pyn of tre or of an hertes horn & stike in an hole of tre f. 80ᵛ þat is bored with | a wymbel, & tak vp þe hony & drawe it 11 about þe pyn ten tymes or xii, til it wexe as hard as it were tempered wex. & do it in a box, & strawe aboue pouder of gyngere, & þis is kendlich mad.

Sloane 121

f. 94 **19** To make gingerbrede. Take goode honye & clarefie it on þe fere, & take fayre paynemayn or wastel brede & grate it, & caste it into þe boylenge hony, & stere it well togyder faste with a sklyse þat it bren not to þe vessell. & þanne take it 5 doun and put þerin ginger, longe pepere & saundres, & tempere it vp with þin handes; & than put hem to a flatt boyste & strawe þeron suger, & pick þerin clowes rounde aboute by þe egge and in þe mydes, yf it plece you, &c.

17. 4 enula] Eimla (*first minim dotted*) MS   6 sauge] *same abbrev.* *follows as in 7. 6 above*
    18. 1 a quart] *om., space left* S1   2 stere] algate stere S1   2–3 with . . . to] *om.* S   3 of tre] *om.* S1;   seth] boille algate S1   3–6 til . . . water &] *missing* As   4 water] *add* that ys cold S1;   þeryn] *add* wyth thy stykke S1   6 with] *add* cold S1   8 medele] styr ham fast togeþer to it be well medled As   9 of tre] *om.* As   10 wymbel] nawgare AsS1
    19. 7 pick] pich MS

Rawlinson D 1222

20 Stewed colops. Take colops of veneson rosted & do in a   f. 2ᵛ
pot. Do þerto wyne & hole spyces & pouder of peper & canel.
Boyl hit vp with a pertye of swete brothe. Sesoun hit vp with
pouder gynger, vyneger & salt, & serue forthe.

21 Sawge. Take gynger, canel, galyngale, clowes; grynde   f. 42ᵛ
þem in a morter. & take a handful of sauge; do þerto, &
grynde hem wel togedres. Take eyren; sethe þem harde. Take
þe 3olkes & grynde with þe sauge. Tempere hem up with þe
vyneger or eysel, or soure ale; þan take þe whyte of þe soden   5
eyren & myce hit smale, & cast þerto. When hit ys tempered
þen take hogges fete or colde flesshe or fysshe & ley hyt in
a dysshe, & cast þys mete abouen & serue forthe.

22 Mynceleek. Take amydoun & braye hyt in a morter; yf
þou haue none, take smale flour of whete; & mylke of almonds. Do þeryn a litel berme or a litel sourdow3. Tempere
hit al togeder, & take a dysshe & make an hole in þe botum &
cole þe myncelek þereþrou3 in oyle or in grece, & take sugur   5
& water & boyl hem togeder, & in þat syryp bothe þe myncelek, & serue forthe.

Oxford, Corpus Christi College F 291

23 Chinche. Tak fayr mylk. Put it þoru a streynour into a   f. 10
panne. Warme it; cast þerto a lytyl rennyng, & þan tak it off
þe feer and stere it togydir & couere it. þan tak a resche þe
lengþe of half a plater, & aboute þis resche broyde oþer
resches crossewyse as þicke as þou may. þanne ley þes | 5
broyden resches on a plater. Cast aboue þe crudde, & pore   f. 10ᵛ
out þe qwhey; þan turne it upsodoun on anoþer plater. Cast
aboue sugyr & gynger & 3eue forþ.

Sloane 1108

24 To make sturgyn. Take þe houghys of vele and caluys   f. 20ᵛ
feete and sethe hem in hony. And whan þou hast soden hem

---

21. 2 take] *add* mylke of almonds or cow mylk *canc.* MS
22. 1 Mynceleek] *trans. of* Myncebek A1
23. 2 off] ouer MS   4 oþer] anoþer MS   8 forþ] forþ3

all to poudre, take þe bonys oute. In case þat þe flesshe be
longe, take it a stroke or ii and put it in a fayre cannevasse
5 and presse it welle. Than take it and lese it fayre in thynne
leches, and not to brode. Take onyons, vynegre, and percelly
and ley þeron, and so serue it forthe.

Arundel 334

p. 307 **25**   A disshe mete for somere. Take garbage of capons ande
of hennes and of chekyns and of dowes and make hom clene
ande sethe hom, and cut hom smal. And take persil and hew
hit smal, and dresse hit in platers and poure vynegur thereon,
5 and caste theron pouder of gynger and of canel, and serue hit
forthe colde at nyght.

24. 4 put] *om.* MS

APPENDIX A

MANUSCRIPTS CITED, BUT NOT GIVEN SIGLA

London, British Library
    Cotton Titus D xx
    Harley 279
    Harley 978
    Harley 2378
    Harley 4016
    Royal 8 B iv
    Royal 17 A iii
    Sloane 121
    Sloane 1986

Oxford, Bodleian Library
    Ashmole 1393
    Corpus Christi College F 291
    Douce 88
    Rawlinson D 194

APPENDIX B

SEQUENCE OF RECIPES IN EACH OF THE *FORME OF CURY* (FC) MANUSCRIPTS

x   = recipe number in individual collection
(x) = appended to recipe
[x] = in table of contents, but missing from collection
*x = beginning of recipe missing
x* = end of recipe missing

A   BL Additional 5016. Roll with table of contents. Recipes are numbered in the manuscript (42 is omitted in the numbering). All recipes on the roll are included in our collection.

B   New York [Morgan Library] Buhler 36. Roll, beginning missing. No table of contents. Recipes are numbered in the manuscript. All recipes are included in our collection.

H   BL Harley 1605, part 3, ff. 98–118^r. Beginning missing. No table of contents. Our numbering. All recipes are included in our collection.

C   Durham, University Library Cosin v. iii. 11, ff. 61^v–72^v. No table of contents. Our numbering. Folios 52–60 contain non-culinary recipes (numbers 143–62). All culinary recipes from this section of the manuscript are included in our collection.

J   BL Cotton Julius D viii, ff. 90^v–104^r. No table of contents. Our numbering (begins with first culinary recipe; preceding non-culinary material is not numbered). All culinary recipes from this section of the manuscript are included in our collection.

W   New York Public Library Whitney 1, ff. 1–12. No table of contents. Our numbering. All recipes from this section of the manuscript except 88 *Elus in sorray*, which follows FC 113, are included in our collection.

P   Aberystwyth, National Library of Wales, Peniarth 394D,

pp. 41–90, 119–20. Table of contents. Recipes numbered
in manuscript. Three groups of non-FC recipes are included: 99–141, except 111 (FC 110), 115 (FC 128),
126 (FC 104); 167–87; 198–229, except 228 (FC 105).
All remaining recipes except 149 *Elys yn dorre*, which
follows FC 113, are included in our collection.

Ar   BL Arundel 334, pp. 275–444. No table of contents.
Our numbering. FC recipes are interspersed throughout
with non-FC recipes and menus. *Elus in sorry*, 103,
again follows FC 113. This collection is much more
distant from A, the base text, than any of the other
MSS. For that reason, variants from Ar are given infre-
quently, only when they offer significant additional
information.

Recipe title (some short forms)	A	B	H	C	J	W	P	Ar
1. Frumente	—	—	—	1	1	1	1	1
2. Blaunche porre	—	—	—	2	2	—	5	5
3. Grounden benes	1	—	—	—	—	—	2	2
4. Drawen benes	2	—	—	—	—	—	3	3
5. Grewel forced	3	—	—	—	—	—	4	4
6. Caboches in potage	4	—	—	3	3	—	6	6
7. Rapes in potage	5	—	—	4	4	2	7	8
8. Iowtes of flessh	6	—	—	8	8	6	11	7
9. Chebolace	7	—	—	5	5	3	8	—
10. Gourdes in potage	8	—	—	6	6	4	9	9
11. Ryse of flessh	9	—	—	7	7	5	10	10
12. Funges	10	—	—	9	9	7	12	—
13. Bruce	11	—	—	10	10	8	13	14
14. Corat	12	—	—	11	11	9	14	15
15. Noumbles	13	—	—	12	12	10	15	16
16. Roo broth	14	—	—	13	13	11	16	17
17. Tredure	15	15	—	14	14	12	17	—
18. Mounchelet	16	16	—	15	15	13	18	21
19. Bukkenade	17	17	—	16	16	14	19	23
20. Connat	18	18	—	17	17	15	20	—
21. Drepe	19	19	—	18	18	16	21	22
22. Mawmenee	20	20	—	19	19	17	22	29
23. Egurdouce	21	21	—	20	20	18	23	38
24. Capouns in councy	22	22	—	21	21	19	24	31
25. Hares in talbotes	23	23	—	22	22	20	25	—
26. Hares in papdele	24	24	—	23	23	21	26	19
27. Connynges in cyuee	25	25	—	25	25	23	28	47
28. Connynges in grauey	26	26	—	24	24	22	27	45
29. Chykens in grauey	27	27	—	(24)	(24)	(22)	(27)	—
30. Fylettes in galyntyne	28	28	—	142	—	24	29	43
31. Pygges in sawse sawge	29	29	—	26	26	25	30	35
32. Sawse madame	30	30	—	27	27	26	31	36
33. Gees in hoggepot	31	31	—	28	28	27	32	37
34. Caruel of pork	32	32	—	29	29	28	33	—
35. Chykens in cawdel	33	33	—	30	30	29	34	—
36. Chykens in hocchee	34	34	—	31	31	30	35	—
37. Fesauntes, pertruches, etc.	35	35	—	32	32	31	36	—
38. Blank maunger	36	36	—	33	33	32	37	26
39. Blank dessorre	37	37	—	34	34	33	38	25
40. Morree	38	38	—	35	35	34	39	30
41. Charlet	39	39	—	36	36	35	40	168
42. Charlet yforced	40	40	—	37	37	36	41	169
43. Cawdel ferry	41	41	—	38	38	37	42	172
44. Iusshell	43	42	—	39	39	39	43	166

	A	B	H	C	J	W	P	Ar
45. Iusshell enforced	44	43	—	(39)	(39)	—	(43)	167
46. Mortrews	45	44	—	40	40	38	44	134
47. Mortrews blank	46	45	—	41	41	40	45	—
48. Brewet of Almayne	47	46	—	42	42	41	46	24
49. Peiouns ystewed	48	47	—	43	43	42	47	42
50. Losyns	49	48	—	44	44	43	48	—
51. Tartlettes	50	49	—	45	45	44	49	—
52. Pynnonade	51	50	—	163	—	45	50	—
53. Rosee	52	51	*1	164	—	46	51	—
54. Cormarye	53	52	2	165	—	47	52	—
55. Noumbles of deer	54	53	3	166	—	48	53	—
56. Loyne of the pork	55	54	(3)	167	—	—	—	—
57. Fyletes	56	55	(3)	168	—	—	—	—
58. Spynee	57	56	4	169	—	49	54	—
59. Chyryse	58	57	5	170	—	50	55	—
60. Paynfoundew	59	58	6	171	—	51	56	—
60a. To clarify hony	(59)	(58)	7	172	170	(51)	(56)	—
61. Crytayne	60	59	8	46	46	52	57	32
62. Vinegrate	61	60	9	47	47	53	58	33
63. Founet	62	61	10	48	48	54	[59]	—
64. Douce iame	63	62	11	49	49	55	[60]	34
65. Connynges in cyrip	64	63	12	50	50	56	[61]	—
66. Leche Lumbard	65	64	—	67	82	—	[62]	64
67. Connynges in clere broth	66	65	—	68	83	—	[63]	48
68. Payn ragoun	67	66	—	69	84	—	[64]	65
69. Lete lardes	68	67	—	—	—	—	[65]	66
70. Furmente with porpays	69	68	13	51	51	57	[66]	89
71. Perrey of pesoun	70	69	14	52*	52	58	[67]	90
72. Pesoun of Almayne	71	70	15	—	53	59	[68]	91
73. Chyches	72	71	16	—	54	60	69	—
74. Lopins	—	—	17	—	55	61	70	—
75. Frenche iowtes	73	—	18	—	56	62	71	—
76. Makke	74	72	19	—	57	63	72	—
77. Aquapatys	75	73	20	—	58	64	73	97
78. Salat	76	74	21	—	59	65	74	—
79. Fenkel in soppes	77	75	24	71	86	68	75	98
80. Elat	78	76	22	—	60	66	76	—
81. Appulmoy	79	77	23	70	85	67	77	—
82. Slyt soppes	80	78	25	72	87	—	78	99
83. Letelorye	81	79	26	73	88	—	79	—
84. Sowpes dorry	82	80	27	74	89	—	80	—
85. Rapey	83	81	28	75	90	69	81	—
86. Sawse Sarzyne	84	82	29	76	91	—	82	—
87. Creme of almaundes	85	83	30	77	92	70	83	111

	A	B	H	C	J	W	P	Ar
88. Grewel of almaundes	86	84	31	78	93	71	84	—
89. Iowtes of almaund mylke	88	85	32	79	94	72	85	92
90. Cawdel of almaund mylk	87	86	33	80	95	73	86	—
91. Fygey	89	87	34	81	96	74	87	93
92. Pochee	90	88	35	82	97	75	88	94
93. Brewet of ayren	91	89	36	83	98	76	89	95
94. Rauioles	—	—	37	84	99	77	—	—
95. Makerouns	92	90	38	85	100	—	90	—
96. Tostee	93	91	39	86	101	—	91	96
97. Gynggaudy	94	92	40	87	102	—	92	117
98. Erbowle	95	93	41	88	103	78	93	—
99. Rysmole	96	94	42	90	105	—	94	—
100. Vyaunde Cypre	97	95	43	89	104	—	95	44
101. Vyaunde Cypre of samoun	98	96	44	91	106	79	96	—
102. Vyaund ryal	99	97	45	92	107	80	97	140
103. Compost	100	98	46	93	108	—	98	—
104. Gele of fyssh	101	99	47	94	109	—	126	123
105. Gele of flessh	102	100	48	95	110	—	228	58
106. Chysanne	103	101	49	96	111	81	142	115
107. Congur in sawse	104	102	50	97	112	82	143*	124
108. Rygh in sawse	105	103	51	98	113	—	[144]	—
109. Makerel in sawse	106	104	52	99	114	83	[145]	—
110. Pykes in brasey	107	105	53	100	115	84	111	125
111. Porpeys in broth	108	106	54	101	116	85	[146]	—
112. Balloc broth	109	107	55	102	117	86	[147]	104
113. Eles in brewet	110	108	56	103	118	87	148	102
114. Cawdel of samoun	111	109	57	104	119	89	150*	—
115. Plays in cyuee	112	110	58	105	120	90	[151]	126
116. Flaumpeyns	113	111	—	—	—	—	(269)	—
117. Noumbles in lent	114	112	—	—	—	—	—	—
118. Chawdoun for lent	115	113	—	—	—	—	—	—
119. Furmente with porpeys	116	114	—	—	—	—	—	—
120. Fylettes in galyntyne	117	115	—	—	—	—	—	—
121. Veel in buknade	118	116	—	—	—	—	—	—
122. Sooles in cyuee	119	117	59	106	121	91	[152]	127
123. Tenches in cyuee	120	118	60	107	122	92	[153]	—
124. Oysters in grauey	121	119	61	108	123	103	[154]	—
125. Muskles in brewet	122	120	63	110	125	94	156	—
126. Oysters in cyuee	123	121	62	109	124	93	*155	—
127. Cawdel of muskels	124	122	64	111*	126	95	157	101

	A	B	H	C	J	W	P	Ar
128. Mortrews of fyssh	125	123	65	—	127	—	115	194
129. Ryse of fische daye	—	—	66	—	128	96	158	—
130. Laumpreys in galyntyne	126	124	67	—	129	97	159	—
131. Laumprouns in galyntyne	127	125	68	—	130	98	160	118
132. Loseyns in fyssh day	128	126	69	—	131	99	161	—
133. Sowpes in galyngale	129	127	70	—	132	100	162	—
134. Sobre sawse	130	128	71	—	133	101	163	121
135. Cold brewet	131	129	72	—	134	102	164	—
136. Peeres in confyt	132	130	73	—	135	104	165	120
137. Egurdouce of fysshe	133	131	74	—	136	105	166	122
138. Colde brewet	134	132	—	—	—	—	—	146
139. Peuorat: veel and venysoun	135	133	75	—	137	106	230	71
140. Sawse blaunche: Capouns ysode	136	134	76	—	138	—	188	72
141. Sawse noyre: capouns yrosted	137	135	77	—	139	—	189	73
142. Galyntyne	138	136	78	—	140	—	190	76
143. Gyngeuer	139	137	79	—	141	—	191	78
144. Verde sawse	140	138	80	—	142	—	192	77
145. Sawse noyre for malard	141	139	81	—	151	—	193	75
146. Gaunceli for gees	142	140	82	—	143	—	194	79
147. Chawdoun for swannes	143	141	83	*112	144	—	195	80
148. Vertesaus broun	—	—	—	113	145	—	—	—
149. Sawse camelyne	144	142	86	116	148	—	196	—
150. Lumbard mustard	145	143	87	117	149	—	197	—
151. Cranes and herouns	146	144	84	114	146	—	—	67
152. Pokok and pertruch	147	145	85	115	147	—	—	68
153. Frytour blaunched	148	146	88	118	150	—	231	—
154. Frytour of pasternakes, etc.	149	147	89	119	152	—	232	—
155. Frytour of mylke	150	148	90	120	153	—	234	—
156. Frytour of erbes	151	149	91	121	154	—	233	—
157. Tourteletes in fryture	—	—	92	122	155	—	235	119
158. Raphioles	152	150	93	123	156	—	236	82
159. Malaches	—	—	94	124	157	—	237	—
160. Malaches whyte	153	151	95	125	158	—	238	—

	A	B	H	C	J	W	P	Ar
161. Crustardes of flessh	154	152	97	127	160	—	240	81
162. Malaches of pork	155	153	96	126	159	—	239	—
163. Crustardes of fysshe	156	154	98	128	161	—	241	—
164. Crustardes of eerbis	157	155	99	129	162	—	242	—
165. Leche frys of fische daye	—	—	100	130	163	—	243	—
166. Leche frys in lentoun	158	156	101	131	164	—	244	—
167. Wastels yfarced	159	157	102	132	165	—	245	—
168. Sawge yfarcet	161	158	103	133	166	—	246	—
169. Sawgeat	160	159	104	134	167	—	247	—
170. Cryspes	162	160	105	135	168	—	(247)	—
171. Crispels	163	161	106	136	169	—	248	—
172. Tartee	164	162	107	137	—	—	249	—
173. Tart in ymbre day	165	163	108	138	—	—	250	112
174. Tart de Bry	166	164	109	139	—	—	251	113
175. Tart de brymlent	167	165	110	140	—	—	252	114
176. Tartes of flessh	168	166	112	—	61	—	253	—
177. Tartletes	169	167	111	141	—	—	254	—
178. Tartes of fysshe	170	168	113	—	62	—	255	—
179. Sambocade	171	169	114	—	63	—	256	—
180. Erbolat	172	170	115	—	64	—	257	—
181. Nysebek	173	171	116	—	65	—	258	—
182. Farsur for pomme dorryse	174	172	117	—	66	—	259	84
183. Cokagrys	175	173	118	—	67	—	260	85
184. Hirchones	176	174	119	*53	68	—	261	86
185. Potte wys	177	175	120	54	69	—	262	—
186. Sac wis	178	176	121	55	70	—	263	—
187. Ruschewys	179	177	122	56	71	—	264	—
188. Spynoches yfryed	180	178	123	57	72	—	265	—
189. Benes yfryed	181	179	124	58	73	—	266	—
190. Rysshews of fruyt	182	180	125	59	74	—	267	—
191. Daryols	183	181	126	60	75	—	268	88
192. Flampoyntes	184	182	127	61	76	—	269	87
193. Chewetes on flesshe day	185	183	128	62	77	—	270	83
194. Chewetes on fyssh day	186	184	129	63	78	—	271	—
195. Hastletes of fruyt	187	185	130	64	79	—	—	—
196. Comadore	188	186	131	65	80	—	272	—
197. Chastletes	189	187	132	66	81	—	273	—
198. Two pecys of flessh	190	188	—	—	—	—	—	—
199. Pur fait ypocras	191	189	—	—	—	—	—	—
200. Blank maunger	192	190	—	—	—	—	—	—

	A	B	H	C	J	W	P	Ar
201. Blank desire	193	191	—	—	—	—	—	—
202. Mawmenny	194	192	—	—	—	—	—	—
203. Pety peruaunt	195	193	—	—	—	—	—	—
204. Payn puff	196	194	—	—	—	—	—	—
205. Clarrey and Braggot	—	—	133	—	—	—	—	—

INDEX AND GLOSSARY

Many of the works referred to in explanatory notes appended to some entries here are given by the name of author or editor, such as Austin, Pegge, Russell, Wilson: see the Select Bibliography for full references. Some works are generally referred to by brief abbreviations; the bibliography should also be consulted for full details on all of these except dictionaries and *DV*, which is listed under Manuscripts (Appendix A). They are:

CB — *Two Fifteenth-Century Cookery Books*, ed. Austin.

DV — 'Trattato de Buone e Dilicate Viaunde', BL MS Add. 18165.

Hodgkin — John Hodgkin's notes to *A Proper New Booke of Cokerie*, ed. Frere.

HV — Platina, *De honeste voluptate*.

LCC — *Liber cure cororum*, ed. Morris.

LdC — *Il Libro della Cucina*.

LSS — *Libre de Sent Sovi*, ed. Grewe.

MED — *Middle English Dictionary*.

MP — *Le Ménagier de Paris*, ed. Pichon, Vol. 2.

NBC — *A Noble Boke of Cookry*, ed. Napier.

OED — *Oxford English Dictionary*.

PPC — *Petits Propos Culinaires*.

T-L — Tobler-Lommatzsch, *Altfranzösiches Wörterbuch*.

V(S) — *Viandier*, Sion MS, ed. Aebischer.

VT — *Le Viandier de Taillevent*, ed. Pichon and Vicaire.

We have made no attempt to cite *all* parallel recipes appearing in other medieval cookery collections since most of them are highly inaccessible.

We have also used the following abbreviations in some entries: TC — Table of Contents (of the MS concerned); t — title, as against words appearing within the recipe itself; n — note, i.e., word appears in a note to the recipe cited. Conjecturally emended forms are marked with an asterisk. We have used

the following to designate languages: A-N — Anglo-Norman;
Fr — French; OF — Old French; OE — Old English; ME —
Middle English; ModFr — Modern French; Lat — Latin; Span
— Spanish.

The glossary does not normally record words still current
in more or less the same sense when the spelling is close
enough to be recognizable in context: *coold/cold, cleer/clear,*
for example. Nor are all variant spellings given for glossed
words. We have not usually commented on such common
alternatives as *y/i/j,* which are listed together; interchange of
u/w as in *cou/cow, pouder/powder* and *ou/au* for *o/a* as in
samoun/saumon/salmon; plurals of *-ys* or *-us* for *-es;* erratic
final *-e* and doubling of consonants, as in *little/litel/littell/
lytyle. Th* and *þ* are listed interchangeably, as are medial *u*
and *v,* written as *u.* The ME letter ȝ, representing sounds
often spelled *y* and *gh,* is placed separately after *g.* Verbs
which may or may not have prefixes of *a-* or *i/y-* are listed
under the base form.

References are selective and may have an arbitrary appear-
ance in that when a word appears more than three times we
have usually noted the first two examples we happened to
notice, whether or not they were the first to appear in the
order printed here. Since many entries are grouped under
headwords regardless of spelling, strict alphabetical order was
not always possible: sage dishes beginning with the word
sawge are grouped under the headword *sauge,* for example,
and thus appear before rather than after *saumon, saundres,*
and *sauery.* But when such entries occur at some distance,
they are cross-referenced. Most titles of dishes and headings
or phrases in French or Latin, such as *Ad faciendum brakott,*
are alphabetized as a whole or cross-referenced under the first
word of the title or phrase. Individual words in such contexts
will not always be glossed separately.

A

a *prep.* at: *al* ⁓ *nyȝt* all night, ⁓ *morwe* in the morning III 24.
abaten *v.* diminish I 7, 9, etc.
abrode *adv.* broadly, i.e. flat II 19n, IV 87.
acorde *v.* blend II 41.
AD FACIENDUM BRAKOTT 'to make braggot': see BRAGGOT.

adoun *adv.* down (off the fire) II 1, 42, etc.

adres, adresse(d) see dres.

aftere *prep.* after: ~ *þat* in proportion to what II 57.

aftermelk *n.* milk made with ground nuts which have been strained from a 'first milk' II 89.

aȝeyn *adv.* again I 63, IV 26.

aȝein *prep.* in I 41.

ah *conj.* but I 56.

aymers *n.* embers IV 73.

ayren see ey.

aysell/eysel *n.* vinegar, usually cider vinegar III 9, IV 117, etc.

al *adv.* all: ~ *þat* until I 41.

alay/alye see lyen.

alegur *n.* malt vinegar IV 117.

alich *adv.* alike III 2.

alkenet *n.* red dye made from the root of a plant so named (or 'orcanet'); a member of the bugloss family II 50, IV 48, etc. (In II 50, either something has dropped out or 'alkenet' is an error for 'amydon'.)

alkyn *adj/n.* ? all kinds, various? I 48.

Almayne *n.* Germany IV 48t, 72t, etc.

alma(u)nd *n.* almond II 33, IV 20, etc.; **alemaun(de)s** *pl.* I 1, 2, etc.; **almaund mylke** ground almonds mixed with broth, water, or other liquid (in I 56 'fat' broth and suet are called for, which would make a very rich 'almond milk' indeed) IV 11, 20, etc.

aloes *n.* stuffed meat rolls, resembling 'veal birds' (< OF 'larks'; cf. *CB* pp. 3, 40, 61, 83) V 1.

aloh *conj.* ? although? I 47n.

als *adv.* as II 29, 30, etc.

am *pron.* see hi.

AMENDEMENT FOR METE . . . see METE TO MUCHE ISALT.

amydon *n.* wheat starch (Lat *amylum*), used to thicken sauces; Gerard reports that a type of spelt called *Triticeum Amyleum, Amyleum Frumentum*, or starch corn, was grown for just this purpose ('amylum' was in very common use in Roman times and is one of the obvious links between Roman and medieval cooking) I 8, 11, etc.; **amnidoun** I 5; **amodyn(e)** III 16, 21, etc. AMYDON I 33 translates *Amydoun* in MS A1, with some confusions and omissions (see also HONY DOUSE); AMIDON TRIED I 60 is a similar pottage named for the thickener: 'tried' usually means 'tested', or 'select', but here it is more likely to derive from Fr *tirer* 'draw' since the amydon is drawn up in almond milk. A notable omission in the translation of I 33 is sugar: the A-N text indicates that the coloured portion of the almonds are to be made so with rose-sugar (see SUGER PLATE). AMYDON TO HOLDEN WATER I 41 mistranslates MS A1's *pur fere amidon par tut l'an a tenyr taunt de tens come vos volez*; *l'an* has evidently been misread as *l'[e]au*. AMYDON V 3 is an almost identical recipe. Cf. *CB* 'For to make amydon' p. 112; *LCC* p. 7; *NBC* p. 101.

(a)mole see *sub* pomys.

and *conj.* if (see *OED* AND 1 IV C 1) III 13/1.

ANESERE I 3 translates *Aneserree* in MS Ro. The last half of the word may indicate an etymological relationship to *Blanc desirree* and *Vert desiree*: the dish appears to be identical except for the use of fried almonds and saffron in place of the pomegranate garnish of the first and parsley colouring of the second, and thus *ane* may be a form of *jaune* 'yellow'.

angeylles/angoyles *n.* eels (A-N *anguilles*) I 19.

an(ne)ys *n.* anise, aniseed III 18, IV 38. ANNEYS IN COUNFYTE V 12, candied anise seeds and other spice seeds.

anoon *adv.* at once, in due course IV 54.

appyl *n.* apple II 40; appleen *pl.* I 9, 18; aplyn/applys II 19, 35, etc.; appeltre apple tree III 31. APPULMOS II 17, APULMOSE II 35, applesauce made with broth and fat on meat days, almond milk and oil on fish days. APPULMOY IV 81 is a version of the fish-day type. Neither is closely related to I 9 POUMES AMOLE (q.v.), though the derivation of the name is probably the same, from OF *moiller* 'moisten, soften'.

aqua ardaunt/ardente *n.* spirits, brandy or aqua vite V 4, 8*. AQUA VITE V 7, distilled spirits. See also ew ardaunt.

AQUAPATYS IV 77, garlic boiled in water and oil. The name is probably derived from Lat *allium* 'garlic' (cf. Span *ajo*). Gerard quotes Galen as advising that garlic be boiled until 'it hath lost his sharpnesse'.

aray *v.* dress, cook IV 9.

archanye *n.* alkenet, q.v.; the He spelling of 'archamye' echoes that of MS Ro, but cf. *VT*, p. 117 (the basic Fr spelling was *orcanet*) I 22.

ardaunt see aqua ~.

armed see enarme.

arn see be.

asay *v.* test V 13, 14.

aske *v.* ? demand?——this may, however, be *ase*, 'make it as a good roast', i.e., put the larded mushrooms on a spit and roast them I 55.

askes *n.* ashes IV 73.

Aster *n.* Easter I 16.

atyre *v.* dress, prepare III 9.

atte *prep.* at (the) II 68, III 24.

auance *n.* avens, an herb (Cogan reports 'good cooks say that it maketh potage black, yet the roots thereof savoureth like unto cloves') IV 8.

aveir de pois *n. phrase* (? expanded abbreviation) avoirdupois in early sense of merchandise (groceries? especially those available from spicers? Cf. *OED*; Greimas, *Dictionnaire de l'ancien français*; and the *Anglo-Norman Dictionary*) V 7n, 17n.

axit *v.* requires; *after þy venesoun* ~——as is necessary for your venison II 57.

B

BACOUND HERYNG Menu 6, baked (i.e. smoked?) herring.

bake flour *n. phrase* flour processed to dissolve easily? III 22.

bakinde *v., pr.p.* baking; probably this means a batter of egg yolk and flour is used to 'gild' the roasting meat while it bakes I 48.

BALLOC BROTH IV 112, BALOUGH BROTH II 92, a fish soup. The II title is more likely to be the original one, even if it is not what was first written in the MS. Other MSS often give 'ballok' or 'balok', but we have also seen 'ballow' and 'ballo' (MSS R and BL MS Sloane 1201). *W* and *kk* were easily confused in the hands of the period (cf. entries for **prews** and **sourdow3**), and since there is no recorded meaning for *ballok* other than 'testicle', which does not seem appropriate for a fish stew, it is more likely that *balowe, balgh* 'bulging' is the word originally meant. The meaning would then seem to be something like a thick, satisfying soup, which this indeed should be. Cf. *CB* pp. 10, 89; *NBC* p. 86.

bataillyng *v., pr.p.* (as if) furnished with battlements IV 197.

be(on) *v.* be I 1, 2, etc.; *3 sg.* V 2, 3, etc.; beoþ I 46; (a)beoþ *pl.* I 31, 44; abeon I 44; ben I 48, II 27, 38; arn II 82, III 13; buth IV 8, 25.

BEEFE Menu 9, beef, probably boiled; cf. **gret vlehs.**

beforne *adv.* beforehand V 13.

benes *n.* beans II 81, III 36, etc. BENES YFRYED IV 189, boiled beans, well drained, fried with onions and garlic. There are similar recipes in the French collections. DRAWEN BENES IV 4, ground boiled beans in broth with onions. GROUNDEN BENES IV 3, despite the name, probably whole beans ground only on the outside to remove the skin; served with bacon. See also FENE BOILES and MAKKE (in which we are told to grind the 'groundon benes').

benyme *v.* detract from V 14.

beor *v.* bear I 54.

BERANDYLES II 27, a strained minced meat in broth differing from COLYS (q.v.) in that beef is used as well as chicken. The resulting soup is highly spiced and garnished with pomegranate seed, which may indicate an ultimate Arabic source.

berm(e) *n.* yeast constituting the froth on fermenting malt liquor, used for leavening IV 205, V 8, 22.

berst(en) *v.* burst IV 71, 179; breste/tobrest II 14, IV 1, etc.

bet *v. imp.* beat I 38, 45, II 80; ibeten *pa.p.* I 54.

bete *n.* beet, i.e. beet greens: the root was not yet in common use in Gerard's time I 47; betes *pl.* IV 8.

BYTORES see BUTORES.

blake *adj.* black I 17, 27, V 7.

blanc/blank *adj.* white (Fr) I 1t, II 29t*, etc.; blaunche II 33, III 1, etc. BLANC DESIRE I 1, BLANK DE SURRY II 29, BLANK DE SYRY II 90, BLANK DESSORRE IV 39, BLANK DESIRE IV 201, BLANDESYRE Menu 7, BLAUNDESIRE Menu 5, BLAUNDES-SORRE Menu 1, BLUNDSORRE Menu 2: bland white pottages based on almond milk, corresponding to MS Ro's *Blanc desirree*. All except II 90, a fish-day version resembling a modern blancmange pudding, contain ground poultry and are thickened with rice flour or amidon. BLANK DESURE II 78, a fish-day dish, bears little resemblance to the others since it is yellow (with egg yolks, cheese, and saffron) and contains cow's milk rather than almond milk. The various spellings may suggest the dish was thought to be Syrian; no doubt it was Arabic in origin. Austin and Serjeantson thought the derivation to be from 'sore' (sorrel) with the meaning 'red', and the *OED* appears to make the same association (*sub* SORRÉ), but this is unlikely when all early versions are uncoloured. Only the atypical Ar recipe cited by Austin contains any colouring near a red shade. Perhaps scholars working on Arabic materials may soon find a better explanation. Referred to as BLANK DE SURE in II 30, BLAUNDESIRE in III 18; cf. *CB* pp. 9, 21, and 84; *NBC* pp. 35 and 105; *LCC* p. 12. BLANCHE BREWET DE ALMAYNE II 13, 'White German Broth', kid or chicken stewed in milk or almond milk; more closely related to the French recipes for *Brouet blanc* (*VT* pp. 7-8, 83, etc.; *MP* p. 165) than to *Brouet d'Alemaigne*: cf. BRUET DE ALEMAYNE. BLANK MAUNGER IV 38, 200; BLOMANGER II 14, 33; BLOMANGER OF FYSCH II 66; BLAWMAUNGER MOLE III 27; BLAWMANGER III 28; BLAUMAUNGER GROS III 29; BLAMAUNGER IN LENTEN III 30: 'white food'. The standard English flesh-day version has ground capon (or chicken) with rice and almond milk; in III 27 the rice is ground (*mole*) into rice flour, and in III 29 the poultry is in chunks rather than ground up (thus *gros* 'large'). French *Blanc mengier* recipes do not always include rice in any form, but do include the garniture of fried almonds usually suggested in English versions. Rice, either whole or in the form of rice flour, is, however, included in two of the very earliest French recipes, those in the treatise of *c.* 1300 printed by Pichon in his edition of *VT*, and in an early Catalonian recipe in *LSS* (*Manjar blanch*, p. 93). This is one of the few medieval English dishes which bears some resemblance to a recipe of Apicius—*Cibarium Album*, mentioned in the *Cibaria Alba* recipe of *HV* (a sweetened sauce with an almond base). But, like so many other medieval courtly dishes, it is probably more directly descended from an Arabic dish. For a brief history of 'blancmange', see C. Anne Wilson in *PPC* 4 (1980), 17-18. BLOMANGER is mentioned in II 34. Cf. *CB* pp. 21, 23, 85, 114; *LCC* p. 9, 19; *NBC* pp. 102-3, 111.—BLAUNCHE PORRE IV 2, 'white leeks' or 'white pottage of stewed vegetables' (Fr *poree blaunche*; see *MP* pp. 139-40, but note that this recipe does not call for adding small birds); *CB* has a *Blanche porrey* to be served with eels (pp. 90-1).—BLAWNCE POUDER V 16, ginger ground with sugar; see also **powdour douce.**

blaunched *v.*, *pa.p.* blanched; for almonds, this means removing the skin III 1, 5.

bliue *adv.* quickly I 46.

blod *n.* blood I 22, 56, etc. The use in I 56 and III 25 may indicate that blood was dried to be kept for future use.

blod *v.* bleed II 68, III 24/2 (1).

blomes *n.* blossoms IV 179; **blausedes** IV 179n.

BLUNDSORRE see BLANC DESIRE.

boillam boil (*v.*) plus *am*, for which see **he.**

boyste *n.* box; the gingerbread is to be put in a container (or shaped into a 'box' form?) V 19.

bolas *n.* bullace plums IV 98.

bolt *v.*? emerge (see *OED* v^2)?—perhaps miswritten *both* 'be' V 1.

boor *n.* boar IV 16. BORYS HEDES Menu 2, HEDE OF þE BORE Menu 1, BORES HEDYS ENARMYD Menus 3, 5, 7, 9: roast boar's head, a favourite entree for the first course of an English feast; 'enarmed'—larded (see **enarme**).

borage *n.* plant formerly in much use as a potherb; the blue flowers are probably what are called for in a salad recipe IV 78.

bord *n.* table I 34, 45, etc.

BOREWYS Menu 9, probably the dish of pork and/or duck or goose in an ale sauce given in *CB* as *Bourreys* (p. 70) and *Bowres* (p. 8), *LCC Bours*, p. 37, and in MS Douce 55 *Bosoun* (fol. 23^v). Austin thought this related to IV 13 and 187, entitled by Pegge 'Bursen' and 'Bursews' (see BRUCE and RUSCHEWYS), but there is no real resemblance between any two of what are three distinctly different dishes, and the A titles of those in Part IV are not the best supported.

bosewes see TARTES ~.

boter(e) *n.* butter I 46, II 38, etc.

bothum *n.* bottom V 12, 16; **bothyn** V 12.

botores *n.* bittern, marsh-fowl related to the heron III 15; see also BUTORES.

bowes *n.* boughs V 11; **bouwes** IV 185 probably means 'bows'.

braan *n.* bran II 69.

BRAGGOT IV 205*, BRAKOTT V 8*, a spiced ale drink, sweetened with honey. The spelling in MS Royal 17 A iii resembles that of *Arnold's Chronicle* ('braket', p. 188) and Cogan, pp. 230-1. The spice quantities in the Royal MS are, to judge by the prices paid by Alice de Bryene in 1419, *c.*2/3 oz. pepper and 1/4 oz. cloves.

bray(e)/brey *v.* pound in a mortar II 1, 11, etc.; (y)**bray(e)d** *pa.p.* I 57, II 59, 82.

BRASEE I 26, translation of *Brasee* in MS Ro; so named because the fish called for is braised. See also PYKES IN BRASEY.

brasyll *n.* brazil wood, an East Indian tree used for colouring V 15.

brauens *n.* brains (?) III 6.

braun *n.* flesh meat I 1, 2, etc.—Pichon thought OF *braon* generally meant organ meat (*MP* pp. 149-50, n. 7), but recognized that white meat was intended in a *Blanc Brouet de Chappons* in *VT* p. 8, n. 2, where he suggested that *brans* was a mistake for *blancs*. However, such evidence as the use of 'braun' in II 29, 'tak ~ of caponys . . . and þe þyes' (cf. II 30, 'tak þe þyys oþer þe flesch of þe caponys')

suggests that the 'braun' of a fowl is breast (white) meat. BRAWNE
FRETURYS Menu 1, meat fritters. BRAWN IN GREDOWSE, see
EGERDUSE. BROKEN BRAWN Menu 2, BROKON BRAWNE
Menu 1, meat, evidently served in pieces.

bre see broyt.

brede n. breadth I 45.

brem n. bream (fish) III 30. BREME Menu 2, ROSTED GRETE
BREMES Menu 8.

bren v. burn V 19; **brennyng** pr. p. II 18n, IV 196; **brende** pa.p. III 13.

breste see berst.

breþ n. air or steam II 2, IV 72. See also broyt.

brewet see bruet and BLANCHE BREWET DE ALMAYNE.

bryddys n. birds IV 2, 21, etc.

brymlent see TART DE ~.

brineus n. blackberries(?) I 38. This spelling, the breneus of J, and the
A-N bramaus of MS A1 are all unrecorded in vocabularies and dictionaries, but the Anglo-Norman Dictionary notes brimeles, bremeles
and the MED brame, bremel, among other forms for 'blackberries':
something of the sort is clearly called for in this recipe.

BRYNEWES* II 16, a stew based on pigs' guts, served with small fritters made of flour and egg white. A meatless (fast-day) version
appears as Brynex in BL MS Sloane 7 and Bryndons in CB p. 15. Cf.
the variant spellings in MSS D and S2 (II 16n). It is possible that the
title indicates that the pale, small 'pellets' on the darker background
were supposed to resemble the seeds of blackberries; cf. brineus.

bringen v. in make ~ I 55, see maken.

broche n. spit, or, if small, skewer II 42, 43, etc.

broyde v. braid, weave V 23; **broyden** pa.p. V 23.

broyt n. broth II 17; **bre** I 63n; **breth** II 59.

bronde n. brand, burning firewood I 40.

BRUCE IV 13 (A BURSEU, Pegge BURSEN, Ar BRUS), Menu 9: a
potage of organ meats (cf. **noumbles**) and leeks. The word may be
a form of 'brewis' in the sense of a broth of meat and vegetables.

bruet n. broth, or meat or other food cooked in broth II 32, 72, etc.;
brewet/browet III 22t, IV 48t, etc. BRUET DE ALEMAYNE I 15,
BROWET OF ALMAYNE II 22, BREWET OF ALMAYNE IV 48,
BRUET OF ALMAYNE Menus 2, 5, 7: 'German broth'. The recipe
in I, from Browet d'Alemaigne in MS Ro, unlike any other recipe for
this popular dish, does not specify the meat to be put into the spicy
sauce. The others are closer to the French recipes: cf. MP pp. 165-6,
172-3, 276; VT pp. 8-9, etc.; CB p. 19; LCC p. 12 (Bruet de Al-
monde); NBC p. 105. BREWET OF AYREN, see EYRYN IN BRUET
sub ey. BRUET OF LOMBARDYE II 32, stew of chicken, thickened
with bread and egg blended with parsley juice, coloured red; closely
related versions in MSS Sloane 7 and 442 say the colouring is to be
done with alkenet. BRUET SALMENE I 17, from Browet Sal-
menee in MS Ro; all other recipes similarly titled in French (Sala-
mine) or English call for an assortment of fish, here omitted, in a

similarly spicy sauce. The name may have an etymological relationship to MAUMENEE, and the recipe for *MUSKELS IN MAMEINE* in MS C (f. 10ᵛ) has a sauce very similar to this one. BRUET OF SARCYNESSE II 55, BRUET SARASEYNS Menu 4, 'Saracen broth': a beef stew bearing no visible relationship to any other dish of similar name in English, French, or Italian collections, although it may be descended from something similar to the *LSS*'s *Carn a la Sarreÿnesca* (p. 188) and makes use of a typical Arabic procedure: cf. C. Anne Wilson in *PPC* 7 (1981), p. 15. BRUET SARAZINEYS BLANC I 18, from *Browet sarasyneys blanc* in MS Ro, a milk-based sauce to which meat or fish was no doubt to be added, also bears no resemblance to any other recipe called 'Saracen' we have seen; cf. SAUNC SARAZINE and *MP*'s *Brouet Sarrasnois*, p. 172, *VT*'s *Sarraginée*, p. 221 (e.g.). BRUET SEEC I 16, from the BROWET SEK in MS Ro: the broth is sharp (*sec*) because of the verjuice. A similar dish appears a number of times in the French collections as *Brouet de Vergus* or *Brouet de Vertjus et de Poulaille*: see *VT* pp. 9, 84; *MP* p. 167; and cf. *CB* p. 27.

ybrulyd *v.*, *pa.p.* broiled II 70.

bruse *v.* grind, crush V 3.

buf(f)/bef *n.* beef II 27, 30, etc.

BUKKENADE II 45, 53, IV 19; VEEL IN BUKNADE IV 121: a stew of variable flesh, veal being most usual. The sauce is also variable: the II recipes have broth thickened with egg yolk and lightly spiced, while those in IV are more elaborate and otherwise thickened. Despite the recipes, the root *buk-* (or *buc-*) of the title signifies the meaning of 'veal dish', as in the well-known modern Italian veal shank dish 'osso bucco'.

bultyng [cloþ] *v.*, *pr.p.* [+ *n.*] [a cloth used for] sieving IV 205.

BURSEN see BRUCE and BOREWYS.

buth see beon.

BUTORES Menus 3, 7; BYTORES ROSTYD Menus 1, 9; roast bittern; cf. botores.

C

caboches *n.* cabbages IV 6, 103. CABOCHES IN POTAGE IV 6, stew of cabbage, onions, and leeks in broth. None of the French recipes correspond closely, although this sort of preparation may be implied under the heading of *poree*, *MP* pp. 139–40; cf. *CB* p. 33, *Caboges*.

calamynte *n.* calamint, an herb V 7.

calwar *adj.* applied to salmon (and sometimes other fish), this may indicate fish fresh enough to be pickled in salt, as modern Swedish *gravlax*, without cooking; see *OED* sub CALVER and the Bosworth-Toller *Anglo-Saxon Dictionary* sub CALWAR and CEALRE IV 101.

cameline see SAWSE CAMELYNE.

canel/kanel(e) *n.* cinnamon, but when contrasted to 'sinamome', as in II 19n, or 'flour of canel', probably cassia bark I 6, 12, etc.

caneuas *n.* canvas III 7; **cannevasse** V 24.

capoun *n.* capon II 6, IV 24, etc.; **chapoun** I 1, 2, etc.; **caponys** *sg. poss.*
II 28; **caponys** *pl.* II 6t, 28, etc. CAPONS Menu 9, CHAPONS
IBAKE Menus 3, 7: baked or roast capons or capons in pastry.
CAPOUNS DORRES Menu 4, 'gilded' roast capons (cf. **endore**).
CAPONES OF HI GRES Menu 1, CAPONES ROSTYD OF HY
GRECE, Menu 2, roasted well-fattened capons. CAPONS IN CAS-
SELYS II 28, an ingenious method of turning the capon into two,
which is referred to (disapprovingly) in *MP* pp. 268-9; 'in casselys'
may mean 'enclosed'. For a possible Arabic source of the method,
see Rodinson, p. 157. Cf. *NBC* p. 36, *To mak two capons of one*,
and p. 116, *Capon in cassolont.*—CAPONYS IN CONCYS II 6,
CAPOUNS IN COUNCY IV 24, COYNES III 23: capon in a sauce
including boiled egg yolks. III 23 adds hen to the capon, and cf. the
similar CHICONES IN MOSE. The yolks would resemble quinces,
'coynes': cf. CONNAT. Cf. *CB* p. 115, *Capon en Counfyt*, and
p. 18, *Capoun in Consewe*; *LCC* p. 24, *Capons in Covisye* (*sic*, but
the *v* is probably a misreading of *n*); *NBC* p. 116, *Capon in Couns.*

care(a)wey *n.* caraway V 4, 5, 12.

CARUEL OF PORK IV 34, pork brains, parboiled, ground, mixed with
egg yolk, and fried. The word 'caruel' (J 'cervel'), OF *cervel* 'brain',
was mistranscribed as *carnel* by Pegge. Brains, which are frequently
called for in the recipes of Apicius—usually boiled and ground, as
one of many ingredients—are relatively rare in medieval recipes. An
exceptional one is boiled brains as a sort of meatball, in a recipe not
unlike some of those of Apicius, found in the 14th-century German
Bûch von gûter spise (see bibliography *sub* Hajek).

caruoun *v., pa.p.* carved IV 158.

casselys see CAPONS IN ∼.

cawdel *n.* smoothly thickened sauce or soup (Fr *chaudeau, chaudel*,
'hot water'; cf. *VT* p. 24, *MP* pp. 88 and 241) II 31, IV 17, etc.
CAWDEL FERRY IV 43, CAUDEL FERRE Menu 5, KAUDEL
FERRE I 5: the latter translates MS Ro's *Caudel ferree*; sweetened,
thickened wine, heated, with beaten egg yolks added—very similar
to Fr *Chaudeau flament*. Since *flament* can mean 'flaming', 'ferry'
may be related to 'fire'. Cf. *VT* p. 24, *MP* p. 241, *CB* pp. 15, 31, 91,
LCC p. 16, *NBC* pp. 32-3, 109.—CAWDEL FOR GEES, see GAUN-
CELI. CAWDEL OF ALMAUND MYLKE IV 90, almond milk made
with wine, sweetened; cf. *CB* pp. 16, 33, 96; *LCC* p. 15; *NBC* pp. 81,
108. CAWDEL OF MUSKELS IV 127, boiled mussels, washed in
wine; some ground and some chopped; the ground mixed with broth
and almond milk plus verjuice and vinegar; all cooked further with
parboiled leek and onions, plus seasonings. Cf. *LCC* p. 47, *Porray of
mustuls.* CAWDEL OF SAMOUN IV 114, salmon with leeks in almond milk thickened with bread.

cerfoyl *n.* chervil (herb) IV 144n.

cerise see **chiryse**.

ceucre see **sucre**.

chapeleyn see PORREY ~.

CHAPELETTES see CHASTLETES.

chapoun see capoun.

charge v. thicken III 21, 22; chargeaunt *adj.* thick III 10, 18, etc.; charchant II 29, 30; charghaunt II 33; chariaunt II 36; chariand II 83, 86.

chargours *n.* flat dishes, platters IV 104.

CHARLET II 20, IV 41: minced pork boiled in a custard-like sauce; thought to be derived from Fr *char* 'meat' plus *lait* 'milk', although no such dish is known in medieval continental French cookery. Cf. *CB* pp. 17, 117; *LCC* p. 11; *NBC* pp. 104, 121. CHARLET YFORCED IV 42, 'charlet' with a sauce of more milk and eggs; cf. *CB* p. 17, *NBC* p. 29.

chasteyns see chestens.

CHASTLETES IV 197, CHAPELETTES Menu 3, pastry castles with towers containing various fillings.

chauden/chaudoun *n.* organ meats (OF *chaudin, chaudun*: *MP* p. 161 defines as liver and lights, etc.) III 6, 13, etc. CHAUDEN III 6, a pottage made with organ meats; CHAUDEN III 12 and CHAWDOUN FOR SWANNES IV 147 make similar use of the giblets of a swan in a sauce, while CHAWDOUN FOR LENT IV 118 is a fastday substitute made from the blood and paunches of fish. The recipes in *VT* pp. 4-5, 80, etc. and *MP* pp. 160-1 are close to that of III 6, as is that in *NBC* pp. 90-1; similar recipes for swan are in *CB* pp. 76-7 and 108, *LCC* pp. 9-10 (printed as *pandon*), and *NBC* pp. 88-9.

chawfour/chawfer *n.* pan IV 170, 181.

CHEBOLACE IV 9, a pottage of onions and herbs with an optional thickening of egg yolks. The TC title is *Erbolace*, relating it to Fr *arboulastre*, but this is probably not the derivation since the Fr dish is fried: the correct title derives, rather, from the onions, 'chibols'— cf. chybolles.

checonys/chicones *n.* chickens II 24, 31, etc.; chekenen I 16; cycchen *sg.* I 32, 56. CHEKENES Menu 4, chickens, probably baked in pastry; CHEKENES IFARSED Menu 5, stuffed chickens, probably roasted; CHICONES IN MOSE III 20, chickens in a sauce resembling that of CAPONYS IN CONCYS in that it includes hard-boiled egg yolks; cf. *NBC Chekyns in Musy*, p. 28. CHYKENS IN CAWDEL IV 35, boiled chicken in broth thickened with egg yolks (cf. cawdel); cf. *LCC* p. 23, *NBC* pp. 114-15. CHYKENS IN GRAUEY IV 29, chickens stewed in broth thickened with almonds (cf. graue). CHYKENS IN HOCCHEE IV 36 (OF *houssié* 'with parsley'): cf. HAUCELEAMYE.

cheite *n.* drippings (OF *cheoite*) III 13n.

cheryes see chiryse.

CHESAN see CHYSANNE.

cheseberien/chiseberien *n.* cherries I 14, 54; chelberyes/cheseberyes IV 59; chyselberyes IV 59n. See also MES OF ~, chiryse.

chestens *n.* chestnuts I 63; chistenis I 32; chasteyns I. 21.

CHEWETES ON FLESSHE DAY IV 193, CHEWETES ON FYSSH DAY IV 194, CHEUETTES Menus 3 and 7, CHEUETTES OF FRUT Menu 8: small pies, baked or fried; the name probably means 'little cabbages' (*choux*, used for modern pastries), indicating that they are small and round. Cf. *CB* pp. 45, 46, 48, 98; *LCC* p. 41; *NBC* pp. 55, 56.

chybolles *n.* spring onions (U.S. 'scallion') IV 14, 78.

CHYCHES IV 73, chick peas roasted in ashes, boiled and seasoned with oil, garlic, saffron, and spices. There is a dimilar recipe in *LdC*.

CHINCHE V 23, junket in the earlier sense of a drained but freshly set milk curd. The *Joncada* recipe in *LdC* p. 78 also calls for milk, rather than the cream which has been said by various authorities to be the basis of earlier junket: perhaps cooks switched to cream somewhat later. A recipe for junket of almonds, presumably a curd of almond milk, appears in the TC of *DV*, but unfortunately the recipe is missing.

chyne *n.* unless the word should be read as 'chyue' and represents the word *shive* 'slice', probably either 'cut, incision' or a particular part of the meat (see *OED sub* CHINE sb[1] 1. c and sb[2] 3) III 11.

chiryse *n.* cherries IV 59; chiryes II 77; cerise I 54; cheryes III 33; cf. cheseberien. CHIRESEYE II 77, SYROSYE III 33, CHYRYSE IV 59: thick cherry pottages; unlike SCIRRESEZ and MES OF CHYSE-BERIEN, q.v., these contain no meat, but IV 59 calls for broth and II 77 and III 33 for grease, so they are not fast-day food and show an origin in common with the meatier cherry dishes.

CHYSANNE IV 106, fried fish with almonds and currents, to be eaten cold; CHESAN Menu 8, probably the same dish, which may derive its name from ME *chis* 'dainty': see *OED*. Apicius has a similar dish called *Patina de Pisciculis*.

chistenis see chestens.

cycchen see checonys.

cypre *adj.* 'of Cyprus', whence a great deal of sugar was imported; the word always occurs here in conjunction with sugar or indicating a notably sweetened dish IV 43, 100t, etc.

cyrip *n.* thin sauce IV 65t; siryppe IV 65.

cirmunteyn *n.* sermountain or hartwort (see *OED s.v.*) V 7.

cyuee *n.* onion sauce, or a dish cooked in such a sauce (OF *civé*) IV 27t, 115t, etc.; seue/syuee I 52t, III 9t.

CYUELES see EMELES.

clanliche(e) *adv.* carefully I 25, 35, etc.; completely I 63.

CLARREY IV 205, POTUS CLARRETI PRO DOMINO V 4, A PYPE OF CLARREY V 6 (< Fr *clarié*): spiced wine, usually sweetened with honey, as against YPOCRAS, usually sweetened with sugar— but some 'clarrey' recipes call for sugar. Not to be confused with claret, a red table wine. Proportions of honey to wine vary from one in two to one in eight; H calls for white wine, which Pichon (*MP* p. 99) thought usual for *claré*, but at least one recipe (in BL MS Sloane 2484) calls for red, and others do not specify which kind, or suggest either will do (e.g. MS A1 f. 119ᵛ). V 4, 'clarrey drink for

a lord', is the second of a series of three: the first, calling for somewhat more elaborate spicing, is *pro rege*, and the third, marginally
simpler, *pro populo*. V 6 is a recipe for a larger quantity; a pipe is a
wine cask of *c*.100 imperial gallons' capacity.

clarry *n.* clary, an herb of the salvia family which Gerard recommends
cooking with eggs (as was done with tansy) IV 180; **sclarie** I 47.

clene *adv.* neatly, carefully I 41, II 46, etc.; completely III 5 (cf. **clanliche**).

icleped *v., pa.p.* 'is called by'; takes a pronoun in the 'dative of interest'
(see *OED sub* ME 2 b) I 45, 57; **clept** III 11; **clepeþ** I 43, 63.

cleue *v.* (1) cut V 6; **cleeue** *pa.p.* IV 63.

cleuyng *v.* (2) *pr.p.* sticking together V 12.

cloute *n.* cloth IV 205; **clowt** II 49.

clowe *n.* clove; **clouwes** *pl.* I 4, 15, etc.; **cloewes** I 16; **cleowes** I 48;
frequently in phrase ~ *(of) gilofre* which means, simply, cloves.

cod(e)lyng *n.* young cod, but may have sometimes been confused with
'ling', a separate species of fish IV 97, 117, 128.

coffin *n.* case or container, usually a pastry shell I 43, IV 166, etc.;
cofyn II 82, V 14, etc.; **cophyn** IV 165.

COYNES see **CAPONYS IN CONCYS**.

coyntis(e)e *n.* cleverness, skill I 54; **coynteliche** *adv.* cleverly I 55.

COKAGRYS IV 183 (A, COTAGRES), KOKETRIS Menu 3: the dish
later generally called 'cokantrice'. A 'new' beast is created by sewing
the top of a cock to the hind-quarters of a pig (*gris, gryse*, a suckling
pig). The creation is stuffed with forcemeat, boiled, roasted, and
gilded (see **endore**); cf. *CB* pp. 40, 115.

COLD BREWET (1) IV 135, **COLD BRUET** Menu 8 (?—see ~ [2] below): cream of almonds (cf. IV 87), dried (i.e., drained), mixed with
mild seasonings, fennel juice, and wine.

COLDE BREWET (2) IV 138, thick almond milk made with wine or
vinegar, mixed with anise, sugar, and green fennel, and spiced, as a
sauce for boiled meat or fowl; similar to ~ (1), but that kind is
apparently to be served on its own. The entry in Menu 8 may mean
either kind.

cole *v.* (1) cool, become cool IV 1, 53, etc.; **kelen** V 3; **kele** 3 *sg.* II 1,
14, etc.; **colde** *pa.p.* V 14/13; **icol(e)d** I 40, IV 107.

cole *v.* (2) strain II 61, V 11, etc.; **colyng** *pr.p.* V 11; **colde** *pa.p.* V 14/2.

coliaundir/colyandre *n.* coriander (seed) V 4, 12, etc.

COLYS II 11, broth enriched by a strained ground meat base, usually
(as here) chicken; a preparation known to later English cooks as
'cullis' (see *OED s.v.*); cf. *VT, Coulis*, p. 167; *MP* p. 242; *CB* pp. 10–
11; *LCC* p. 20; *NBC* p. 112.

colops *n.* cutlets, scallops of meat V 20.—Cf. *NBC* p. 93; later references to 'collops' in England suggest they were made with bacon,
and the two references in *Piers Plowman* (B. VI. 367 and C. XVI.
67) may or may not imply bacon. However, Skeat's notes and
glossary in the 2 vol. ed. (Oxford, 1886) and the references there
cited make it clear that collops were as often slices of venison, and

were distinguished from the type of slice called 'steaks'; one reference states that they were beaten before cooking, and, since the first
Piers Plowman reference implies that collops took special skill in
cooking, they may well have been similar to the modern 'scallop'
or *scaloppine*, whatever meat was used.

colowre *n.* colour II 32; *poudre of* ~ colouring powder III 18: but this
is probably an error, with colouring substituted for a spice, since the
'saundres' mentioned immediately before would suffice as colouring.

comade *n.* mixture used as a filling IV 116.——Hodgkin thought this
word might be related to Spanish *comedar* 'glutton', and suggested
the meaning 'fit for an epicure'; possibly, though, it means 'that
which is eaten' in contrast to the pastry case, which was often not
eaten. COMADORE IV 196, a filling of ground fresh and dried
fruits, cooked in oil before it is enclosed in pastry and fried.

comet *v.* come I 54; comyn *pa.p.* II 77.

comfery *n.* comfrey, herb formerly much used to treat wounds (Pegge
reported that its roots are 'of a glutenous nature') IV 198.

comyn *n.* cumin (spice) I 61, II 7, etc. COMENEYE I 59, COMYN
II 39, sauce named for the cumin seasoning, although the II recipe
omits it: 'amydoun wiþ flowre of rys' should probably read 'comyn
with amydoun'. The Fr *cominée* recipes all specify meat or fish in
the sauce; cf. *VT* pp. 5–6, 20, etc.; *MP* pp. 161–2; *NBC* p. 27.

COMPOST IV 103, relish or chutney made of root vegetables, fruits,
vinegar, honey, and spices, among other things, as preserves. A version of this can be found in Apicius, Lib. I, xxiv: turnips preserved
in honey and vinegar, with or without myrtle berries or mustard and
salt. Cf. *MP* pp. 243–7, *CB* pp. 12–13 and 87–8, *NBC* p. 100.

concys see CAPONYS IN CONCYS.

co(u)nfyt(e) *n.* comfit; sugar coating; confiture; or simply sugar syrup
IV 38, 136, etc.

CONGUR Menus 6 and 8, conger; method of cooking unspecified.
CONGUR IN SAWSE IV 107, conger boiled in a sauce of bread,
herbs, spices, garlic, and vinegar.

con(n)ynges *n.* rabbits IV 19, 27, etc. CONYNG ROSTYD Menus 2, 9;
CONYES ROSTYD, Menu 5: roast rabbit. CONNYNGES IN CLERE
BROTH IV 67, rabbit in a strained broth of wine, water, and vinegar;
cf. *CB* p. 80. CONNYNGES IN CYUEE IV 27, rabbits in sauce of
fried onion, bread, broth, blood, and vinegar; cf. *VT* pp. 10, 85, etc.;
MP p. 169; *CB* p. 20; *LCC* pp. 20–1; *NBC* p. 112. CONNYNGES IN
GRAUEY IV 28, CONYNGGYS IN GRAUEY II 10: rabbit stewed
in a broth thickened with almonds; see grauey and cf. *CB* pp. 18, 80;
LCC p. 8; *NBC* p. 101.

CONNAT IV 20, CONNAUNCE Menu 9, quinces ('connes') stewed in
grease with honey, egg yolks, and almond milk; served sliced, presumably cold. The title is similar to *Cotignac, MP* p. 247, but that is
a preserve. Cf. *CB* pp. 106–7, *Chared coneys*, the preserve type, but
also reference in *Charde-wardon* pp. 12, 88, to a type with egg yolks
added; *NBC* pp. 81–2, *Charwardon*.

cool *n.* cole, kale?——cabbage, but which member of this family is impossible to determine IV 8.

cophyn see coffin.

corance, coraunte see reyseyns of ∼.

CORAT IV 14, **CORATE** Menu 9: organ meat (cf. **noumbles**) cooked in broth with herbs and onions, thickened with egg yolks and verjuice. The name may be derived from 'heart', Fr *coeur*.

corf *v.* carve I 41, 42, etc.; (i)**coruen** *pa.p.* I 6, 27, etc.

CORMARYE IV 54, roast pork in a sauce of wine, garlic, pepper, coriander, and caraway; name may be derived from one of the spices.

cormoraunz *n.* cormorants, large sea birds III 15.

corne *n.* grain in the sense of best quality wheat; *flour of* ∼ translates *flur triée de forment* in I 9, *flur demeyne* in I 34.

cornes *n.* either a vessel, probably horn-shaped (see *OED sub* CORNET and CORNUTE), or a carelessly written 'corner' V 12.

CORNUDE LORU3E Menu 1: if 'loru3e' is a miscopying of 'lounge', as seems likely, this may be 'corned' (i.e., salted) tongue; see *OED sub* CORN v. II. 3). That the first instance cited is 16th century does not invalidate a presumption that the word may have been used earlier. Tongue is elsewhere called *longe* (II 43), Fr *langue*.

cose *v.* sprinkle (? translates A-N [a]*rose*) I 46.

costmaryn *n.* costmary (herb); in Gerard's time used to flavour ale IV 144n.

COTAGRES see COKAGRYS.

cote *v.* cut V 12/36.

COUDRE EN TENS DE NOIS I 10, 'fruit of the hazel-tree in nut season', from *Coudree en temps de nois* in MS Ro; sauce made with hazelnuts.

couertour *n.* cover (top crust) IV 116.

councy see CAPONYS IN CONCYS.

counfy see ELES IN ∼.

counfite see confyt.

cours *n.* layer (see *OED sub* COURSE n. 29) IV 84n.

COUWE DE ROUNCIN I 42, translation of *Couue de Rouncin* in MS A1; the first element of the name suggests a relationship to *MP*'s *Queue de Sanglier*, meaning 'boar's tail' but also used for other meats prepared with a similar spicy sauce: see pp. 179, 236, and cf. II 44, REW DE RUNSY.

cowche *n.* layer II 84.

cowche *v.* lay down III 1, IV 26, 104.

cowsloppys *n.* cowslips (Gerard says 'the leaves are used among potherbs') IV 8n.

CRAYTOUN II 24, **CRYTAYNE** IV 61 (A CROTOUN), **CRETEYNE** Menu 4: chicken in a sauce made with milk, the only common ingredient linking the early French and English recipes, although there is no milk in two *Cretonée* recipes in *VT* pp. 149-50 and almond milk is sometimes substituted. *T-L* and other authorities derive the name from a word meaning 'lard' or 'pork crackling', but neither is

involved in any of the English versions, and the frying called for in
MP pp. 159, 160 and various *VT* recipes (pp. 5, 80-1, etc.) is no
different from the process for many other dishes. Cf. *LCC* p. 8,
NBC pp. 28, 101.

CRANE III 15, CRANYS & HERONS II 3, CRANES AND HEROUNS
IV 151, CRANYS ROSTYD Menu 1, CRUNES ROSTYD Menu 2:
roasting and serving the relevant birds. The III recipe uses woodcock
as an analogy; note that woodcock does not appear separately here,
but was much consumed in the period; to this is appended brief
notes on the roasting of plovers, mallards, and other game birds.
Cf. *CB* pp. 78, 116; *LCC* p. 35; *NBC* pp. 61-2.

CREM & BOTORE OF ALMOUNDES III 5, CREME OF ALMAUNDES
IV 87, CREM OF ALMAUNDES Menu 6, thickened confection of
almond milk curdled with vinegar, to which the IV recipe adds sugar.
Cf. *CB* p. 20 ('Crem de Colure'), *NBC* pp. 42-3.

CRESTEROLE (J CRYSTEROLE) I 34, translating *Crosterole* in MS
A1; but the latter calls for the fast-day version of the cakes to be
made with almond milk, not fried almonds. The name may indicate
the crossing of the two colours of paste (Fr *croisé*); cf. *CB* p. 46.

CRETEYNE/CRYTAYNE/CROUTOUN see CRAYTOUN.

CRISPELS IV 171, thinly rolled pastry cut into rounds and fried,
served with honey, possibly in piles with honey between layers; cf.
LdC Crispelli.

CRYSPYS II 26, IV 170, crêpes, pancakes (OF *crespes*) or fritters; cf.
MP p. 226, *VT* pp. 124-5, *CB* pp. 44, 93.

croppes *n.* sprouts, tips III 10.

crouh(h)e *n.* crock (spelling unnoted in *OED*) I 40, 47, etc.

crudde *n.* curd V 23; cruddes *pl.* IV 179.

crudde *v.* curdle IV 41n.

CRUNES ROSTYD see CRANE.

crustardes *n.* open tarts resembling the modern quiche, usually containing a thick, often egg-based, filling of a type which is liquid uncooked
but solidifies and crusts over: hence *crustard* IV 161t, 163t, 164t.
CRUSTARDES OF EERBIS IV 164, greens ground with walnuts,
mixed and cooked in water and verjuice, in a pie shell over partly-
baked fish *or* mixed with ground boiled egg yolks—presumably still
in a tart; cf. *MP* p. 218, *Tourte*, *VT* p. 41. CRUSTARDES OF
FYSSHE IV 163, open tart of fish, some fried and some stewed in
almond milk with currants, prunes, and the cooking liquid, spiced;
VT's *Flaons et tartes en Quaresme* have some similar basic ingredients
(no dried fruits) but the fish is to be ground. Cf. also *CB* p. 55,
Crustade Ryal. CRUSTARDES OF FLESSH IV 161, pie (covered,
despite title) of stewed poultry with currants, seasonings, and eggs
beaten with the broth; for quiches with similar fillings, cf. *CB*
pp. 50-1, 55, 74; *NBC* p. 54. CRUSTEDE Menu 8, 'crustard' of
unspecified type, but it would have to be meatless. See also GRETE
CROSTUDE.

culdore *n.* colander, strainer II 25, 27.

CULINARY NOTES V 1, notes on such matters as soaking raisins and parboiling onions.

culpoun *v.* cut up III 19.

cumpas *n.* extent, measurement IV 197.

cury(e) cookery II *heading*, IV *head note*. (See Introduction, p. 18.)

curlewes *n.* curlews, a wading water-bird III 15, IV 37. CURLEUS Menu 5, CURLES Menu 7, CURLEWS ROSTYD Menu 1, (roast) curlews.

CUSKYNOLES I 45, translating KUSKYNOLE in MS A1, small pastries with a fruit filling. The name is probably derived from *rissoles*, variously spelled in OF. The diagram, similar to that in MS A1 (which is divided into nine parts), indicates how to cut the pastry into cakes, not how to fold it, as the wording suggests. The version of MS L is in *CB* pp. 112-13, under the editorially added title of 'Ryschewys close'. Cf. *MP* pp. 225-6, *CB* pp. 93, 97.

cwe *n.* cow V 2; kyne *pl.* II 1, 13, etc.

D

damysyns *n.* damsons (plums) IV 163, 175; damasines IV 100n.

DARYOLS IV 191, Menus 3, 6, 8; DARIOL OF CREM Menu 4; DARIOL OF ALMAUND Menu 8: custard tarts. *Darioles* appear on several of *MP*'s menus, but no recipe is given; the 15th-century edition of *VT* has a terse and rather unclear one. A recipe in MS Bodley F 291 (*Dareals*) specifies one quart of cream and forty egg yolks to make twenty tarts, so they were evidently quite small, as is also indicated in *HV*'s recipe for *Diriola* (filled with egg yolk, milk, sugar, and cinnamon); cf. *CB* pp. 47, 53, 55-6, 75; *LCC* pp. 38-9; *NBC* p. 56.

DATYS IN COMPASTE Menu 1, preserved dates; cf. COMPOST.

DAUCE EGRE see EGERDUSE.

dawes *n.* days I 41.

de *prep.* of (Fr) I 15, 27t, etc.

decoccioun *n.* decoction (see *OED s.v.*) V 12, 13, 14.

dee *n.* die; deez *pl.* I 6; dysys II 15; *lyche a* ~ into dice IV 158.

defaute *n.* lack (Fr); *in* ~ *of* instead of IV 26.

deys *n.* high table I 54.

de(e)l(e) *n.* amount, portion III 20, IV 116 etc.; dole I 34, 45, 57.

deliet see lyen.

demembre/dimembre *v.* dismember II 31, 57.

deore *adj.* precious I 54; deoree *v., pa.p.*? made precious? I 49.

departe *v.* divide III 26.

desire, desorre see BLANC ~.

despyne see VIAUNDE ~.

DYACRE I 22, translation of *Diacre* in MS Ro; capon meat in a sweetened almond milk sauce, coloured red. Cf. *VT* p. 126, *Dyapré*; Pichon and Vicaire note that *diapré*, 'diapered', is a word used in heraldry signifying an ornamental (generally floral) pattern. Perhaps the effect is gained here by the use of the 'losenges' called for among the ingredients.

di(h)ʒte *v.* prepare III 11t, 24t, V 6t; **diʒ(h)t** *pa.p.* III 13, 15.

dysch/disshe *n.* dish II 6, V 21, etc.; **dihs** I 46, 54.

dysys see **dee.**

A DISSHE METE FOR SOMERE V 25: this simple dish of giblets, etc., appears in *MP* as *Menus de piés*, p. 145, and in *VT* as *Menus d'Oies*, p. 15, but spices are not called for in the French recipes, which do not say that this is to be served cold.

ditayn(e) *n.* dittany, herb with a sharp-tasting root, treated by Gerard together with horseradish IV 148, 180.

do(n) *v.* do; putt; add I 31, 53, etc.; *imp.* I 63; **ido(n)** *pa.p.* I 1, 4, etc.

dof *v.* do off, remove (cf. 'doff') IV 104.

dole see **del.**

dolyf *n.*, *poss.* of olive II 65, III 9, etc.; **doliue** III 17.

DOMEDES IN PASTE Menu 1, possibly a variety of fruit (pear?) dumpling or pastry, like the next item on the menu.

dorry see SOUPES ∼ and cf. **endore.**

DOUBLE MORTREUS I 8, translating *Double Mortrews* in MS Ro; an apparently meatless sweet dish in which 'losenges' are likely to be slices of sugar candy rather than noodles. There is no obvious reason why these 'mortrews' (Fr *mortels*, something ground in a morter: cf. MORTRELLUS) are 'double'.

douce see **powdour douce.**

DOUCE IAME IV 64, capon braised in a sweetened milk sauce with herbs and pine nuts. This seems to be a descendant of the dish called AMYDON, q.v., named for the amydon thickening: *amidoun* > **ami douce* > **douce ami* etc. Some later spellings, such as Ar's *Bouce Jane*, compound the confusion.

doust *n.* dust; *grinde it al to* ∼ grind it to a fine powder IV 46.

dow(e) *n.* dough I 24, II 88, etc.; **dowh** IV 95.

dowes *n.* doves V 25.

DRAGONE I 20, from MS Ro's *Dragonee*, a sweetened pottage of capon in almond milk, named for the 'dragon's blood' colouring (see **sanc dragoun**); cf. SANC DRAGON, a similar dish without capon.

drauh *v.* draw I 49, 56.

(y)drawe *v.* (1) *pa.p.* beaten or strained; blended IV 4, 28, etc. DRAWEN BENES see **benes.**

drawe *v.* (2) cut up IV 6n., 200; **(y)drawe(n)** *pa.p.* IV 106.

dr(u)e *adj.* dry I 41, II 57, etc.

dr(u)e(n) *v.* dry I 43, 44, etc.; **dryyd** *pa.p.* II 89.

DREPE IV 21, DROP Menu 3, parboiled birds finished in almond milk with fried onions; the etymology is unknown. Cf. *CB* pp. 30-1, *Dropeye.*

dres(se) *v.* arrange for serving I 37, 38, etc.; **drescee** I 35; **dresch** III 26, 27, etc.; **adres** I 36; **adressed** *pa.p.* I 21, 27, 58.

dressur *n.* dresser, sideboard I 56.

drong *v.*, *pa.p.* drunk, absorbed II 55.

droppe *v.* dredge, baste II 28.

drue see **dre.**

E

eerys see erys.

EGERDUSE II 60, EGGE DOWS II 51, DAUCE EGRE III 17, EGUR-
DOUCE IV 23, EGREDOUNS Menu 3, EGREDOUNE Menu 7,
EGURDOUCE OF FYSSHE IV 137: 'sweet-and-sour' dishes (Fr
aigredouce). BRAWN IN GREDOWSE Menu 1 is flesh (possibly boar
is intended) in such a sauce; IV 23 calls for white flesh-meat and all
the others for fish, except II 51, which is unique in giving only the
sauce—but not in omitting the sugar: later recipes are equally for-
getful. No such name appears in *VT* or *MP*, but similarly named
dishes are still current in Italy and sweet/sour combinations appear
frequently in the *LSS* and the *Baghdad Cookery-Book*. Cf. *CB*
pp. 31, 71, 113.

egge *n.* edge V 19.

EGRET ROSTYD Menu 2, roast small heron.

ey *n.* egg I 44; (h)eyryn *pl.* II 5, 15, etc.; ayren I 8, 9, etc.; eyre III 32.
EYRYN IN BRUET II 23, BREWET OF AYREN IV 93, soup of
eggs, water, milk, and cheese. See also POCCHEE and PENCHE OF
EGGES.

eir *n.* air V 8; see also erys.

eysel see aysell.

elena campana *n.* the herb elecampane; the root was used medically
and, in Gerard's time, in a candied form IV 80; enula campana V 17.
ELAT IV 80, egg mixed with boiled, ground elecampane; probably
similar to *Tansy*, a popular dish of the period not represented in the
collections used here, made of eggs and the herb tansy.

eles *n.* eels I 43, IV 113t, etc.; helys II 84, 92. ELES IBAKE Menu 8,
baked eels, probably in pastry. ELES IN COUNFY III 1, eels in
broth (OF *confit*, broth) with pine nuts: a more elaborate dish than
any in French and Italian collections. ELYS IN BRUET II 74, ELES
IN BREWET IV 113: while the former calls for ale rather than wine
and omits onions, and the latter omits herbs, both appear to be versions of SOREE, q.v.

elren *n.* elder (tree) IV 179.

EMELES I 46, translating *Emeles* in MS A1. The French name seems to
indicate that these cakes are an enriched variety of the *Alumelle frite
au sucre* of *MP*, p. 208, and that the word is thus etymologically
related to 'omelet'; note, however, that 'Cyuele', the spelling indicated in l. 5 here, is also used by L: cf. *CB* p. 113.

enabbe see habben.

enarme *v.* lard III 11; enarmud *pa.p.* II 3; enarmyd Menus 3, 5, 7, 9;
armed IV 151.

endor(r)e *v.* gild, i.e. apply a finish tinted gold (or some other colour)
II 42, IV 195; endored *pa.p.* Menu 6; endort Menu 1; indorretes
Menu 4.

enula campana see elena campana.

erbes *n.* herbs IV 9, 14, etc.

ERBOLACE see CHEBOLACE.

ERBOLAT IV 180, a baked custard (or omelet) of eggs and herbs in butter; name apparently goes back to Fr *arboulastre*, a word of obscure origin—perhaps from the herbs in most versions, but others have few or none and some are not omelets, either. Cf. *MP* pp. 206–8, 209, 227–8; *VT* pp. 157–8; *CB* pp. 54, 76; *NBC* pp. 58–9.

ERBOWLE IV 98, bullace plums (hence, apparently, the name) stewed in wine, strained, sweetened, spiced, and thickened.

eren *adj.* iron V 14.

e(e)rys *n.* ears II 56, IV 105, 185; eyr II 44; eren I 42.

ERMINE I 29, translation of *Ermynee* in MS Ro; almond milk is no doubt understood as the basis of this food, probably named 'ermine' because of its whiteness, but since the ending *-mene* (variously spelled) appears on such other dishes as MAUMENE and SALMENE a connection with the fur of this name cannot be assumed without question.

erne see renne.

ert *n.* hart, deer III 6.

erthe *n.* earth or earthenware IV 20, 22, etc.; herþe II 58; yerth IV 105n.

esy *adj.* easy; ~ *fyre* slow fire, low heat IV 68, V 11; esely *adv.* gently IV 36; eselich IV 116.

ESPYNE see SPINETTE.

ete(n) *v.* eat I 40, IV 106, etc.

eurose *n.* rosewater IV 179.

ew ardaunt *n.* spirits, aqua ardaunt, q.v. IV 197.——The idea seems to be to serve the 'castle' flambé, as is called for in one Ar recipe, no. 139 (a rich version of 'mawmenny'), which adds at the end, 'putte thereon a litel aqua vite and quen hit is dresset in dysshes as hit is before sayde thenne light hit with a wax candel and serue hit forthe brennynge'.

EXPLICIT DE COQUINA QUE EST OPTIMA MEDICINA (end of II): 'Here ends (the work) on cookery, which is the best medicine.'

EXPLICIT DOCTRINA FACIENDI DIUERSA CIBARIA (end of I): 'Here ends the treatise on making various foods.'

EXPLICIT SERUICIUM DE CARNIBUS; HIC INCIPIT SERUICIUM DE PISSIBUS, II between 59 and 60: 'The service of meat ends; this begins the service of fish.'

F

fayle *v.* fail; *if þou ~ þerof* if you do not have any of that III 30.

fallyþ (to) *v.* (it) befits, is proper to II 84.

fanne *v.* winnow IV 119.

fars(ure) *n.* forcemeat, ground meat or meat substitute used as a filling or for meat balls, etc. (cf. force) I 27, IV 51, etc.; fassure I 45, 54; fassyng I 27. FARSUR TO MAKE POMME DORRYSE AND OþERE þYNGES IV 182, mixture of ground pork, seasonings, currants, for meat balls or use in other recipes; from Fr *pomme dorée* 'gilded apple', which the meatball would resemble if finished with saffron-coloured batter. See also POMMEDORRY; cf. *MP, Pommeaulx*, p. 222; *VT* pp. 119-21; *CB* pp. 14-15, 31, 34, 38; *LCC* p. 37; *NBC* p. 120.

fassen/yfassed *v.* apparently *pa.p.*s of the verb force 'stuff', but this does not make sense in either case; perhaps the meaning is 'pitted' because pitted cherries and grapes would be hollowed out as if to be stuffed I 54, 57.

fasten see TWO PECYS OF FLESSH, FOR TO MAKE TO ~ TO-GYDER.

fasticade see **festicade**.

FAWNE III 36, pottage made with bean leaves and blossoms; the name is probably related to Fr *fève* 'bean'.

FELETTES INDORRETES Menu 4, gilded pork filets; cf. **fyletes** and **endore**.

FENE BOILES II 81; *fene* is clearly a mistranslation of an original *fèves* 'beans' (Fr), the basis of this sweet dish, a sort of pudding of ground beans, almond milk, wine, honey, and raisins.

fen(n)el/fenkel *n.* fennel IV 78, 79, etc. FENKEL IN SOPPES IV 79, fennel and onions boiled in water and oil, poured over toast 'sops'; there is a similar recipe in *LdC*.

fe(e)r(e) *n.* fire II 59, 75, etc.; **fur(e)** I 40, 47, etc.; **vure** I 56; **fuyre** IV 196.

fere *n.* company; *y* ~, *in* ~, together III 1, IV 65, etc.

ferre, ferry see CAWDEL FERRY.

fesauntes *n.* pheasants IV 22, 37. FESAUNTES Menus 3, 5, 7, 9; FESANTES ROSTYD Menu 1; FESAINTIS ROSTYD Menu 2, roast pheasant. FOR TO BOILE FESAUNTES, PERTRUCHES, CAPOUNS AND CURLEWES IV 37, boiling the fowl in seasoned broth.

fest(e) *n.* feast, festival II 77, Menus 1 and 2.

festicade/festigade *n.* pistachio nuts (Arabic *fustaq*), but the suffix *-ade* suggests a preparation made from the nuts—perhaps chopped nuts I 4, 27, 28.

fetherfoy *n.* feverfew (herb) IV 180n.

FYGEY II 62, IV 91, fig pudding with raisins. The IV recipe includes ground almonds and honey, while that in II is based on breadcrumbs and directs one to grind the figs; the latter is given as it appears in L because the D scribe absentmindedly repeated EGERDUCE (II 60) instead of copying the right recipe. Cf. *CB* pp. 24, 94-5, 113; *LCC* (*Fygnade*), pp. 42-3; *NBC* p. 119.

fyle(t)tes *n.* filets (of pork) IV 30, 57, 120. FYLETES (of Pork) IV 57, defined in a *nota*. FYLETTES IN GALYNTYNE IV 30, 120 (given in A recipe heading, IV 30, as OF GALYNTYNE), partly-roasted pork filets finished in a mixture of bread, blood, broth, and vinegar; the more elaborate version adds onions, herbs, wine, grease, and raisins, but omits blood. Cf. *CB* pp. 8, 82; *LCC* p. 31; *NBC* pp. 89-90.

fyn *v.*, *pa.p.* finished; as a technical term applied to beer, wine, and mead, cf. Boorde's *Dyetary* (EETS ES 10) p. 256, 'If the bere be wele served, and be fyned and not new'; also p. 257 *re* mead, and Simon's *Guide, sub* BEER, p. 681, 'filtered or fined before being drunk'. The meaning is not absolutely clear in relation to the *OED*'s definitions of 'fine'; perhaps 'clarify' (*v.*)/'clear' (*adj.*)? V 6, 8, etc. FYN MEADE & POYNAUNT V 10, spiced mead. Despite the initial directions, no recipe calling for cooked apples actually occurs in the vicinity of this one. The quantity of spices called for would work out to something like 2 oz. of pepper and 1/4 oz. cloves: this would not make a very spicy drink, considering the 34 gallons of other ingredients.—fyned in IV 196 is probably a scribal error for 'fryed' and/or 'founded': see found.

fynelich *adv.* extremely IV 200.

fyngerbroede *n.* the breadth of a finger III 19.

flamme *v.* baste: see *OED sub* FLAMB IV 157, 171.

FLAUMPEYNS IV 116, FLAMPOYNTES IV 192, Menus 3, 5, 6, 8; pastry filled with a pork filling and decorated with fried pieces of the same pastry, 'points', which indicates that the second recipe gives the etymology: OF *flaon, flan* 'tart' + 'poyntes'. A 'Flaumpoynt' recipe in MS Bodley CCC F 291 calls for pork costing 2 or 3*d.*, cheese 1*d.*, and 20 eggs. Since a whole pig (slaughtered) cost 2*s.* but pigs, like eggs, were smaller than today's, this works out to *c.*5 lbs. each pork and cheese. Cf. *CB* p. 53.

fle *v.* flay II 92, III 1, etc.; **flawe** *pa.p.* II 69; **fleyn/flayn** II 72, 74.

flen *v.* fly III 2.

florissh *v.* garnish, decorate IV 38, 61, etc.; **floriche** IV 129; **flour** IV 24; **floris** (?) I 55.

FLOWNYS IN LENTE II 86: the filling for these tarts is pieces of thick almond mixture in more almond milk, plus figs and dates. *Flaons* or *Flans* in *VT*, pp. 31, 108, etc., and *MP*, pp. 216–17, invariably consist of eel or other fish and seem to indicate open tarts as against covered ones, although this is nowhere stated. Cf. *CB* pp. 51, 56, 73; *LCC* p. 39.

fl(o)ures *n.* flowers I 11, 23, etc.; **flour of canel** is probably 'good quality' cinnamon, not 'ground to flour', since we are told to use it whole IV 22.

foile *n.* foil, leaf IV 51, 95, etc.; **foyles** *pl.* IV 50, 157, etc.; ~ *of dowh(3)* piece of thinly rolled pastry IV 51, 95, etc. *Foille de pastee bon sarrays*, first sentence of I 27, represents Ro's 'feuille de paste bon farois'—'leaf of pastry well filled'.

FONEL see FOUNET.

force *v.* (1) stuff (OF *farsir*); (2) often in sense of 'reinforce', 'strengthen', i.e. 'season' or 'sauce'; see also fassen (and cf. fars) III 3, IV 6, etc.; **fors** IV 178; **forsy** II 38; **enforce** III 22, 23; **yforced** *pa.p.* IV 42t, 45; **enforced** IV 45t; **yfarced** IV 167t.

FORMETE see FURMENTY.

fo(u)rnes/furneys *n.* stove V 11, 12, etc.

forse *n.* importance V 12.

fort see **vorte** and **powdour fort.**

for to *adv.* until II 33; **fort þat** IV 200.

found/funde *v.* melt, dissolve, mix; Fr *fondre* IV 96, 143; **yfoundred** *pa.p.* IV 63.

FOUNET (AB FOUNELL) IV 63, lamb or kid with poultry in egg-thickened almond-milk; evidently from OF *foun* 'young animal' (cf. 'fawn').

FREYSCH SAMOUN Menu 8, method of cooking unspecified, but cf. SAMOUN FRESCH ENDORED AND ROSTED.

FRENCHE IOWTES IV 75, boiled (dried, no doubt) white peas, strained, with herbs, onions, oil, and seasonings (cf. IOUTES). The dish resembles *MP*'s *Potage de pois vielz*, fish-day version, pp. 135-6.

FRESCH LAUMPREY III 24, directions for lamprey pastries; cf. *CB* pp. 51-2, 98-9, 100; *LCC* p. 38; *NBC* pp. 49-50; *VT* pp. 18-19, etc.

frissiaus *n.* strawberries (MS A1's *freseus, fraseus*) I 37. FRESEE II 47, FRESSE I 37, translating *Fresee* in MS A1; a meatless version of FRESEYES I 13, translating *Fryseye* in MS Ro; named for the fruit. Cf. *CB Strawberye*, p. 29.

fritur *n.* fritter, fried cake (sense often pl.) I 46t; **frutours** II 26; **freture** III 15. FRETOUR Menu 7, FRETOWRYS Menu 1, are probably apple or cheese fritters, the most popular varieties. FRYTOUR OF ERBES IV 156 is made from a batter flavoured with chopped herbs; cf. *VT* p. 42. FRYTOUR BLAUNCHED IV 153 is not what we would call a 'fritter' today but a filled pastry, fried, then baked in a syrup of wine and honey; possibly this is Menu 8's FRUTOUR BLAUNCHE. FRUTURS (1) II 19 is the most common of medieval English fried delicacies, apple fritters; FRYTOUR OF PASTERNAKES, OF SKIRWITTES, & OF APPLES IV 154 calls for root vegetables as alternatives (or supplements?) to apples. FRYTOUR OF MYLKE IV 155 and FRETOUR OF MYLK Menu 8 are the cheese type, made of fresh curds and egg—the recipe in MS Ashmole 1393 adds flour, probably correctly, and specifies a mixture thick enough to cut into pieces; it resembles a 'ravioli' recipe in *LdC* p. 39. For the apple type of fritter, cf. *CB* pp. 44-5, 73; *LCC* pp. 39-40; and for the cheese variety, *CB* pp. 43, 73-4 (*Longe Frutours*).

FROYS II 18, fried cake of minced meat (OF *fraise* < *frire* 'fry'); cf. *VT* pp. 10-11, 86, etc.; *CB* pp. 45, 86; *LCC* p. 50.

FRONCHEMOYLE (As FRAWNCHEMOYLE) II 15, pudding cooked in a sheep's maw; name from Fr *franchemule* 'the second stomach of a cow'. See *MP* pp. 129, 132n7; cf. *CB* p. 39, *LCC* pp. 36-7, *NBC* pp. 119-20.

frot *v.* rub II 58*, 76, 77.

FRUMENTE see FURMENTY.

frut *n.* fruit III 2, Menu 6; **froytes** *pl.* V 15.

FRUTURS (2) II 40 is not a fritter (cf. ~ (1) *sub* **fritur**) but a potage containing apple blossoms; possibly named for the fruit tree from which the blossoms are taken.

FUAUS I 38, translating a note in MS A1 appended to *Fresee* on how to make 'the same without strawberries'; apparently blackberries (A-N *bramaus*) are substituted. The title word may be based on *bramaus*, or on one of the words in the heading to the recipe, which appears in A1 as *Ici enseygne coment l'em ferra saunz fraseus*.

fugurre *n.* figure I 45.

fulþ *n.* filth; of fish, entrails I 43, **vulþe** I 1.

funde see found.

funges *n.* fungus, mushrooms IV 12. FUNGES IV 12, mushrooms and leeks in broth; while we have not found a French parallel, an almost identical recipe for 'fungi' occurs in the *LdC.*

fur, fuyre see fer.

FURMENTY II 1, FRUMENTE IV 1, a dish of boiled, hulled wheat, resembling a modern wheat porridge or pilaff; other recipes for this common dish here are FORMENTY ON A FICHSSDAY II 89, FURMENTE WITH PORPAYS IV 70, and FORMETE V 2. FURMYNTE IN VENESOUN appears on Menu 1, FRUMENTE WITH VENESOUN on Menu 3, and VENESOUN WITH FURMYNTE IN POTAGE on Menu 2. The metathesized spelling *frumente* appears in MS C and some later versions. Cf. *VT* pp. 15-16, 92, etc.; *MP* pp. 210-11; *CB* pp. 6-7, 17-18, 70, 105; *LCC* p. 7; *NBC* pp. 86-7, 100.

G

gad(e)re *v.* gather III 7, IV 87; **igedered** *pa.p.* I 35; **gaderyd** II 46.

galynga(le) *n.* galingale, a plant whose root constitutes a spice resembling ginger II 10, 40, etc. While English cooks may have made some use of *Cyperus longus*, the 'English galingale', Gerard reported that the kind 'commonly in shops called Galingale' was 'true galingale' of the type called *Galinga minor*, imported from China in his day; this is the type still available from speciality herb and spice suppliers.

galyntyne *n.* (1) jellied juices of meat or fish is the basic meaning (Fr *galantine, galatine*, Lat *galatina*) but since this was further thickened with bread crumbs and spiced, the term was transferred to the sauce IV 130t, 131t (?).——It is not clear that any of the recipes included here are of the basic type: GALANTINE, I 51, makes no specification, and note that III 24 FRESCH LAUMPREY is to be served cold but the 'galentyn' hot. This may or may not mean that the fish was kept in a jellied state until it was served, at which time the jellied sauce was heated up. (Cf. CBH's article ' "To boille the chiknes with the marybones": Hodge's Kitchen Revisited', in *Chaucerian Problems and Perspectives*, ed. E. Vasta and Z. P. Thundy (South Bend, 1979), pp. 149-63. Hodgkin also concluded that 'in galentyne', as against 'galyntyne sauce', meant 'in gelatine'.) **galentyne** (2) a spiced sauce thickened with breadcrumbs, usually containing galingale— probably as a result of false etymology; in some MS versions of IV 131 the two words are confused II 68, 69, etc. ~ (3) alternative name for the spice(s) alone or with breadcrumbs II 30, 31, etc. GALYNTYNE IV 142, sauce resembling the Fr *cameline*; cf. *MP*

p. 230, *VT* pp. 32-3, 109, etc.; for English 'Galyntyne sauce', cf. *CB* pp. 77-8, 108-9; *NBC* p. 77.

gar *v.* make, cause to V 13, 14.

garbage *n.* giblets V 25.

garette *n.* ham, hock (A-N *garette*, ModFr *jarret*) I 31.

garlec *n.* garlic IV 36, 78, etc.; *grene* ~ the green shoots, not the bulb.

GAUNCELI FOR GEES (AB CAWDEL ~) IV 146, sauce made from milk and flour seasoned with garlic and saffron; Fr *Jance à aulx, gance aillie* 'yellow garlic sauce': see *VT* p. 34, *MP* p. 234, and cf. *CB* pp. 77 ('sermstele'), 110; *LCC* p. 29.

gawdy grene *n.* + *adj.* a yellowish-green obtained from the plant weld (OF *gaude*) IV 115.—A recipe for paint of this colour in BL MS Harl. 2253 substitutes pennyroyal or iris, plus verdegris, to achieve this colour, but we may hope verdegris was not used to dye food.

gedere see **gadre**.

GEES IN HOCHEPOT II 22* and **GEES IN HOGGEPOT** IV 33 differ slightly in that the former is more-or-less braised while the latter is stewed. A recipe for *Hochepot de Volaille* in *MP*, p. 163, says this should be made with tough, lean geese, for the fat ones are roasted; the recipe in *VT*, pp. 9, 84, and *V(S)* 88, does not specify the fowl. The name apparently derives from OF *hochier, hogier* 'shake, stir': the pan would be shaken or stirred to keep the meat from sticking in a recipe calling for very little liquid such as II 22. *T-L* identifies this dish as containing turnips, which is not the case in any early recipe we have seen. Cf. also *CB* p. 18, *LCC* p. 32.

GELEE I 25, translating *Gelee* in MS Ro, fish, cooled, to jell in its own broth; other jellied fishes here are **GELE OF FYSSH** IV 104 and **GELE** on Menu 8, a fish-day menu. **GELY** II 56 and **GELE OF FLESSH** IV 105 are meat jellies; **METE GELEE** II 36 calls for either meat or fish, and the **GELE** of Menus 2 and 4 may be of either kind. Cf. *VT* 17-18, 94, etc.; *MP* 218-20; *CB* pp. 25, 26, etc.; *NBC* p. 42.

gelofre see **gilofre**.

genger see **gyngeuer**.

gentilich *adv.* gently, nobly I 55.

GENTIL ROST I 48, 'noble roast'. There is a blank left in the MS where the title should have been; it would probably have specified the food to be roasted. If 'goustard' is a form of the word 'gustard' listed in the *OED*, this may be roast bustard, but the recipe is unclear in other respects, too: it is called a 'rost', but directions call only for boiling and skinning whatever-it-is. The mixture of egg yolks, spices, and flour called for at the end would probably be used as a glaze in finishing the meat on a spit.

ges *v.* see **gon**.

gilofre/gelofre *n.* clove I 17, 48, etc.; *cloves of* ~ cloves (OF *girofle*); in V 13, clove pinks (flowers).

gyngeuer/gyngyuyr *n.* ginger II 5, 24, etc.; **genger** I 11. **GYNGERBRED** (1) V 18, confection resembling taffy or toffee candy, referred to as

gyngebred in I 21, 28; not to be confused with the cake-like variety, GINGERBREDE (2) V 19, made from breadcrumbs boiled in honey with spices: not the modern cake, but more like it than the confection. (Cf. *CB* p. 35.) GYNGEUER IV 143 is a sauce of vinegar, ginger, salt and bread: cf. *VT Jance de Gingembre*, p. 34; *CB* p. 77, 109; *LCC* p. 52; *NBC* p. 77.

GYNGGAUDY (A GYNGAWDRY) IV 97, dish based on fish livers and pouches, coloured green and named for the 'gaudy green' colour (cf. **gawdy grene**). The recipe is similar to a Fr *Brouet Vergay* [Gaudy Green] *d'Anguilles*; cf. *VT* pp. 20, 97; *MP* pp. 171-2; *CB* pp. 16, 94.

gleyre *n.* egg white IV 60, V 15.

gobet(t)es *n.* pieces II 60, III 1, etc.; **gobouns** I 19, 43, 50.

(i)goboned *v., pa.p.* cut into gobbets I 9.

gon *v.* go II 1, 2, etc.; **ges** *3 sg.* V 12.

goustard *n.* flavour? (from Fr *gout?*)—but cf. note on GENTIL ROST I 48.

gowrdes *n.* gourds IV 10.—The particular vegetable of this family used in the 14th century probably resembled a modern vegetable marrow or winter squash, to judge by the method of cooking. The name *courge* in *MP* suggests the vegetable as likely ancestor of the modern *courgette* (zucchini) squash. Gerard's idea of 'gourds' seems to be what we call by that name today, not an edible vegetable; while he also shows 'pompions' (pumpkins) and cucumbers, which were and are sometimes cooked, he has nothing which looks like a vegetable marrow or its close relations. However, some members of this family were used as vegetables in early Arabic cooking: see the *Baghdad Cookery Book*, pp. 38 ('gourd'), 206 ('cucumber', 'gourd'), and 207 ('pumpkin-shell').—GOURDES IN POTAGE IV 10, squash stewed in broth with onions, ground pork, and egg yolks. *MP* p. 148 gives a somewhat simpler recipe, but two in the *LdC* pp. 8-9 are much closer to this.

graue(y) *n.* sauce ('gravy') usually, in English recipes, based on almond milk II 79t, IV 28, etc.—The word is thought to be based on OF *graine* 'meat'—note that $u(v)/n$ are difficult to differentiate in most MSS and both *grane* and *grave* are printed in *VT* and *MP*—but this etymology is not really satisfactory. GRAUE ENFORSE II 79, the almond milk sauce usually found in English recipes, here 'enforced' with boiled egg yolks and cheese. Cf. CHYKENS IN ~ (*sub* checonys), CONNYNGES IN ~.

grece(e)/gres *n.* grease, fat I 33, 46, etc.

gre(u)dil *n.* griddle I 45, 55; **gredyrn/grydere** I 26, II 25, etc.

GREDOWSE see EGERDUSE.

greyns *n.* seeds I 57, 59, etc.; **graynys** II 27; **greyn** *sg. form but pl. in meaning* III 27; ~ *de parys*, spice seed of the genus *amomum Melequetta*, closely related to cardamom and sometimes called cardamom (Fr *graine de paradis*) III 10, 25, etc.; **greynes**, with no pomegranate or other type specified, means the same V 4, 5, etc.—Pichon, ed. of *MP*, though *graine* might also sometimes mean cloves.

greyþe(n)/graythe *v.* prepare (see *OED sub* GRAITH) I 47, 48, etc.

greke *adj.* Greek, used of a sweet type of wine which actually came from Italy and also spelled **creke, crete, cryk, qyk** (in variants) IV 65, 102, 103.

greles *adj.* cut or ground in small pieces; elsewhere OF *grele* is translated 'ygrounden' (cf. ModFr *grêle*) I 8, 22.

grete *adj.* large; ~ *mynced* chopped or minced coarsely IV 4; **gret vlehs** large meat, translating Fr *grosse char*, which *VT* makes clear generally meant boiled pork, beef, or mutton (see p. 3) I 7, 12, etc. GRETE FLESSHE appears on Menus 1 and 2. GRETE BIRDES ROSTYD Menu 1, roasted larger game birds. GRETE CROSTUDE Menu 1, a large open tart: for possible types, see **crustardes**. GRETE ELES Menu 6: method of cooking the eels unspecified but cf., e.g., ELYS IN BRUET. GRETE LUCES ISODEN Menu 8, boiled luce (fish). GRETE TARTES Menu 1, may have been similar to the crustards, but for other types see TART DE BRY etc. **gretnesse** *n.* size II 59.

greudil see **gredil**.

grewel *n.* oatmeal (or, sometimes, barley) porridge IV 5, 88t; **gruel** I 40. GREWEL FORCED IV 5, oatmeal (?) boiled in meat broth and mixed with ground pork; cf. *CB* pp. 6, 70; *LCC* pp. 20, 47; *NBC* p. 88. GREWEL OF ALMAUNDES IV 88, oatmeal with almond milk; cf. *MP* pp. 242-3, *V(S)* p. 95, *LCC* pp. 14-15, *NBC* p. 107.

gryce *n.* pig II 16n.

grydern see **gredil**.

grotys *n.* groats II 11.

GROUNDEN BENES see **benes**.

grout *n.* malt V 8.

gum araby *n.* + *adj.* gum arabic (see *OED sub* ARABIC) V 15.

GURNARD Menu 6, a saltwater fish; **gurnardes** *pl.* IV 118.

ȝelk *adj.*? *a* ~ *warm* lukewarm? V 6.

ȝelkes see **ȝolc**.

ȝeolue (J **ȝol**) *n.* Yule, the Christmas season (the dish is specified as suitable for Lent in MS A1) I 43.

ȝest *n.* yeast IV 154, 156.

ȝeue/ȝef give I 4, 56, etc.; **gyf** II 68, 69, V 12; **gyffes** *2 sg.* V 12.

ȝoelu/ȝolou *adj.* yellow I 3, 4, etc.

ȝolc *n.* yolk I 44; **ȝolkus** *pl.* I 53, 54, etc.; **ȝelkes** III 4, 6, etc.

H

habben *v.* have I 32; **han** I 48; **habbe** *3 sg.* I 11; **enabbe** *neg. 2/3 sg.* have/has not I 48.

HAKKE IFARSED Menu 8, stuffed hake? The context makes any gloss dubious, but this must be a fish-day dish.

hakken *v.* chop I 56; **hac/hak** *imp.* II 11, 12, etc.; **hakke** II 5*, 23, etc.; **(i)hakked** *pa.p.* I 47, II 10.

HALEKAYE I 57, a parti-coloured confection of almond milk and sweet ingredients; the name is probably descended from Arabic *halwā* (marzipan or 'Turkish Delight') or *halāwāl* 'sweet dish': cf. Rodinson, pp. 103 and 139.

halue *adj.* half I 34, 57.

ham see **hi.**

HARYS IN CIUEE II 8: hare in onion sauce, a dish very close to the Fr recipes for *Civés de liévres, VT* p. 10, *MP* p. 169; cf. *CB* p. 18, *LCC* p. 21, *NBC* p. 113. **HARES IN PAPDELE (A PADELL, C PAPADE)** IV 26, hares stewed in a sauce of broth with wafers or losyns, q.v. The name may have been associated with 'pap', but the titles of the same recipe in *LCC, Harus in Perdoylyse,* p. 22, and *NBC, Haires in pardelos,* pp. 113–14 (TC *perdolous*) suggest, rather, a derivation from Fr *perdu*: 'smothered hare', perhaps. **HARIS IN TALBOTAYS** II 9, **HARES IN TALBOTES** IV 25: recipes characterized by the use of blood in the cooking broth; the title of the parallel recipe in *LCC, Hares in abrotet,* p. 21, TC *albrotetus,* is glossed by the editor as 'in a browet'; cf. also *NBC* p. 113, *Haires in albroturs.*

HASTLETES OF FRUYT IV 195, **HASTELESTES OF FRUT** Menu 8: 'haslet'—meaning, basically, a small piece of meat, generally organ meat, spit-roasted—counterfeited of a mixture of dried fruits and almond paste (OF *hastelet*). **HASTELETTES** Menu 9 are probably of the same type. Cf. *LCC* pp. 37–8, *NBC* p. 120.

hatte *n.* apparently the froth ('hat') on the top of boiling liquid, but note that in some MSS it is replaced by the pronoun *hit* IV 60.

hatte *v.* is called I 33, 34, etc.

HAUCEGEME I 6, translating MS Ro's *Haucegeme*: minced veal in a sauce coloured red.

HAUCELEAMYE I 31, translating MS Ro's *Hauseleamye* (with two unfortunate mistakes: see notes); chicken in a green sauce. The first element of the name is OF *houssie*, which *MP* tells us means, in culinary terms, garnished with parsley: see *Brouet houssie,* pp. 163–4, and cf. *VT* p. 151. Cf. **CHYKENS IN HOCCHEE**, a version of the same dish; another appears in *HV* as *Puleus in Aoresta* 'pullet in verjuice'.

heam see **hi.**

hed(e) *n.* head I 27, IV 56; **heuyd** II 28. **HEDE OF THE BORE** see **BORYS HEDES.**

heyryn see **ey.**

HEYROUN III 13, directions for dressing a heron; more elaborate than those of II 3 and IV 151, **CRANYS & HERONS. HEROUNS** appear on Menu 3 and Menus 1 and 2 list **HERONES ROSTYD.**

held(e)/hyld *v.* pour II 91, III 17, etc.; **yholode** *pa.p.* covered IV 133n.

helde *v.* hold, keep IV 197.

helys see **eles.**

hem see **hi.**

hennyn/hennys *n.* hens II 5, 11, etc. **HENNYS IN BRUET** II 7, chicken in cumin sauce; cf. *MP* pp. 161–2, *Comminée de Poulaille; VT* pp. 5–6, 81; *CB* pp. 18–19; *LCC* p. 22; *NBC* p. 114.

heppe *n.* rosehip III 37; **heppes** *pl.* III 37, IV 86; **hympes** IV 86n.
HEPPEE III 37, a pottage of rosehips, with rose petals as garnish;
the title PEPERYNGE in MSS S1 and C is a corrupted form.

her see hi.

herdeles *n.* hurdles II 57.

(i)here *v.* hear I 54.

hereseve/hersyue *n.* hair (i.e., fine) sieve II 11n, 61, V3.

HERONES, HEROUNS see HEYROUN.

HERT ROWTE (Pegge) see HIRCHONES.

hertes *n.* hart's V 18.

herþe see erthe.

hese *poss. adj.* his, its III 35.

hete *n.* heat V 7, 12.

heten *v.* heat I 63; **hete** *imp.* V 6; **hett** *pa.p.* III 5.

heuyd see hed.

he(o)wen *v.* cut up I 61, 63; **hewe(n)** *imp.* II 22, 42, etc.; **heuw** I 56,
62; **hewe** *pa.p.* II 9; **tohewen** I 51.

hi *pron.* they II 27; **he(o)m** *dat. acc.* them I 42, II 2, etc.; **heam** I 42;
am I 31, 42, etc.; **ham** II 24n; **hom** V 25; **her** *poss.* their IV 125,
126; **hare** IV 124.

Hic incipiunt diuersa seruicia tam de carnibus quam de pissibus (heading
of II): 'Here begins (a work on) various services, of meats as well as
fish.'

hye *adj.* high V 12; **hyar** *comp.* V 12; *of ~ gres* very fat Menus 1 and 2.

hier *n.* hair I 27.

hilde *v.* flay, remove skin IV 112, 122.

hym *pron.* him (it) *or* them IV 95: the context does not make this clear.

hympes see heppe.

HIRCHONES (A HERT ROWCE / TC HERT ROWS / Pegge HERT
ROWTE; J VRCHONS) IV 184, YRCHONS Menu 7: 'urchins'
(hedgehogs, OF *herichon*), sausages shaped like hedgehogs, with
pastry quills. Cf. *VT* p. 128, *MP* p. 269, *CB* p. 38.

hit *pron.* it I 1, 4, etc.

HOCCHEE see CHYKENS IN ~.

HOGGEPOT, HOCHEPOT see GEES IN ~;
HOISTREYE see OYSTERS IN CYUEE.

hoke *n.* hook V 14.

hokke *n.?* plant?—see *OED sub* HOCK, but there is no way of telling
whether the reading here is correct I 47.

ho(o)l(e) *adj.* whole I 56, II 69, etc.

hold(e) *adj.* old IV 183, 205.

(i)holden *v., pa.p.* held back, withheld I 19.

hole *n.* hull I 63; **holys** *pl.* II 1, 2, IV 1; **hulkes** IV 3.

holye *v.* hull V 2.

holke *v.* hollow IV 167; *pa.p.* with a hole (like an upside-down funnel),
perforated IV 181; **yholed** IV 39.

hom *n.* home II 57; see also hi.

hong(e) *v.* hang II 49, IV 68; **yhonged** *pa.p.* I 41.

HONY, TO CLAREFY IV 60n, a note on the clarification of honey appended to recipe for PAYNFOUNDEN in some MSS of IV.

HONY DOUSE II 80, a parti-coloured rice and almond milk pottage, sweetened with sugar and not, as the title seems to imply, with honey; it greatly resembles HALEKAYE and AMYDOUN, other parti-coloured pottages, and the name is probably derived from the latter, misunderstood because the basic 'amidon' thickening has dropped out (cf. also DOUCE IAME). The coloured sugar called for is probably rosewater-sugar candy, coloured pink or red: see SUGER PLATE, V 13.

hool see hol.

hoot *adj.* hot III 24, IV 24, V 9.

hostrees/hoystres *n.* oysters I 62, 63.

houel *n.* part of the still apparatus (cf. *MED sub* HOVEL (d)) V 7.

houghys *n.* hocks V 24.

hout *adv.* out I 41.

hulkes see hole.

hwareuore *conj.* wherefore I 47.

hwaryn *adj.* wherein I 1.

hwyte(e) *v.* blanch, peel I 33*, 56; ihwyted *pa.p.* I 33; qwyte I 3, 57.

hwuch *pron.* which I 32.

I/Y

iame see DOUCE IAME.

yevyn *adv.* evenly IV 1 n: 'not to moche' is a gloss on this.

yfere see fere.

ilk(e) *adj.* each, every V 12, 14.

YMAGES IN SUGER V 15, directions for molding candy shapes.

ymbre day *n. phrase* ember day, one of the fast days which mark the four seasons of the Christian year IV 169, 173.—Dairy goods were permitted on fast days out of Lent at this time.

Incipit liber utilis conquinario, heading of III: 'Here begins a book useful for cookery.'

inde *adj.* indigo, blue colouring I 7; ~ *wawdeas* 'indebaudias' (see *OED sub* INDE) V 15.

indorretes see endore.

inouȝ *adj.* enough V 6, 10; ynoh I 41; ynow II 49, III 2, 12.

inwyt *n.* mind, wisdom I 54.

yoyse see ius.

ioutes *n.* pot-herbs or pottage of pot-herbs I 47, IV 8t, etc. IOUTE DORE I 47, 'golden herbs', boiled greens seasoned with saffron, grease, and pepper. IOWTES OF (P, WITH) ALMAUND MYLKE IV 89, chopped greens and herbs in almond milk. The French collections have a similar recipe (*Porée de Cresson*) but specify only cress; a closer recipe is *Erbe Minute* in *LdC*, p. 84; cf. *VT* pp. 32, 108; *MP* pp. 140-1. IOWTES OF FLESSH IV 8, chopped greens and herbs in broth—a variant of the Fr *Porée de Cresson* is similar to this, as are other recipes for *porée* in *MP*. Cf. also *LCC* pp. 47-8.

YPOCRAS IV 199 and V 5: the recipes give only the spicing to be used to make this sweet, spiced wine; few specify the type of wine to be used, but Cogan's recipe calls for either white or red and a medieval Spanish one calls for a mixture of both. *MP*, p. 273, says to 'melt' the sugar in the wine over the fire, mix in spices, then strain until it is clear red. For similar directions, cf. Russell, pp. 125-8.

yrchons see HIRCHONES.

irne *n.* iron; *roost* ~ gridiron IV 110.

yrth see erthe.

ysop(e) *n.* hyssop (herb) II 54, III 19, etc.

issu *n.* entrails III 12.

ius *n.* juice I 39, II 32, etc.; yoyse IV 182n.

IUSSEL II 21, IUSSHELL IV 44, basically a boiled mixture of eggs and broth, but breadcrumbs appear in most recipes; probably so-called from the 'juice' in the sense of broth. No extant French recipe is so titled, but there is a similar untitled recipe in *VT* p. 42, and one called *Iusculum* in *HV*. IUSSHELL ENFORCED IV 45 embellishes the dish with the same milk and egg sauce recommended for CHARLET YFORCED, q.v. Cf. *CB* p. 87, *LCC* p. 11, *NBC* pp. 26-7, 87, 104-5.

K

kake *n.* cake I 34, 45.

kanel see canel.

KAUDEL FERRE see CAWDEL FERRY.

kechen *n.* kitchen III 13.

keyntlich see queyntliche.

kele see cole.

kendlich *adv.* properly, by nature III 24, V 18.

keneschype *n.* sharpness I 10.

kerf/kerue *v.* carve, cut II 29, 30, etc.; koruen *pa.p.* III 30.

kernelis *n.* kernels, seeds II 83; kyrnels IV 149.

kyt/ket *v.* cut II 19, 55, etc.

KOKETRIS see COKAGRYS.

krase *v.* break V 16.

L

lay see lye.

layour see lyour.

LAMPRAY FRESCH IN GALENTYNE II 68, **LAUMPREYS (P FRESH LAMPREY) IN GALYNTYNE** IV 130, **GALANTINE** I 51: lampreys, boiled or roasted, served in a spicy sauce, probably mostly to be served cold (jelled) as is clearly indicated in the *VT* recipe (pp. 19, 96, etc.) which not only directs us to stir it *jusque ad ce qu'il soit refroidié*, but contrasts this recipe with *Lamproie fresche à la saulce chaude*: but the two types may well have been confused in England. Cf. also *MP*'s *Lamproie Boulie*, p. 193; *CB* p. 32; *LCC* p. 25; *NBC* p. 117. **LAMPREYS IN BRUET** II 70, broiled lamprey in a sauce, base unspecified here but cf. *Lamproie fresche à la saulce chaude*, *VT* pp. 18-19, 95-6, etc.; cf. also *CB* p. 99, *Sauce pour lamprey*.

LAMPREYS IROSTED Menu 8, roast lamprey. See also FRESCH
  LAUMPREY (a pastry) and SALT LOMPREY IN GALENTYNE.
la(u)mprouns *n.* small river lamprey (OF *lamproions*) IV 131, 163.
  LAMPROUNS Menu 6, method of cooking unspecified. LAUM-
  PROUNS IN GALYNTYNE IV 131, a rather simpler and more basic
  recipe than LAUMPREYS IN GALYNTYNE. See also SEUE OF ~.
langdebef *n.* a plant of the bugloss family, used as a salad, vegetable, or
  potherb IV 8.
LANGETTES Menu 3, probably either small tongues or something
  shaped like such, as the modern French cakes called *langue du chat.*
lardes *v., pa.p.* (?) larded (or 'lard them'?) I 55.
larduns/lardons *n.* lardons, pieces of fat (cf. *OED s.v.*) I 55, II 3, 43.
LARKYS ROSTYD Menus 1, 2: roast larks. LAUEROK Menu 3,
  LAUEROKYS Menus 5, 7, 9 are probably all roasted.
lasse *adj.* less V 7.
lat *v.* let II 1, 14, etc.; latyn *pa.p.* II 68.
launprey *n.* lamprey III 24; lomprey II 70. Cf. LAMPRAY....
leche *n.* slice IV 66t; leches *pl.* II 15, V 24; lesys II 71. Cf. leshe. LECHE
  FRYS (A LESSHES FRYED) IN LENTOUN IV 166 are, despite
  the title, neither sliced nor fried, but are very close in ingredients
  to *MP*'s *Rissolles* for Lent, p. 225; chopped fruits, spiced, with almond milk and oil, as a tart filling. LECHEFRES Menus 4 and 8
  may be of this type, as are certainly LECHEFRES OF FRUT Menu
  6, but cf. LECHE FRYS OF FISCHE DAYE (CJP OF CHESE),
  IV 165: tarts of cheese, butter, and egg yolk baked in a pastry shell,
  again neither sliced nor fried. Cf. *CB* p. 75, *NBC* p. 59. An ultimate
  ancestor may be represented in *LSS* pp. 174-5, *Lesques de Fformatge
  gras*, slices of cheese in a yeast dough, fried. LECHE LUMBARD
  IV 66, a spiced boiled pudding of pork, dried fruits, and eggs, in a
  sauce of wine and almond milk; cf. *CB* pp. 35, 92-3; *NBC* p. 34.
led *v.* take II 57.
(y)leesshed see lesh.
lef *n.* leaf or petal I 36; leues *pl.* I 12, 24, etc.—I 24 translates a recipe
  in MS Ro, which calls for 'leaves' of pastry emplanted, not strewn.
lef *v.* leave II 57.
left *v.* lift III 5.
ley *v.* lay II 68, 69, etc.; see also lye.
leynþe *n.* length I 45.
leyue *n.* layer IV 84.
leke *prep.* like V 12, 16; lyche IV 158.
lekys *n.* leeks IV 2, 6, 82.
lemes *n.* limbs, legs III 20.
lenton *n.* Lent IV 166t; leynt(e)en I 34, 45, 46.
les(e) *v.* rinse II 14, 66, 67.
lesh(e) *v.* slice IV 66, 68; lese V 24; yleesshed *pa.p.* IV 20.
LETE LARDES IV 69, LETELORYE IV 83, MYLK ROST II 25: milk
  and egg custard, enriched with lard, chilled to be sliced; Fr *lait lardé*;
  see *VT* pp. 123-4, *MP* pp. 224-5. Ar's title for IV 69, *Leche Lardys,*

demonstrates the ease with which etymologically correct names became confused. Cf. *CB* pp. 17, 35–6, 85–6, 92; *LCC* p. 13; *NBC*
pp. 87–8, 106.

let(u)ys *n.* lettuce IV 8n, 78n.

leues see lef.

leuyþ *v.* remains II 25, III 5.

lewe *adj.* lukewarm II 69*, IV 101n; l(e)uk III 5, 28.

lyche see leke.

lye(n) *v.* mix I 35, 51, etc.; ley *imp.* II 6; (a)lay/(a)lye I 35, IV 33, etc.;
alyth II 45; (i)lied *pa.p.* I 18, II 62, III 21; deliet *imp.* make it mixed
I 61.

lyes *n.* lees, dregs V 7; remains of the embers IV 73n.

lyf hony *adj.* + *n.* raw honey, 'live' in the sense of 'in its native state'
(see recipes for MEDE and FYN MEADE) III 3, V 8, etc.

lynger *adj.* longer IV 197.

l(a)your *n.* thickening IV 30, 33, etc.; laye III 24; lyure I 23.

ly(u)re *n.* flesh I 44, II 5, etc.; see also lyour.

loches *n.* loaches, small freshwater fish IV 163.

LOYNE OF THE PORK IV 56, defined in a *nota.*

LONGE DE BUF II 43, beef tongue; the recipe corresponds to *MP*'s
Langue de beuf vieil, p. 177, except that the French version is not
'gilded'. *NBC*'s *Longe de bef*, p. 30, is a different dish (stuffed tongue
slices).

LONGE FRETURYS Menu 2; for recipe see *CB* pp. 43, 73–4, and cf. fritur.

longe peper *adj.* + *n.* variety of pepper considered superior to black pepper V 4, 5, etc.

LOPINS IV 74, lupins, lupines, as a pulse vegetable; Gerard reports that
they were boiled to remove bitterness, seasoned with fat, and eaten
with 'pickle'; Markham, who apparently thought them identical with
lentils, considered them fit only for animal fodder. In Roman times
they seem to have been used for human sustenance on occasion, but
primarily as fodder, fertilizer, and for medical purposes. *HV* includes
two lupine recipes, one of which advises cooking the stalks in the
same way as asparagus.

lopister/lopuster *n.* lobster II 66, 75. LOPISTER II 75, lobster roasted
in the shell.

lorere *n./adj.* laurel, bay II 56.

loruȝe see CORNUDE ~.

los(e)yns/losenges *n.* sweet confection, likely to be the sugar-candy
'lozenge' familiar today I 8; otherwise more often noodles, as modern
lasagna IV 26, 50, etc. LOSYNS IV 50, noodles in broth with cheese;
a contemporary Italian recipe in *LdC* is virtually identical. Cf. *CB*
Lesynges de Chare, pp. 44, 82 (with meat filling, to be fried).
LOSEYNS IN FYSSH DAY IV 132, noodles in almond milk sauce;
cf. *NBC* pp. 80–1.

luk see lewe.

LUMBARD MUSTARD IV 150, ground mustard seed mixed with honey,
wine, and vinegar; mentioned in IV 103.

lute(l) *adj.* little I 31, 36, etc.

luz *n.* luce, a fish I 32. See also GRETE LUCES ISODEN.

M

mageran *n.* marjoram (herb) IV 144n.

maken *v.* make, cause to be I 54, 55; mak(es) *imp.* I 24, 35, etc.; makyd/makyþ *pa.p.* II 69, 86; (y)mad I 29, 45, V 18; *make bringen* is one of several phrases in I 55 we cannot explain: it should probably be directions for chilling lard until it is hard enough to cut into pieces for larding.

MAKEREL IN SAWSE IV 109, mackerel poached in wine and verjuice with mint and other herbs; the broth used as a sauce. Cf. *NBC* p. 75.

MAKEROUNS (A MACROWS) IV 95, macaroni, but note that it was made in flat noodles, not tubular forms. One of the menus in *MP*, p. 101, may include noodles as *nieulles*, but Pichon though this *merles* 'blackbirds'.——On the history of pasta, see Charles Perry in *PPC* 9 and 10.

MAKKE IV 76, cooked beans, finely ground, mixed with wine and garnished with fried onions.

MALACHES IV 159, swine's blood, diced lard, flour, salt, and meal (oatmeal?) mixed and baked in a pie shell; this version, presumably the basic type, does not occur in MSS A and B. MALACHES (AB MYLATES) OF PORK IV 162, MULACHES OF POORK Menu 9, are filled with pork, eggs, grated cheese, and pine nuts. MALACHES (AB MYLATES) WHYTE IV 160 has a simple egg filling which is not actually white, since saffron is demanded.

ma(u)lard *n.* mallard, a type of wild duck IV 145; malardis *pl.* III 15. MALARD Menus 5, 9: no doubt roast mallards. MALLARD IN CYUEY II 52, mallards stewed with onions; cf. *CB* p. 14.

male marow *adj.* (or *n.*) + *n.* marrow IV 203.——Hodgkin explained this passage as 'take the marrow of an ox; when extracted from the marrow bone it comes out in solid form, there being a thin skin containing the marrow itself; this skin is to be removed, leaving the pared marrow whole; this is then to be cut up into small pieces . . .' (p. 95). However, *male* appears to be an A-N spelling for *moele* 'marrow' in one MS we have seen (Bodley Auct. F 31, f. 67ᵃ) and the phrase may be simply redundant.

manerlich(e) *adv.* in a mannerly fashion III 2, 8, etc.

mare see SOUPE ~.

Mars *n.* March (Fr) I 31.

MAUMENEE I 7, translating *Maumenee* in MS Ro; MAUMENE II 30; MAWMENE III 25; MAWMENEE IV 22; MAWMENNY IV 202; MAMMANE Menu 5: a dish of meat, usually minced poultry, in a spiced sauce of wine and/or almond milk——usually wine and ground almonds. Austin (p. 136) suggests a derivation from Fr. *malmener*, 'the meat being teased small'; however, the name is very similar to Arabic *ma'muniya*, a sweet dish usually including chicken: see Rodinson, p. 139. The recipe for *Malmonia* in *DV* follows that for

Bramagiere (i.e., BLANK MAUNGER) and is differentiated from it by directions that it is to be coloured yellow with saffron and lemon or orange juice; the colour of the English version varies, being blue ('ynde') in I 7, yellow in II 30 and IV 202, and presumably black or brown in III 25, which calls for blood as a colouring. Cf. *CB* pp. 22, 88-9; *LCC* p. 26; *NBC* p. 118.

maunger see BLANK MAUNGER.

mawe *n.* stomach, i.e. stomach membrane used as a sausage-case IV 184.

me see mon (for use in I 38 etc.).

meddlen *v.* mix I 51, 55; **medel/meddle** *imp.* I 49, 54, etc.; **ymedled** *pa.p.* I 11.

MEDE V 9, mead; see also FYN MEADE.

mederyiu *n.* midriff—diaphragm? III 6.

meischid *v.* mashed V 8.

mel *v.* melt or stick together V 12; **(i)melte** *pa.p.* melted IV 95.

mele *n.* meal II 49, V 16, etc.

meluel *n.* cod III 26.

menden *v.* correct, improve I 51.

meng(e) *v.* mix, blend I 49, II 32, etc.; **myng** II 30, IV 69.

merlyng *n.* whiting (fish) III 26. MERLYNG YFRYED Menu 6, fried whiting.

mes *n.* dish, food I 48, 49, etc. MES OF CHYSEBERIEN I 54, 'a dish of cherries', with meat and eggs, which bears only slight resemblance to such other cherry dishes as SCIRRESEZ and CHIRESEYE.

mes(se) *v.* serve, generally in the sense of placing in dishes to serve one to four diners (the number assigned to a 'mess' varied according to ranks, local custom, etc.) II 1, 2, etc.

imeset see myce.

mete(e) *n.* food, not necessarily meat I 29, 32, etc. METE GELEE see GELEE. METE OF CYPREE see VIAUNDE DE CYPRE. METE TO MUCHE ISALT I 40, translating *Kaunt un viaunde est trop salé*, MS A1; AMENDEMENT FOR METE þAT YS TO SALT II 49: neither is the same recipe as that which appears in *VT* p. 29, *MP* p. 262. Cf. *CB* p. 112. METE VERNIS III 10, pottage of ground white meat made 'vernis' (green, apparently) with an extract of vine leaves and shoots. If *vernis* should be read as *vervis*, it is possible that the herb vervain is intended; the creeping variety might be considered a vine.

myce/myse *v.* mince (OF) II 8, 15, etc.; **(a)myced** *pa.p.* II 44*, III 1, etc.; **imeset** IV 54n.

myche(ll) *adj.* much II 49, IV 200, V 14; **moche** II 57; **muchel** I 47, 51, V 3.

myd(d)es *n.* middle IV 183, V 19.

mie *n.* crumb(s) I 52.

(y)myed *v.* crumbled II 35, 78, etc.; in I 48, 51, contexts seem to demand 'mixed'; cf. also myce.

myȝt/miht *v.* may, can I 44, 57, etc.

MYLATES see MALACHES.

mylberyes see mulbery.

(a) **myle wey** *n. phrase* the time it takes to walk a mile III 7.

MYLK ROST see **LETE LARDES.**

mylne *n.* mill IV 3n.

MYNCELEEK V 22, translating MS A1's *Myncebek*; NYSEBEK IV 181; NYRSEBEK Menu 6: a simple fritter containing yeast or sourdough. The inexplicable name may be of Arabic origin (sourdough —not to mention rotted bread—figures fairly frequently in early Arabic recipes). *Nese Bekys* in MS Harl. 279 (*CB* pp. 45–6) is an elaborate unleavened version, with a filling of figs and fish.

mynen *v.* mince? (cf. **myce**) I 53.

myng see **meng.**

mysceliche *adj.* mixed, beaten? (possibly derived from OF *meslée*, but cf. **myce**) I 48.

moche see **myche.**

mo(y)ld(e) *n.* mould V 15; **moolde** IV 185; **moldys** *pl.* V 15.

mole see **BLAWMANGER** ~ *sub* **blanc**; cf. **amole** *sub* **pomys.**

molour *n.* hand-mill (from Fr *moulin*?) I 48.

mon *pron.* one, the indefinite 'they' I 51; **me** I 38, 43, 63.

MONCHELET see **MOUNCHELET.**

moni(e) *adj./pron.* many I 17, 45, 47.

monnes *n.* man's I 27.

MORRE, MORREY see **MURREE.**

MORTRELLUS II 5, a boiled dish of finely ground food in broth etc., named for the morter used in preparation: usually of meat or fish, but not, apparently, always: cf. DOUBLE MORTREUS. MORTREWS IV 46 is the same version as II 5; for other types, see MORTREWS BLANK IV 47; MORTREUX OF FISCH III 26; MORTREWS OF FYSSH IV 128; MORTREUX OF LUNGES III 8; and (probably) MORTRELLUS BLANC*, an untitled recipe erroneously appended to II 47 which strongly resembles IV 47. This common medieval dish appears as *Morterol* in the *LSS*, whose ed. claims a Catalan or Provençal origin for this dish (p. 133).

mor(o)we *n.* (next) morning II 33, III 24, etc.

mose see **CHICONES IN** ~. *Sub* **checonys.**

mossels *n.* morsels I 42, 44.

mosserouns/musseruns *n.* mushrooms I 53. MOSSEROUNS FLORYS I 55: 'mushrooms garnished' or 'as a garnish'; this recipe is far from clear, but it is for a type of grilled mushrooms, gilded with egg yolk.

MOUNCHELET (A MONCHELET) IV 18, a stew of veal or mutton with herbs, onions, etc., thickened with egg and verjuice; name may be derived from a spelling of *mouton*, sheep or mutton.

mow *v.* may V 15.

MULACHES see **MALACHES.**

mulbery *n.* mulberry II 37; **mulburus** *pl.* II 37; **mylberyes** IV 102;—generally used as a colouring.

MULE I 63, probably Fr *moules* 'mussels' although none are specified in the recipe (cf. **potten**). No other shellfish recipe we have seen calls for chestnuts, but that some shellfish or other is in question is indicated by the reference to the preceding recipe.

MURREE I 32, translating *Morree* in MS Ro; MURREY II 37; MORREY II 85; MORREE IV 40; MORRE, Menu 7: the dish in II is a preparation of mulberries, which give it its name (see *OED sub* MURREY), but the others are sauces coloured to look like mulberry sauce, with varying meat, fish, or fruit ingredients. Cf. *CB*, pp. 19, 28.

muskels/muskles *n.* mussels IV 125, 127. MUSKLES IN BREWET IV 125, mussels in broth with bread thickening, vinegar, and onions; cf. *MP Civé de moules* p. 277; *VT* p. 108; *CB* pp. 24, 90; *NBC* p. 78. See also MULE, CAWDEL OF ~.

musseruns see mosserouns.

N

na(u)ȝt see noȝt.

nast *v.* have not I 59, 62.

neowe *adj.* fresh I 27.

nesche *adj.* raw (or soft) I 54.

NEW LOMBARD Menu 2, possibly a version of LECHE LUMBARD q.v., or *Crustard Lumbard*, for which see *CB* pp. 51, 74.

NEW NOUMBLES OF DEER IV 55, venison organ meat (cf. noumbles), presumably stewed.

nimen *v.* take I 48, 52; nim *imp.* I 31, 33, etc.

NYSEBEK, NYRSEBEKE see MYNCELEEK.

noed *n.* need I 56.

noȝt/noght *adv.* not II 42, 49, etc.; na(u)ȝt II 37, IV 1.

noynte *v.* anoint V 15.

noyre *adj.* black IV 141t, 145t.

nombles see noumbles.

(i)noriced *v.* ripe I 44.

nost *n.* oast, kiln IV 3.

notemugges *n.* nutmegs V 4, 5, etc.

notis *n.* nuts II 89.

nou *adv.* now I 47, 52, etc.; now that I 55 (?).

noumbles *n.* organ meat ('umbles': heart, liver, kidneys; OF *nombles*) IV 13, 15, etc.; nownbols II 12n. NOMBLES II 12, NOUMBLES IV 15, stew of organ meat; NOUMBLES IN LENT IV 117 is a fast-day version made of fish blood etc.

nouþer *adj.* neither IV 69.

NUROLES (J RUROLES) FARSEYS I 53: while the recipe has several difficulties, it seems to be a boiled dumpling made of minced capon and egg yolk.

O

o *prep.* out of V 7.

obleys *n.* wafers, thin cakes of pastry (Fr *oublie*) IV 26.

of *prep.* off III 5, V 13.

offall *n.* parts of the meat carcass generally discarded IV 61, 147; since the former is to be coloured with saffron, the recipe is probably for flesh meat, not organ meats—which could be described as offal; but the latter is a 'chawdon', which invariably calls for organ meat, and 'offal' must include such parts as feet and neck as well as giblets since there are bones to be removed.

oftor *adv.* more often II 37.

oy(n)gnons *n.* onions I 15, 42, etc.

OYSTERS IN CYUEE IV 126, oysters in onion sauce; HOISTREYE I 62 is the same but does not preserve the full Fr title. Cf. *MP* pp. 174, 277; *VT* pp. 22, 98, etc.; *CB* pp. 100-1. OYSTERS IN GRAUEY IV 124, OYSTRES IN GRAUE Menu 6, oysters simmered in wine and their own liquor; broth is thickened with almonds and rice flour. Cf. *CB* pp. 13, 100. OYSTRYN IN BRUET II 73, oysters in broth, may be a version of the French *Comminée* with cumin omitted; cf. *CB* p. 23, *LCC* pp. 53-4.

olde *adj.* old II 42; perhaps an error for hole 'whole'; cf. **hold**.

oneliche *adv.* ? into single (small?) pieces? I 55.

onys *adv.* once II 37, III 18, 29.

onoward *adv.* above, on top (of a prepared dish) IV 26.

ooþerdele *n.* the rest IV 178.

or *adv.* before V 1.

orage *n.* orach, a leafy plant; Gerard reported it was generally eaten boiled IV 8.

oþe *prep.* in the I 27, 45.

oþer/oþur *conj.* or I 13, 37, etc.

otyn *adj.* oaten II 11.

ouerstepid *v.* well cooked (or overcooked?) IV 112.

ouwher *adv.* anywhere I 47.

P

payn *n.* bread IV 68t, 204. PAYN FOUNDEW IV 60, fried and 'drowned' bread (cf. **found**) in a syrup of wine, raisins, honey, sugar, and spices; cf. *CB* pp. 42, 83, and *NBC* p. 46. PAYN PUFF IV 204, PAYN PUFE Menu 2, a confection resembling PETY PERUANT (q.v.) but richer. Hodgkin suggested that 'payn' here is a corruption of 'pan' and that this should be understood as a light fritter made in a pan, but a recipe for the dish in MS Ashmole 1393 suggests, rather, that one makes a 'loaf' of pastry—for which the ingredients are cream, flour, egg yolks, and sugar—wrapped around the rich filling; the loaf is baked and would be something like a modern strudel. It would be 'bread', then, in a playful sense, because formed into a loaf. PAYN RAGOUN IV 68, a confection of sugar, honey, and nuts, sliced so that it presumably resembles bread slices; cf. *CB* p. 112; a version appears in *HV*.

payn(d)emayn *n.* best quality white bread IV 43, 61, etc.; *flour of* ~ best white flour IV 43.—Usually thought to derive from *panis dominis* 'lord's bread', but some medieval sources suggest that the best quality flour was called 'mayne' and that thus the name was understood as 'bread made of mayne flour'. Another bread of similar quality was *manchet*: perhaps *mayne* + *cheat* 'loaf'.

papdele, padell see HARES IN ~.

par *v.* pare I 56, II 19; **parade** *pa.p.* IV 203; *hole* ~ removed from the bone in one piece.

parchemin *n.* parchment I 34.

parys see **greyns**.

passen *v.* pass, sift, I 50; in I 55, possibly an incorrect or otherwise unrecorded form of 'pierce'; if a form of 'surpass', the meaning would have to be 'make clean'.

pa(a)st *n.* pastry or dough I 34, II 88, etc.

pasternak *n.* root (vegetable) IV 103; **pasternakes** *pl.* IV 154.—Gerard notes that the botanical name of both parsnips and carrots is *pastinaca.*

paume *n.* palm (of the hand) I 45.

(y)paunced *v.*, *pa.p.* decorated IV 63n.

paunches *n.* stomachs IV 117, 118.

pece *n.* piece IV 198; **pese** V 14; **pecys** *pl.* IV 10, 198t; **peses** V 12.

peeres see **per**.

PEGONES ROSTYD Menu 2, roast pigeons. PEIOUNS YSTEWED IV 49, pigeons stuffed with garlic and herbs, stewed in spiced broth with grease and verjuice; cf. *LCC* p. 14, *NBC* p. 107.

peyre *n.* pair (of) V 14.

peys *n.* pea V 12; **pise** *pl.* II 2t; **pisyn/pesoun** II 2, IV 71, etc. PISE OF ALMAYNE II 2, PESOUN OF ALMAYNE IV 72: peas 'German style' (boiled, strained, with almond milk and rice flour); cf. *CB* p. 114.

peyuere *n.* pepper I 39, 51. PEYUERE EGRESSE I 39, translates *Pevre gresse* in MS A1, 'sour pepper' sauce; an almost identical sauce is *MP*'s *Poivre aigret*, p. 232; cf. *VT* p. 33n7 and *V(S)* p. 99.

PEKOKES AND PARTRICHES III 14, PECOKYS AND PERTRIGCHIS II 4, POKOK AND PERTRUCH IV 152: versions of the same recipe for roasting and serving peacock and partridge. PEKOKYS ROSTYD (ENDORT in 1) and PERTERYCHES ROSTYD appear on Menus 1 and 2; PERTRICH on Menus 3, 5, 7, 9; PERTRICH IBAKE (probably meaning in pastry) Menu 4; cf. *LCC* pp. 29-30.

peletre/peletur *n.* pellitory, herb with a hot, pungent root; the Spanish variety was most highly esteemed IV 107, 148; **pellydore** IV 21.

pelotys *n.* pellets II 16, 42; **pelettes** IV 116.

PENCH OF EGGES II 38, a dish resembling both EYRYN IN BRUET and POCHEE but rather richer and more elaborate than either; identical to *VT*'s *Brouet d'oefs et du fromage*, p. 23, and *MP*'s *Bruet Vert*, p. 172, except that it omits green herbs. 'Pench' may be related to 'poach'. Cf. *CB* p. 24.

penes see **pynes**.

PENYDES V 14, a candy; mentioned as an ingredient I 33, 57.

penys *n.* pennies, i.e. small pieces? II 19.

penne *n.* pen in the sense of feather? II 28, IV 119.——Pegge suggested a feather used as a sort of whisk, or 'pin' in the sense of a cylindrical piece of wood, as in 'rolling pin', in his note to the IV recipe; the former seems more likely in both cases.

peoper *n.* pepper I 47, 61, etc.; peper/piper II 5, 6, etc. Pepper in apple fritters: Wilson points out that the Romans put pepper in everything, including very sweet dishes: 'This was not illogical, for pepper is not in itself either sweet or savory, but simply pungent' (p. 277).

per *n.* pear V 15; perys/peeres *pl.* II 82, IV 32, etc.; *peoren* I 24, 32, 45. PEERES IN CONFYT (Ar WARDUNS IN SYRUPPE) IV 136, pears cooked in red wine with mulberries or saunders as a colouring; cf. *CB* pp. 7, 87. PERES IFARSYD Menu 3, either stuffed or mashed pears.

perboyle *v.* parboil III 19, IV 2, etc.; parboyled *pa.p.* III 14, 15.

perce *v.* pierce III 5.

PERCHYS Menu 2, PERCHYS IN GRAUE & GELE Menu 8: perch (fish); for recipes see **grauey** and GELEE.

percil/persile *n.* parsley I 16, II 54, etc.; persele II 74; percelly V 24.

perree see RAMPAUNT ~.

perrey see porre.

perte *v.* part V 14.

pertie *n.* portion I 4, 14, etc.; party II 2; pert(y)is *pl.* II 38, 80, 86; *beon* ~ *wiþ/to* accompany I 29, II 34.

pertruch *n.* partridge IV 152; pertruches *pl.* IV 37; pertrichys II 31, 56; partriches III 2; see also PEKOKES AND PARTRICHES.

pese see pece.

peskodde *n.* peapod IV 66.

pesoun see peys.

PESSON Menu 2, peas?——cf. peys.

pestels *n.* legs, almost always used of pork IV 57. PESTELL OF PORKE ISODE Menu 9, boiled leg of pork.

PETY PERUANT IV 203, small, rich pastries containing a filling of dried fruits with beef marrow and egg yolk. Hodgkin explained as *petit provaunt* 'small provision', i.e. provender, nutriment. The recipe is much like CUSKYNOLES, q.v. The recipe in MS Ashmole 1393 also calls for a paste of flour and egg (cf. PAYN PUFF) and calls for frying the cakes and serving as fritters. Cf. *CB* pp. 50 (*Pety Pernolles*), 51, 74.

PEUORAT FOR VEEL AND VENYSOUN IV 139, sauce of bread mixed with broth and vinegar seasoned with salt and pepper: 'pepper sauce', ModFr *poivrade*. Cf. *VT* pp. 34, 193, *Poivre noir*; *MP* p. 233; *CB* p. 110; and PEYUERE EGRESSE.

PYANY III 2, 'a peony', poultry dish garnished with peony petals and seeds. Peony seeds as a seasoning are mentioned in *Piers Plowman* (B. V. 312).

pyes *n.* magpies III 2; pye *sg.* possibly also 'magpie', but more likely pie: possibly used to indicate pastry filled with mixed ingredients as against a 'pasty', which usually had one principal filling ingredient IV 193.

PIGGES Menu 7, PYGGYS ROSTYD Menus 1 and 2, roast pork, probably suckling pigs. PYGGES IN SAUGE/SAWSE SAWGE see SAWGE *sub* **sauge.**

(i)piht *v.* placed, inserted I 3, 21.

PYK Menu 6, PYKE Menu 2, pike (fish). PYKES IN BRASEY IV 110, grilled or roast pike in a wine-based sauce; the name probably means 'grilled': see *OED sub* BRAZE v². Cf. *CB* p. 101, *NBC* pp. 34-5, 79.

pyl/pill *v.* peel II 69, IV 77.

PYMENTE V 17, spiced and sweetened wine with herbs.

pynes/penes *n.* pine (pignolia) nuts III 1, 3, etc. PYNADE II 91, III 3; PYNITE I 21, from *Pynetee* in MS Ro; PYNNONADE IV 52: sweet dishes named for the pine nuts which are an essential ingredient, except that almonds have been substituted in the II recipe. In other respects these are quite different recipes, although there is a vague resemblance between the recipes in II and III. Cf. *CB* pp. 34-5.

pype see CLARREY.

pise, pisyn see peys.

plays *n.* plaice (fish) III 26, IV 104, etc. PLAYS IN CYUEE IV 115, fried plaice in sauce of bread, broth, vinegar, and spices, tinted green; no onions are mentioned, although the name of the dish suggests they should be a prominent ingredient.

plaunt *v.* plant, or garnish with whatever is to be emplanted on the dish IV 116; iplaunted *pa.p.* I 27; plauntede IV 63.

plawe *v.* boil III 29n; pley V 2.

plece *v.* please V 19.

plomtre *n.* plum tree III 31n.

pl(a)umen *n.* plums I 49.

pluuers *n.* plovers III 15. PLOUERYS ROSTYD Menu 1, PLOUERS Menus 3, 5, 7, roasted plovers.

POCHEE IV 92, poached eggs in a milk-based sauce thickened with egg yolks; cf. *Lait de Vache lié, MP* p. 175.

poeren *v.* pour? perhaps 'pour off the broth in which it was cooked' I 53.

poynaunt *adj.* pungent, well seasoned V 10t.

poyne *n.* handful, A-N *poyne* (MS A1; cf. ModFr *poignée*) I 36.

poite *n.* petre; *salt of* ~ saltpetre II 58.

poke *n.* stomach (of a fish) IV 97.

(i)polled *v., pa.p.* chopped? (translates Fr *moudrée* 'ground', and cf. *OED sub* POLL v. I. 1) I 6, 7.

pomys *n.* apples V 10. POUMES AMOLE I 9, translating *Poumes ammolee* in MS Ro, 'softened apples'; POMMYS MORLES II 63 is the same dish; cf. also APPULMOS. Cf. *CB Pommesmoile*, p. 113.

pomme garnet see poume gernet.

POMMEDORRY II 42, POUM DORROGE II 59, 'gilded apples' made of meat balls dredged with egg yolk. The dish appears in *VT* p. 120 and *MP* p. 222 as *Pommeaulx*; see also FARSUR FOR POMME DORRYSE; cf. *CB* p. 38, *LCC* p. 37.

porpays/porpeys *n.* porpoise IV 13, 70, 111. PORPEYS IN BROTH IV 111, prepared in the same way as 'noumbles of flessh with oynouns',

i.e. in broth, wine, vinegar, bread, onions (and blood?). PORPEYS
IN GALENTYN Menu 6, cf. **galyntyne.**

porre/perrey *n.* vegetable dish IV 2, 71; all French authorities give both
legume-based purees of this name and dishes of chopped greens, usually including leeks; **porrettes** young leeks or green onions, scallions
(Lat *porrum*) IV 78. PERREY OF PESOUN IV 71, boiled (dried?)
peas, strained, with onions, oil, seasonings: similar to *MP*'s *Potage de
pois vielz*, fish-day version, pp. 135-6; cf. IV 75, and *CB* pp. 32, 83;
LCC p. 44. PORREY CHAPELEYN II 88, onion soup with pre-fried
pastry dumplings made to look like onion rings; probably named for
the onions.

PORREYNE II 76, a thick, sweet pottage based on plum juice: note
that 'prunes' do not necessarily mean dried fruit, which would hardly
do here; cf. ERBOWLE, a somewhat simpler but spicier plum pottage. The name appears to be a form of 'porridge', so that this may
be the oldest extant version of 'Plum-porridge'.

possenet *n.* small pot I 1, IV 32, 54; **pos(t)net** II 26, III 12.

potage(e) *n.* pottage, stewed or braised dish at least partly cooked in
the liquid from which the sauce is made I 40, IV 6t, etc. POTAGE
OF RYS II 67, rice with almond milk; cf. RYSE OF FISCHE DAY.
A French version is in *VT* pp. 157, 190-1, 204, and *MP* pp. 214-15;
cf. *CB* p. 114.

pot(t)el(l) *n.* a two-quart container IV 22, V 5.

potstyk *n.* stick for stirring V 18.

potte suger *n. phrase* ordinary cooking sugar, as against 'clarified' con-
fectioners' sugar V 12, 13.

POTTE WYS (A POTEWS) IV 185, POTWYS Menu 7; 'in the manner
of pots', i.e. forcemeat made up to resemble flower pots. The recipe
occurs in *VT* pp. 128-9, called *Potz d'Espaigne*; cf. *CB* pp. 53, 93.

potten *n.* possibly scallops (Fr *petoncle*; see *OED sub* PETUNCE)
but more likely 'pots of mussels', which is what this must actually
be (see MULE) I 63.

potus *n.* drink (Lat) V 4, 5. POTUS CLARRETI see CLARREY. POTUS
YPOCRAS see YPOCRAS.

poule de mars *n. phrase* spring chicken (Fr) I 31.

POUM DORROGE see POMMEDORRY.

poume gernet/pomme garnet *n.* pomegranate I 1, IV 86, etc.; **powmys
gernatys** *pl.* II 27; **poum gernetes** III 27.

poumes see **pomys.**

powche *n.* stomach (of a fish; cf. **poke**) IV 97n.

powdour/poud(e)re *n.* powder, ground spices I 7, IV 6, etc.; **powdres**
pl. II 17; ~ **marchant** prepared mixture of ground spices (cf. ModFr
quatre épices and such mixtures as 'pickling spices', 'spices for apple
pie', etc.; we have not found a recipe for the mixture) IV 2n, 116;
~ **douce** mild mixture of ground spices, probably often containing
sugar, although some suggested substitutes have none; in general,
douce mixtures contained cinnamon but not pepper IV 2, 6, etc.;
~ **fort** strong mixture of ground spices, generally including pepper

and/or cloves; we have not found a recipe, but suggested substitutes, and the name, make its nature clear IV 12, 13, etc.

powdur *v.* season IV 2; **ipoudred** *pa.p.* I 19.

pownas *adj./n.* evidently a colour, either blue or purple (from the turnesole) and probably purple since Ar has a separate provision for blue (from **ynde**, q.v.) IV 69.

prew(s) *n.* apparently a scribal error for *prikkes*, misreading *kk* as *w*, in some MSS of IV 184, and for *bouwes* in IV 185 (by influence of the previous recipe?): MS R gives 'pynes of past' in its recipe for *Vrchons*.

prikkes *n.* pricks, in the sense of a hedgehog's quills IV 184.

prymorole/premerole *n.* primrose III 34, 35. PRIMEROLE III 34, pottage flavoured with primrose petals and decorated with blossoms.

prunys *n.* plums II 76.

pul *v.* pluck II 52.

purslarye *n.* purslane, a scrubby herb IV 78.

put *v.* put; ~ *hem to, it among* add it to V 7, 8, etc.

Q

quayle *v.* shake IV 170.

QUALYS ROSTYD Menus 1, 2, roasted quails.

quartroun *n.* quarter V 18; **quartes** *pl.* I 56.

queyntliche/keyntlich *adv.* carefully IV 181, 185n, 197.

quest *v.* crush I 39.—The *OED* has no citation for this verb before the 17th century and marks etymology as 'unknown' but it translates *quassez* in MS A1 and is certainly ModFr *ecrasez*.

quyk *adj.* alive III 13.

QUYNSYS IN PAST Menu 1, baked or boiled quince dumplings; for recipes, see *CB* pp. 51, 97–8.

qwen *adv.* when I 31, 44, etc.

qwhey *n.* whey V 23.

qwyt(e) see **wyt**.

QWITE PLUMEN I 49, pottage of white plums, with (apparently) hard-cooked eggs.

R

RABATYS ROSTYD Menu 1, RABETES ROSTYD Menu 2, roast young rabbits.

rafens *n.* radish (Lat *raphanum*) IV 103 (also given as **radich** II 91).

ragoun see PAYN ~.

raysouns see **reysyns**.

ramme *v.* used where CJ give 'take'; it is difficult to be sure what 'to ram up' chickens implies—perhaps drain them thoroughly and press them together, to hold their shape neatly? IV 35n.

RAMPAUNT PERRE I 24, translating *Rampant Perree* in MS Ro, cooked pears decorated with pastry lions 'rampant', i.e. (apparently) figures of standing lions cut from pastry, baked and 'gilded', and inserted in the serving dishes in standing position: a simple 'subtlety'.

ramphens *n.* either rampion or a form of **raphens** (radish), q.v. IV 103n.

rapes *n.* turnips; white turnips were still the standard in Gerard's time, although he knew of others IV 7, 103. RAPES IN POTAGE IV 7, stewed turnips and onions in broth; cf. *MP Navets*, p. 144.

RAPHIOLES (AB RASYOLS) IV 158, **RAPHIOL IBAKE** Menu 9: meat balls (pig's liver, cheese, egg, etc.) enclosed in a caul and baked in an open crust, with eggs added later. While the name resembles RAUIOLES, the principle is quite different; this may be, rather, derived from the kind of fried meatballs called *rissoles* (cf. *MP*'s *Rissolles en jour de char*, pp. 225–6).

RAPY II 61, **RAPEE** II 87, **RAPEY** II 50, IV 85, Menu 8, **RAPES** III 18: it is not clear what, if anything, these recipes—none of which call for turnips—have in common. II 61 is fried fish in a spiced sauce; II 50, III 18, and IV 85 are pottages of dried fruits; II 87 contains both fish and dried fruit. *Rapee, VT* pp. 10, 85, etc., and *MP* p. 168 is fried meat in a bread-thickened sauce of which an optional ingredient is currants. There is no one ingredient or procedure common to all of these: possibly the original dish of this title is *Saulce Rappee, VT* p. 177 and *MP* p. 237, a sauce for meat in which something (bread in *VT*, grapes in *MP*) is ground; in this case the words may be derived from *raper* 'scrape, grate'. Within II 61 and 87, 7 spelled *rape*.

rastichipe see rest.

RAUIOLES (C RAUCOLES) IV 94, ravioli; this also turns up in the French menus in *MP* pp. 93, 95, 97, although Pichon transcribed the *v* (written as *u*) as *n*. The recipes for *Raviuoli bianchi* in *DV* are similar to the IV recipe, but those in *LdC* are not modern ravioli but fritters of various sorts. A similar recipe for *ravieles* appears in MS A1.

raumpauns *adj.* rampant, standing (on the lions' hind legs) I 24.

rawnes *n.* roe (of a fish) IV 128.

real *adj.* royal I 32; **ryal** IV 102t.

REFLES Menu 4, possibly RAPHIOLES, q.v., or a related fritter such as CUSKYNOLES; the menu's 'of' may be erroneous and a separate dish meant.

regges *n.* ridges; in the case of rose hips, membranes are probably meant III 37.

reyn(e) *n.* rain II 58, V 14.

reysyns/resons *n.* grapes or raisins; in the case of recipes translated directly from A-N, the first meaning is often probable I 5, II 62, etc.; **reysouns/raysouns** II 81, IV 16, etc.; ∼ *of coronse/coraunte* currants II 42, IV 16, etc.

reme *n.* surface IV 105n.

remnaunt *n.* remnant; *and þe* ∼ for the rest, to finish them IV 171.

renne *v.* run III 5, 7, etc.; **ryne** IV 195; **erne** IV 182; **ronnen** *pa.p.* III 5.

rennyng *n.* rennet V 23.

require de carnibus ut supra 'see under meats, above' II 85.

rescett *n.* receipt, recipe V 4.

resche *n.* rush V 23.

RESMOLLE see RYSMOLE *sub* **rys.**

RESQUYLE Menu 2, probably a rice dish (cf. RYSMOLE).

rest *adj.* rancid (see *OED sub* RESTY a^2) II 58; **rastichipe** *n.* rancidness I heading following 56. RESTYNG OF VENISOUN, FOR TO KEPE FRO II 57, salting venison. RESTYNG OF VENISON, TO DO AWEY II 58, how to salvage rancid venison.

rether *n.* ox II 43, IV 15.

rew *n.* rue (herb) IV 78.

REW DE RUNSY II 44, the same dish as COUWE DE ROUNCIN, q.v., but, like the source of the latter in MS A1, it does not say to chop or grind the meat.

ryal see **real.**

rygh *n.* a fish, probably the rochet or red gurnard, called *ruget, roget,* or *rouget* in some sources listed in the *OED* IV 108. RYGH IN SAWSE IV 108, fried fish, almonds, and currants in a sauce of almond milk, garlic, verjuice, and seasonings: cold.

ryne see **renne.**

Rynysshe wyne *adj. + n.* Rhine wine IV 102 n.

ry(y)s(e) *n.* rice I 1, 3, etc. RYSE OF FISCHE DAY IV 129, rice cooked in almond milk; cf. POTAGE OF RYSE. RYSE OF FLESSHE IV 11, rice cooked in meat broth; cf. *VT* p. 19. RYSMOLE (A RES-MOLLE) IV 99, RYS MOYLE II 64, 'softened rice'; cf. APPULMOY.

RYS ALKERE II 83, since rice is not a distinguishing ingredient of this fruit mixture, the name seems to be a corruption of another word or words.

RYSSHEWS OF FRUYT IV 190, meatless rissoles of ground fresh and dried fruits; cf. *MP*'s *Risolles en Karesme,* p. 225; *CB* pp. 93, 97.

ryth *adv.* right, very IV 87n.

ro(o) *n.* roe deer II 54, III 19, IV 16. ROO BROTH II 54, III 19, IV 16: venison or boar boiled in wine and water; *VT* has a similar recipe for 'venison of boar', p. 80.

roch(e) *n.* rock, loaf sugar II 14n, IV 187n; **troch** IV 187n(?).

roches *n.* roaches (fish) IV 106.

roge *n.* a fish, probably the same as **rygh** (q.v.) III 26n.

ronnen see **renne.**

rose(e)n *n.* roses I 12. ROSEE I 12, I 36, II 41 and 47, Menus 6, 8; ROSYE III 32: all later versions derive from the recipes in Ro and A1 and all contain, and/or are coloured to resemble, rose petals.

roset see **sugre** ~ *sub* sucre.

ROSYN ROSTHENES Menu 8, possibly a type of roast fish.

rote *n.* root I 39, V 17, etc.; **rotys** *pl.* II 91; in I 39, a mistranslation of *raysine* 'grape vine'.

roundeles *n.* round slices, circles I 58.

ruayn chese *adj. + n.* autumn cheese, made after the cattle had fed on the second growth, called 'rewen' or 'rowen' in various sources IV 50, 174.—This was apparently a semi-soft cheese, but not as soft as a ripe modern Brie: one recipe says to grate it. It appears to be the same cheese called *fromage de gaing* in France; Pichon, *VT* p. 14, n. 3, identifies Pont-l'Évêque as an example.

RUSCHEUES III 4, RUSCHEWYS (A BURSEWS, H HERUN SEWES)
IV 187: rissoles of ground meat, fried, although the III recipe omits
this direction. The recipes differ little from *MP*'s *Rissolles en jour de
char*, p. 225.

S

SAC WIS (A SACHUS, C SAKKYS) IV 186, SACWYS Menu 7: 'in the
manner of sacks', forcemeat modelled in canvas sacks to look like
the sacks themselves.

sadly *adv.* slowly V 12.

saym/seym *n.* fat, grease, probably often in sense of clarified lard (cf.
Liber de diversis medicinis, ed. M. S. Ogden, EETS OS 207, p. 71,
cited by C. Anne Wilson in *PPC* 13, 1983, p. 29) I 42, 48, etc.

SALAT IV 78, green salad.

salmene see BRUET ~.

SALT LOMPREY IN GALENTYNE II 69, probably a dish to be served
hot, in contrast with LAMPRAY FRESCH IN GALENTYNE.

SAMBOCADE IV 179, open tart of cheese curds with egg whites, sugar,
and elder blooms (< Lat *sambucus* 'elder'); cf. *HV Torta Sambucca.*

SAMOUN FRESCH ENDORED AND ROSTED Menu 6, 'gilded' (cf.
endore) fresh roast salmon.

sanc dragoun *n.* 'dragon's blood', Fr *sang dragoun*, a plant used for red
colouring. According to Gerard, the dock called bloodwort, but see
also *OED sub* DRAGON'S BLOOD; and *sandragon*, an English spelling listed in the *OED*, may seem close enough to the **sandres** (q.v.)
specified for red colouring in many recipes for the two to have
been confused. SANC DRAGON I 30, which translates *Sang Dragoun*
in MS Ro, is named for the colouring; this differs from the similarly
named DRAGONE in omitting capon and using different spices.

SANDALE II 34, ground white meat in a sauce of broth thickened with
egg, presumably named for the 'sandres' colouring. The red (or
orange/yellow with saffron) would serve as a contrast to the white
BLOMANGER (cf. *sub* blanc) with which the recipe advises serving
this.

sa(u)ndres *n.* red sanders, a wood used for colouring; considered a variety
of sandalwood, but not to be confused with the fragrant variety (see
also entry for **sanc dragoun**) II 34, III 18, etc.

sarray see *Foille de pastee sub* foile.

sarse *n.* sieve IV 150.

SARTES Menu 2, possibly an error for *Tartes?*

sauche *n.* sauce III 20.

saueray *n.* savory (herb) IV 8, 32, etc.

saug(e) *n.* sage I 43, II 54, etc. SAWGE V 21, PIGGES IN SAWSE
SAWGE IV 31, PYGGES IN SAUGE Menu 4: cold meat or fish in
a sauce of boiled egg yolk, sage, and vinegar; cf. *VT* pp. 20, 94, 155,
and *MP* pp. 215-16; *CB* pp. 28, 72. SAWGE YFARCET IV 168,
ground boiled pork mixed with egg and breadcrumbs, spices, and
pine nuts, made into small balls wrapped in egg batter and fried. MS

A reverses the order of this recipe and the next (SAWGEAT), although the titles occur in the usual order in the TC; Pegge apparently assumed that the TC was correct, and reversed the order of the titles but not of the recipes. Thus the recipes in his edition (and Warner's) are incorrectly titled. SAWGEAT IV 169, eggs seasoned with sage added to fried sausage, or, 'in ymbre day', cooked with butter. On title and order, see above; neither recipe resembles *CB*'s *Sauoge*, despite Austin's note ('compare "*Sawgeat*" . . .').

SAUMON GENTIL I 50, 'noble salmon', poached (?), in a lightly spiced sauce (including ground bones?).

SAUNC SARAZINE III 16, SAWSE SARZINE IV 86, a pottage of almond milk and rice flour coloured red and garnished with pomegranate seeds, to which the IV recipe adds rose hips: these characteristics testify to its genuine 'Saracen' background. While the IV title sounds more natural in modern terms, the III title is no doubt correct, indicating that the dish is the colour of blood (cf., e.g., SANC DRAGON). On the association of red food colouring with Saracen cookery, see C. Anne Wilson in PPC 7 (1980), p. 118.

SAWSE BLAUNCHE FOR CAPOUNS YSODE IV 140, sauce of ground almonds in verjuice, seasoned with ginger; cf. *CB* p. 110, *LCC* p. 28. SAWSE CAMELYNE IV 149, ground currants, walnuts, bread and spices, mixed with vinegar. The French *cameline* recipes do not call for nuts or currants (ingredients which occur in at least one other English recipe, that of the *LCC*—which is as a whole probably based largely on *The Forme of Cury*); all recipes for cameline we have seen call for cinnamon, including the French *aulx camelins* 'garlic cameline', which differs from other garlic sauces, such as *aulx verts*, only in including cinnamon (no other spice). We therefore believe the name is derived from *canel* 'cinnamon', not from its brown colour (the colour of a camel, Hodgkin suggested) or an herb, as the *OED* suggests. No recipe we have seen contains herbs of any kind, and the herb called 'camel' commented on by Gerard appears to have been unpalatable, in view of his advice to administer it to induce vomiting (as a cure for worms). Cf. *CB* pp. 77 (*Sauce gamelyne*), 109; *LCC* p. 30; *NBC* p. 48; *MP* pp. 230-1; *VT* pp. 32-3; *HV·Condimentum Camellinum*. SAWSE MADAME IV 32, stuffing for goose of fruits, herbs, and garlic, plus wine and spices to make it into the sauce. A sauce for goose of this name occurs in a group of recipes added to the *Viandier* in the 15th-century (printed) edition printed by Pichon (p. 176), but its ingredients are completely different. SAWSE NOYRE FOR CAPOUNS YROSTED IV 141, capon liver, ground with bread and spices, mixed with verjuice and capon drippings. A recipe for sauce for capon in *VT* p. 136 is close to this, but is thickened with egg yolks rather than bread; cf. also *CB* p. 110. SAWSE NOYRE FOR MALARD IV 145, made of bread, blood, vinegar, ginger and pepper, and the malard drippings; cf. *CB* p. 110, *LCC* p. 27. SAWSE SARZYNE see SAUCE SARAZINE.

scalys *n.* shell (of a lobster) II 75.

schald(e)/skalde *v.* scald II 11, IV 85, etc.

schallyd *v.*, *pa.p.* shelled II 73.

schawe *v.* shave, scrape II 43.

schepys *n.* sheep's II 15.

scher see sher.

schyuerys *n.* slivers, slices II 25, 86.

schyuis *n.* slices II 38, 65n.

(i)schredde *v.* shredded IV 6n.

schul(l)en *v.* shall I 1, 7, etc.; schul/schal *3 sg.* I 1, II 4, etc.; schalt *2 sg.*
I 32, 48, etc.; schul *2 pl.* I 53; sud *pa.* V 12.

SCIRRESEZ I 14, from *Sirisee* in MS Ro, named for the cherries used
as a sauce for meat; similar dishes are MES OF CHYSEBERIEN,
CHIRESEYE (and CHYRYSE, etc., *sub* CHIRESEYE).

sclarie see clarry.

scome *n.* scum V 11.

scome *v.* skim V 9, 10.

scure *v.* scour, scrub I 61; score III 6.

sedys *n.* seeds V 12.

seec/sek see BRUET ~.

seie *v.* say V 7.

seym see saym.

Seint Iohn St. John's; the feast day is June 24 I 41.

seyz *v.* strain II 25, 27; seye V 3.

self/selue *adj.* same II 5, IV 7, etc.; seoluen *pl.* I 62.

seoluere *n.* silver I 54.

seoþþen, seþe *adv.* see syþ.

serpell *n.* whild thyme IV 144.

seþe/seeþ *v.* simmer or boil II 40, IV 3, etc.; seoþen I 53; zeoþen I 47,
53, etc.; seoþ/zeoþ *imp.* I 56, 61, etc.; seyt II 1; ysoden/izeoden
pa.p. I 16, 44, etc.; sothen III 10, V 13, etc.; sethynge *pr.p.* III 34,
V 13.

seue/syue *n.* sieve II 76, 77; see also cyuee.

SEUE OF LAMPROUN I 52, river lamprey in onion sauce; cf. cyuee.

sew(e) *n.* juices, broth or sauce II 38, III 9, etc.

s(c)her *v.* cut II 25, 63; schorn *pa.p.* II 71.

Si dificiat sugir 'if sugar is lacking' V 5.

(y)sih *v.*? see? I 55.

sinamome see canel.

synycle *n.* herb understood as a flower which appears here in error (see
SUADE) I 44n.

siryppe see cyrip.

SYROSE see CHIRESEYE.

sit [to the pot] *v.* stick (to the pot) IV 200, V 18.

syþ/siþþyn *adv.* then II 2, 60, etc.; seþe/soþþe(n) I 34, 35, etc.

syuee see cyuee.

skyrwittes *n.* root vegetable resembling parsnips; Gerard says they are
sweet and may be eaten raw or cooked IV 7, 154.

sklyse *n.* spatula, flat utensil for stirring IV 60, V 19.

sle *v.* slay IV 130.

slytte *v.* slit (but A's *slype*, peel off the outer layer, may be correct) IV 13. SLYT SOPPES IV 82, sliced leeks in broth with toasted sops (cf. soppes).

smacche *v.* taste I 28.

SMAL ROST Menu 4, probably a leg of pork or mutton: not poultry, but a small cut of flesh meat.

smale ale *adj.* + *n.* weak ale IV 116.

smallage *n.* wild celery V 7.

smartliche *adv.* briskly I 48; smertyly V 12.

SNYTES Menu 9, snipes (birds) or a species resembling them; see *OED* *sub* SNITE.

SOBRE SAWSE IV 134, SOBER SAUU3 Menu 8, a sauce for fried fish of spiced wine thickened with ground raisins and bread.

sodyn, ysode see seþe.

softe *adv.* gently I 51.

(i)soken *v.*, *pa.p.* soaked I 41.

soler *n.* cellar II 57.

somdel *adj.* some, a portion of IV 179.

sone *adv.* quickly I 48, 55.

sonne/sunne *n.* sun II 57; zunne I 41.

sooles *n.* soles (fish) IV 122; solys II 72. SOLYS IN BRUET II 72, grilled sole in sauce of bread and ale; this should probably have cumin in it (cf. HENNYS IN BRUET and *MP* pp. 160, *Cretonée à jour de poisson*, and 162, *Cominée à jour de poisson*). SOOLES IN CYUEE IV 122, poached sole in a sauce of onions, broth, and bread; seasonings include honey.

soppes *n.* sops, generally toasted pieces of bread IV 79t, 82t, etc.; sowpes II 65t, IV 84t, 133t. SOWPYS DORRY II 65, SOWPES DORRY (P SOPPIS IN DORRE) IV 84, sops in wine with almond milk (IV) or fried onions (II); probably 'golden' because of the toasted bread (hardly 'glazed', as glossed by Austin), but see comments on SOUPE MARE below; cf. *CB* p. 11. SOWPES IN GALYN-GALE (A OF GALYNTYNE) IV 133, toast in a syrup of wine, galingale, sugar, and salt.

SOREE I 19, from *Sorree* in MS Ro, is the dish called *Soringue d'an-guilles* in *MP* p. 173 and *VT* pp. 21-2, 154, but is *V(S) Sorvigne* (p. 94), which may point to the wine in the recipe as an important part of the name; cf. *V(S)* p. 87 (including n. 30) also. The Ro recipe says the colour is 'sorree': sorrell in the sense of red? But this may be an idea arising from the name rather than vice versa, for none of the French recipes of this group is coloured red. (Cf. BLANK DESIRE.) Cf. *CB* pp. 22-3 (*Elys in Gauncelys*), 89; *NBC* p. 34. A similar modern dish is the French and Belgian *anguille au vert*.

sotilteis *n.* 'subtleties' were usually foods made to look like something else: e.g., birds covered with their feathers to look 'alive' and sugar sculptures of human figures etc.; often produced for each course of a great feast V 1 heading. SOTELTE, SOTELTEYS appear on Menus 1, 2.

soþþe(n) see syþ.

(i)souced v. soaked I 27.

soupe n. soup, in the sense of a liquid mixture; a 'strong' soup of wine and sugar must be a sweet syrup I 56, 58t. SOUPE MARE I 58: the 'soup' may be either 'superior' (see *OED sub* MORE, *adj.*) or 'famous, beautiful' (see MERE, *adj.*); it is, however, very similar to SOWPYS DORRY (q.v.), although not all dishes of this name contain onions. Evidently there is some confusion in these terms, but it is possible that 'mare' was misread as 'dore' or vice versa. Cf. the confusion of SOREE/DOREE I 19n. and MURREE/TURREE I 32n.

sourdowȝ n. leavening, yeast dough saved to leaven the next batch of bread V 22; sowre dowe IV 181: the reading of *sowre dokkes* in MSS A and B no doubt arises from a confusion of *w* and *kk*; cf. entry for prews.

southrenwode n. southernwood, herb said to have a sour taste IV 180.

sowe v. sew IV 32, 183.

sowpes see soppes.

sowple adj. supple, i.e. soft and pliant? IV 158.

(i)spandled v. splat, spread out flat (A-N *espandlé*, ModFr *épandre*) I 26.

spatur(e) n. spatula, flat spoon V 13, 14; spatyl(le) V 12.

specerie/spicerie n. spices, usually a mixture I 7, 17, etc.

speces n. spices I 17, 35, etc.

spende v. use IV 150.

spete n. spit I 52, II 28; spite III 15.

spykenard n. an herb; see *OED* IV 199, V 5, 6.

SPINETTE I 11, translating SPYNETE in MS Ro; ESPYNE I 35, translating *Espinee* in MS A1; SPINE II 46; SPYNEE III 31, IV 58: a pottage named for the hawthorne blossoms (A-N *aube spyne*) which distinguish it. Cf. *CB* pp. 25, 29.

spinoches n. spinach IV 78n, 188. SPYNOCHES YFRYED IV 188, parboiled spinach with the water pressed out, braised in oil; cf. *MP* p. 141.—On the 'saracen' origin of spinach, and of this recipe, see C. Anne Wilson in *PPC* 8 (1981), 23–4.

spryng v. sprinkle IV 87; spreing V 2.

stampe v. beat V 15.

stat n. state, condition I 40.

steles n. stalks IV 185.

step(e) v. steep III 2, 29, etc.; stoppit/stepyd *pa.p.* II 69, 71, etc.

ster(e) v. stir III 25, 28, etc.; stury II 26, 32; istured *pa.p.* I 49; steryng(e) *pr.p.* V 12, 13, 14.

STEWED COLOPS V 20, braised cutlets (of venison); cf. colops.

STOKFYSSH Menu 6, dried fish; for recipes see *CB* pp. 100, 109.

stole n. stool, stand V 13.

stonden v. stand I 41, V 3; stonde *3 sg.* V 8, 9; ~ by be thick with IV 135; stondyng *pr.p.* very thick, as against 'renning', runny IV 81, 83, etc.

stop(pe) v. stuff IV 36, 49.

stoppit see step.

storchoun see STURIOUN.

streberyen *n.* strawberries I 13.

strey(ȝ)en *v.* strew I 1, 11; **strey(e)** *imp.* I 35, 58, etc.; **strawe** II 31, 79, etc.; **istreyed** *pa.p.* I 13, 22, etc.; **istreed/istried** I 4, 12, 14.

streinþe *n.* strength I 5, 9, etc.

streme *v.* stream, form a 'thread' V 12.

stude *n.* place I 1.

(i)stured, stury see stere.

STURGYN V 24, a version of the recipe called *Esturgon contrefait de Veel* in *MP* p. 200 and *Esturgon de chair* in *VT* p. 163; mock-sturgeon, but the French recipes call for boiling the meat in wine and vinegar, not honey, which may be an error in the English MS, which still specifies serving the cold 'sturgeon' with vinegar.

STURIOUN Menu 6, sturgeon. This fish was supposed to be reserved for royalty at one time; the 'Traité de Cuissin écrit vers 1300', e.g., states 'Esturjon est 1 pesson real', *VT* p. 220; but note that the counterfeited kind cannot be intended on this menu, which is for a fish-day. STORCHOUN II 71, boiled sturgeon; French recipes also call for boiling this fish, but most specify it is to be eaten cold. Cf. *MP* p. 199, *VT* pp. 30–1, 107, etc.

SUADE I 23, translating *Swade* in MS Ro; SWAU II 47: a dish named for the elderflower which is the distinguishing ingredient. Continental OF forms of this word for elder included *seu, seut,* and *seuch*; the glossary of MS Harl 978 (f. 24^r—*c.*1264), in a list which usually gives an A-N gloss before the ME word, glosses *sambucus* as 'sueþ/ swew, ellarne'. SUOT BLANC I 44, translating *Suet Blanc* in MS A1, is basically the same dish: chicken or fish in a sauce flavoured with elderblossoms, fresh or dried (note that elderflowers are still preserved dry). 'Grapes' seems to be an error, made under the influence of errors in the French: principally, the scribe of MS A1 wrote the 'une' of *une sucche* 'an elder' with an extra minim, so that it appears to read 'vine'. The recipe in MS L is in *CB*, p. 112; whoever produced the L recipes was equally misled by the French scribe and appears to have read *une sucche* as 'vine vermile'.

sucre(e) *n.* sugar I 1, 2, etc.; **sucur** I 11; **ceucre/ceugre** III 1, 3, etc.; **sugur cypre** *n.* + *adj.* imported, high quality sugar, whether or not from Cyprus, a common source of sugar in this period; another was Crete, which was thus known as 'Candia' IV 43, 123, etc. SUGER, TO CLARIFIE V 11, a sort of basic sugar candy, called for in other confectionary recipes. SUGER PLATE V 13, sugar candy, optionally —but probably usually—flavoured with rosewater and coloured red; referred to as **sugre roset** in III 22.

sud see schulen.

sumdell *adv.* somewhat IV 52.

SWAN, TO DIȜTE III 11, how to dress, roast, and serve a swan; cf. *CB* p. 78. SWANNES Menus 3, 7, 9; SWANNES ROSTYD Menu 1; SWAN ROSTYD Menu 2.

SWAU see SUADE.

swerden *v.*? answered? i.e., told?—if so, the meaning depends on a recipe not included in this collection; if it is a verb, the 'to' should be joined or hyphenated, but since little is clear here, almost any punctuation may be misleading I 55.

swete *n.* suet I 56.

swete *adj.* sweet, fresh I 16, II 1, etc.; in I 31, a translator's error.

swetemete oyl *n. phrase* probably oil of a type appropriate to sweet-meats, but possibly oil made from sweet (nut) 'meats': cf. the use of oil of almonds in the next recipe V 14.

swyng *v.* (1) beat, mix II 20, IV 41, etc.; swonge *pa.p.* III 23. (2) put—briefly—over II 52.

T

talbotays/talbotes see HARIS IN ～.

talwe *n.* tallow, fat II 15.

TART DE BRY IV 174, open tart filled with fat cheese of the type imported from Brie, or ruayn (q.v.), with egg yolks and seasonings. **TART DE BRYMLENT** IV 175, a tart (or pie—this recipe says to cover it) filled with ground apples, pears, and dried fruit, with wine and sugar plus boiled fish and spices, baked with more dried fruits (and/or nuts) on top; brymlent = *brim* in the sense of 'full'? **TART IN YMBRE DAY** IV 173, open tart filled with onions, herbs, and breadcrumbs or (more likely) soft, fat cheese, mixed with eggs, butter, seasonings, and currants; this was a combination considered suitable for fast days out of Lent (cf. ymbre day). **TARTEE** IV 172, an open tart filled with ground pork, dried fruits, small birds, eggs, and seasonings; cf. *CB* pp. 47 (*Tartes de chare*), 52, 74–5; *NBC* p. 52; and **TARTES OF FLESSH** below. **TARTES** Menus 5, 6, 7, type unspecified, but if the immediately preceding *crem* in 5 is a clue, possibly **DARYOLS**, q.v. **TARTES BOSEWES** Menu 3, this may be the name of a tart or two words: 'bosewes' may be the same as **BOREWYS**; cf. the spelling *Bosoun* of MS Douce 55. **TARTES OF FYSSHE** IV 178, eels and salmon stewed in almond milk and verjuice, with the sauce (broth) thickened with more almonds and the fish boned, all but the midpiece of the eel ground, with bread and seasonings, to make a stuffing for the eels; the rest is mixed with the thickened broth and poured over; baked in a shell. **TARTES OF FLESSH** IV 176, tart filled with boiled pork, ground, with boiled eggs, grated cheese, small birds, and young rabbits, chopped. Cf. **TARTEE**, which differs in including dried fruit. **TARTYS IN APPLIS** II 82, open tart of apples and other fruits; a similar tart, containing onions, covered, is in *VT* (15th-century section) pp. 174–5. **TARTYS OF FYSCH OWT OF LENTE** II 84, tart of eels in a custard base of cream and cheese, foods not allowed in Lent; this is called **TARTE JACOPINE** in *VT* (15th-century) pp. 173, 174; cf. also *MP* p. 217. **TARTLETES** IV 177, boiled veal, ground with boiled eggs and dried fruits and nuts, as a filling for small open tarts.

TARTLETTES IV 51, an entirely different recipe from **TARTLETES**

above; of the variant spellings, C's *Torteletys* is closest to what is probably an Italian original: *tortelletti*. Paste dumplings boiled or fried, with a filling of ground meat or a meat substitute such as dried fruits; referred to as **turteletes** in IV 94. *DV* has several *tortelletti* recipes.

te *prep.?* to? (cf. vort) I 53.

techeþ *v.* teaches I 38.

teeles *n.* teals (small river ducks) III 15. TELYS Menu 9, TELYS ROSTYD Menu 1, TELIS YBAKE Menu 5; baked or roast teal.

temper/tempre *v.* mix, modify by mixing with something else I 35, II 1, etc.; (i) tempred *pa.p.* I 32, 45.

TENCHE IN SYUEE III 9, TENCHES IN CYUEE IV 123: the III recipe is a true 'civy', with onion sauce, but that in IV calls for a sweet syrup in which onions are omitted and dried fruits added; cf. *CB* p. 23, *NBC* p. 80.

tese *v.* shred II 66n; yteysed *pa.p.* IV 22.

TEST DE TURT I 27, translating MS Ro's *Teste de Tourt;* TESTE DE TURT I 43, translating *Teste de Turke* in MS A1: 'head of a Turk' (Saracen). In I 27, directions are given for making a 'face' of ground pistachio nuts, tinted variously, on the basic tart; this effect is not explained in I 43, but is probably to be assumed here too, since the rubric indicates this to be a festive dish for the fish days in the Christmas season, although the A-N describes it as suitable for Lent. A simpler version of the latter recipe in MS L is entitled *Teste de Cure* (in *CB*, p. 112).

þanne *adv.* then II 57, IV 38.

þarmys *n.* guts, intestines II 16.

þat *conj.* so that, until, in such phrases as *seeþ hem ~ þey be tendre* II 2, IV 24, etc.

þekke *adj.* thick V 2.

þenne *adj.* see þynne.

þeos *adj.* this I 45; *pl.* I 31; þoes I 1; I 1, 32.

þeoueþorne *n.* generally means the blackberry bush, but is also confused with hawthorne (see *OED sub* THEVETHORN), which is what is meant here: the A-N recipes call for *flurs d'aubespyne* I 11, 35.

þes *adv.* thus IV 60.

þyes/þyys *n.* thighs II 29, 30.

(i)þikked *v.* thickened I 14.

þilke *adj.* this I 31, 40, etc.

þynne *adj.* thin; in the case of cooled water, any sediment would presumably settle to the bottom II 57, 88, etc.; þenne II 32; þunne I 34.

þoes, see þeos.

thorne *n.* hawthorne III 31.

þoruout *adv.* throughout V 6.

þor(o)w/þoro *prep.* through II 11, 17, etc.; þur(g)h I 44, IV 3, etc.

þre(o) *adj.* three I 45, II 57, 58.

þredde/thridde *adj.* third II 60; *~ pert* a part one third of the total amount II 60, III 28, etc.

thriddendele/þriddel *n.* a third part IV 68, 138; in 105, probably 'one third each'.

þrin *adv.* therein I 3, 6, etc.

þron *adv.* thereon I 59.

thur(g)h see **þorow.**

to *adj.* two II 66.

to *conj.* till II 26.

tobrest see **berst.**

tofore/tovoren *prep.* before I 54, 63, IV 53n.

togider *adv.* together V 6, 19, etc.; **togedres** V 21.

tohewen see **hewen.**

TORTE Menu 9, probably TARTEE (spelled *Torte* in C).

TOSTEE IV 96, toasted bread in a spiced syrup of wine and honey; the garnish of pieces of ginger is no doubt preserved (candied) ginger. Cf. *VT* p. 122.

tou(w)ayl *n.* towel I 40, 41; II 80; **twayle** III 5; **tuel** III 24.

toun cressis *n. phrase* garden cress, as against watercress, which grows wild IV 78.

TOURTELETES IN FRYTURE IV 157, a rissole of ground figs in pastry, fried and eaten with honey; this seems to be a sweet variant of TARTLETTES, q.v.

tovoren see **tofore.**

towh *adj.* tough IV 181, 196n.

tre *n.* tree II 56; wood V 12, 18; **treen** *adj.* wooden V 18.

TREDURE IV 17, a caudle of eggs, crumbs, and broth, with saffron; *MP* has a similar soup, not given a specific title, under the heading of *Souppe despourveue* (i.e., for unexpected guests) p. 146. Name from the golden colour; *tres dorée?*

(i)tried *v.* tested, select I 9, 10, etc.—*MP* suggests that the way to 'try' cinnamon is *à la dent*, with one's teeth. See also AMIDON ~.

troch see **roche.**

tuel see **touayl.**

turbet *n.* turbot (fish) I 43, IV 104. TURBOT Menu 8, method of cooking not specified.

t(o)urnesole *n.* herb used for colouring food and fabrics pink or purple; Gerard says the French dyed linen rags with it and these rags were sold in England to be used as a food dye IV 69, V 13.

turt see TESTE DE ~.

turteletes see TARTLETTES.

twayle see **touayl.**

tweydel *n.* a second part, i.e. half as much; Pegge's gloss of 'two parts' cannot be right when the alternative is a 'þriddell of vynegar', which is much sharper and would be used in a smaller quantity IV 138.

twey(n)e *adj.* two II 12, III 26.

twyse *adv.* twice IV 50; **twies** V 8.

TWO PECYS OF FLESSH, FOR TO MAKE TO FASTEN TOGYDER IV 198, to glue pieces of meat with comfrey juice (cf. **comfery**).

U

uat *adj.* fat I 53.

unc(e) *n.* ounce V 4, 5, etc.

upsodoun *adv.* upside-down V 23.

utter *adj.* outer IV 1n.

V

vacchen *v.* fetch; *let* ~ have fetched I 48.

vach *v.* pour I 39.

vache *v.* pick, gather I 39.

vche *adj./pron.* each I 41, 45, 47; vchon/uchan each one I 1, 45.

veel/vele *n.* veal I 6, 32, etc. VEEL IN BUKNADE see BUKKENADE. VEEL IROSTED Menu 7, roast veal.

veet *n.* feet I 42.

veld *v.* fold (Fr *plier*) I 45.

velle *n.* skin I 48.

VENESOUN ROSTYD Menus 1, 2, 3, roast venison. VENESOUN WITH FURMYNTE see FURMENTY.

veorst *adv.* first I 55.

ve(y)r(re) *adj.* fair, good I 41, 47, etc.; veyre *adv.* well I 41, 43, etc.

VERDE SAWSE IV 144, green sauce, Fr *saulce verte*: ground herbs and spices in wine and vinegar, thickened with bread. The recipe in *VT*, p. 33, resembles this closely, and a 12th-century ancestor is in Nequam's *De utensilibus*, but the recipe goes back at least to Apicius, who gives a number of similar sauces for fish; cf. *CB* pp. 77, 110; *NBC* p. 77; and many later—and no doubt earlier, too—cookbooks.

verhe* *v.* work, do (MS *verhs*) I 44.

verious *n.* verjuice, liquid of acid fruits such as sour grapes and crab-apples (Fr *verjus* 'green juice') IV 14, 17, etc.; vergus I 16, 31.

vernage *n.* a wine IV 136.—This generally refers to a strong, sweet Italian wine, but there is a recipe so titled in MS Harl 2378 for making an unsweetened spiced wine, colour unspecified.

vernis see METE ~.

verre see ver.

ver(h)s *adj.* fresh (? not clear in all cases) I 48, 49, 54.

VERT DESIRE I 2, translating *Vert desiree* in MS Ro, a green version of BLANC DESIRE, using parsley for colouring; mentioned in I 29.

VERTESAUS BROUN IV 148, herbs, bread, and verjuice; the only reason we can see why it should be 'brown'—in contrast to regular green sauce (VERDE SAWSE)—would be that dried herbs are to be used.

veruayn *n.* vervain, an herb not in general culinary use today IV 180.

vessalage *n.* something worthy of a nobleman I 54.

VYAUND RYAL IV 102, Menu 3: sweetened wine, spiced and thickened with rice flour, coloured red with mulberries or saunders; cf. VIAUNDE DE CYPRE; *CB Vyaund de ciprys Ryalle*, p. 21, and *Vyande Ryalle*, p. 32. VYAUNDE CYPRE OF SAMOUN IV 101, salmon in almond milk thickened with rice flour, presumably with enough sugar to be on the sweet side, as is all this family of recipes; cf. *CB* p. 28. VIAUNDE DE CYPRE I 28, translating *Viaunde de Cypre* in MS Ro; VYAUNDE CYPRE IV 100; METE OF CYPREE I 56; VIAUNDE OF CYPRE III 21: 'sweet food' because of the sugar ('cypre') represented in I 28 by the confection gyngebred. Always an exceptionally sweet dish. One later version (Ar 141) calls for 4 lbs. sugar to 11 lbs. of dates and pine nuts, with a sweet wine base; cf. *LCC* pp. 8–9, *NBC* p. 102. VIAUNDE DESPYNE I 4, translating MS Ro's *Viaunde d'espyne*, is not to be confused with SPI-NETTE and the related recipes calling for hawthorne blossoms: this contains the relatively exotic pistachio nut, and the title may mean 'food of Spain'. It is probably not sweet, like other 'Viaunde' dishes here, as no sugar is mentioned. It strongly resembles *Fustaqīya* in the *Baghdad Cookery Book*, p. 197.

vi(c)hs see vische.

VINEGRATE (AB VYNEGRACE) IV 62, Fr *Vinaigrette*, pork in a sauce of wine, vinegar, and onions; there are similar recipes of this title in *VT* p. 7, *MP* pp. 164–5.

vynegre/veneger *n.* wine vinegar I 57, II 71, etc.; wyneger II 51, 69.

vyngres *n.* fingers I 45.

viol *n.* vial V 7.

violet *n.* violet *leaves* are probably meant, although the flowers were also used in salads and pottages IV 8. VYOLET III 35, VYOLETTE Menu 1, pottage containing violets, with more flowers as a garnish; cf. *CB* pp. 23, 29.

vische *n.* fish I 26, 32, etc.; vi(c)hs I 19, 26, 44.

vlehs *n.* flesh, meat I 7, 11, etc.; vlesche I 56.

vn *art.* a, Fr *un* I 51.

vnce see unce.

vnchis *n.* inches V 6.

vndo *v.* cut open, i.e. clean out the guts III 11.

vnneþe *adv.* scarcely, only with difficulty IV 20n, 67n.

vnto *prep./conj.* until II 2.

volatils *n.* birds I 27.

vor *prep.* in order I 35, 52, etc.

voresayde *v.* foresaid I 44.

vorsche *adj.* fresh I 19.

vort(e) *adv.* in order to I 5, 9, etc.; fort I 7.

vorþ *adv.* I 49, 50, 57.

(i)vounden *v.* found I 32.

vrchoun *n.* hedgehog IV 184.

vþur *adj.* other I 56.

vulþ see fulþ.

vure see fer.

vurst *adv.* first I 56.

W

wafrouns *n.* wafers IV 26.

waisshe *v.* wash IV 3; **wahs** I 43; **wasch** II 2, 12, etc.; **ywaschen** *pa.p.* I 41; in I 27, translates *plumee*, 'cleaned', probably in the sense of 'pitted'.

walm *n.* boiling; *ones a* ~ let it boil up once III 18.

wan(ne) *adv.* when II 25, 38, etc.

warly/warliche *adv.* carefully IV 22, 196.

wastel (bred) *n./adj.* high quality white bread (cognate with ModFr *gâteau*) I 36, 37, etc.; **wastelys** *pl.* II 30. WASTELS YFARCED IV 167, hollowed loaves of white bread stuffed (cf. **force**) with a mixture of crumbs with eggs, tallow, spices, and currents; tied up and boiled.

wat *adj.* what II 45.

weder *n.* weather V 14.

weel *adv.* well III 32.

welkes see **woelkes**.

welle *v.* boil, bring to a boil II 23; **welled** *pa.p.* IV 53n; **ywol** (in contrast with *rostyd*, unlikely as it seems that larks would be boiled) II 31.

werce *n.* work V 1.

were *adv.* where II 58.

wete/wite *n.* wheat II 1, 89.

wex *n.* wax V 18.

wexe *v.* grow II 25, V 18.

wheyȝe *n.* whey IV 155, 179.

whyte grece *adj. + n.* lard or similar animal grease IV 38, 49, etc.

wyl *v.* desire II 51; **wole** V 9; **wolt** *2 sg. subj.* I 41; **woldest** III 30; **wold** *3 sg. subj.* V 14; **ywylned** *pa.p.* I 47.

wyle *n.* while II 2, 49.

wymbel *n.* gimlet V 18.

wymmon *n.* woman (or women, *pl.?*) I 27.

wynde *v.* wring, twist IV 154n, 158.

wyndewe *v.* winnow IV 3.

wyrke *v.* work V 12, 17.

wise *n.* manner, fashion IV 7.

wyt(e) *adj.* white II 6, 14, etc.; **hwit(e)** I 1, 48, etc.; **wyth** II 48; **qwyte** I 3, 11, etc.

wyte *n.* white of egg II 6, 25, etc.; **wytys** *pl.* II 16, 20, etc.; **hwyte** I 48. See also **wete**.

wyte *v.* (1) keep, preserve; see *OED sub* WITE v.² I 62. (2) know V 16.

wodekok *n.* woodcock III 15. WODECOK Menus 3, 7; WODCOKKES Menu 9; WODECOKES Menu 5: woodcocks, doubtless roasted.

woelkes *n.* whelks (shellfish) I 61. WOELKEYE I 61, whelk pottage; cf. *NBC* p. 100. WELKES Menu 6, whelks, in pottage or not.

(y)wol see **welle**.

wole see **wyl**.

womb(ee) *n.* stomach I 47, II 15.

won *n.* quantity IV 18, 23n, etc.; wan IV 53n.

wort *n.* malt used to make beer, so-called before or during fermentation V 8, 10.

wose *n.* juice IV 198.

wrye *v.* cover IV 73; wreh I 41; ywryen *pa.p.* I 25.

wryng *v.* wring, often in sense of 'strain' II 32, 37, etc.; ywronge(n) *pa.p.* I 32, II 76.

wroght *v.* made V 12; wroȝte V 17.

Z

zeoþ, zeoþen see seþe.

zunne see sonne.